AN UNNATURAL METROPOLIS

AN

UNNATURAL

METROPOLIS

WRESTING NEW ORLEANS FROM NATURE

CRAIG E. COLTEN

LOUISIANA STATE UNIVERSITY PRESS

BATON ROUGE

DESIGNER: Andrew Shurtz   TYPEFACE: Adobe Caslon, Nelvetica Neue
TYPESETTER: G&S Typesetters, Inc.   PRINTER AND BINDER: Edwards Brothers

Library of Congress Cataloging-in-Publication Data

Colten, Craig E.
An unnatural metropolis : wresting New Orleans from nature / Craig E. Colten.
p.   cm.
Includes bibliographical references and index.
ISBN 0-8071-2977-1 (alk. paper)
1. Human ecology—Louisiana—New Orleans Metropolitan Area.   2. Urban ecology—
Louisiana—New Orleans Metropolitan Area.   3. Wetland ecology—Louisiana—New
Orleans Metropolitan Area.   4. River engineering—Louisiana—New Orleans
Metropolitan Area.   5. Flood routing—Louisiana—New Orleans Metropolitan Area.
6. Water levels—Louisiana—New Orleans Metropolitan Area.   7. New Orleans
Metropolitan Area (La.)—Social conditions.   8. New Orleans Metropolitan Area (La.)—
Environmental conditions.   I. Title.
GF504.L8C65 2004
304.2′8′0976335—dc22
2004008640

Published with support from the Louisiana Sea Grant College Program, a
part of the National Sea Grant College program maintained by the National
Oceanic and Atmospheric Admisistration of the U.S. Department of Commerce.

TO TOM AND JANE COLTEN

for introducing me

to the most peculiar city

of New Orleans

CONTENTS

Acknowledgments xi

Abbreviations xv

INTRODUCTION: The City and the Environment 1

1. Water Hazards 16

2. Remaking the Environment 47

3. Inequity and the Environment 77

4. Environment Comes to the Fore 108

5. Combating New Flood Hazards 140

6. Reintroducing Wetland Environments 162

EPILOGUE 187

Notes 193

Index 237

FIGURES

I.1. New Orleans's local setting 3

1.1. Topography of New Orleans 18

1.2. Levee development to 1812 21

1.3. Flooded area, 1849 27

1.4. New Orleans in 1863 37

1.5. Drainage machine, ca. 1860 41

2.1. Nuisances, cemeteries, parks, and sanitary districts 49

2.2. Street drainage 55

2.3. French Quarter cistern 62

2.4. City Park, ca. 1900 74

3.1. Urbanized territory, 1900 84

3.2. Drainage system expansion, 1900–1940 85

3.3. Drainage system features 86

3.4. African American population, 1900 88

3.5. Trees planted on St. Roche Avenue, 1901 92

3.6. African American population, 1910 93

3.7. African American population, 1920 95

3.8. Areas without sewers, 1923 98

3.9. African American population, 1930 101

3.10. New Orleans Floral Trail, 1949 102

3.11. Aerial view of oak-shaded boulevard 103

3.12. African American population by census tract, 1940 104

4.1. Agriculture Street Landfill neighborhood 111

4.2. Sign of protest 121

4.3. Industry and water use along the Mississippi River, 1969 132

5.1. Broadmoor drainage system 148

5.2. Raised house in Broadmoor neighborhood 150

5.3. East bank drainage system, 1951 156

5.4. West bank drainage districts 157

6.1. Wetland exhibits and preserves 164

6.2. Swamp tour boat 170

6.3. Alligator exhibit at the Audubon Zoo 172

6.4. Development approaches Bayou Sauvage wetland, 1964 181

ACKNOWLEDGMENTS

THE LONGER I work at this enterprise we refer to as scholarship, the more
I appreciate the important contributions of others in my work. Not just the
direct influences, but the subtle and less obvious encouragements one re-
ceives along the way. While I point out the more apparent players here, it
in no way diminishes my gratitude to those whose contributions were less
apparent but made this endeavor so satisfying.

First, I want to thank Stephanie Shaw, who was my research assistant
for a considerable period of time while I was teaching in Texas and helped
me get this project underway. She carried out tedious but essential library research on several topics, and our joint efforts helped me work through some
of the sticky problems I encountered in New Orleans. Additionally, she offered insightful comments on drafts of this work. Joy Adams energetically
scoured through historical government documents, Reno Cecora investigated urban forestry, and John Welch (at LSU) assembled information on
air conditioning. I am deeply grateful to these research assistants.

Several editors and colleagues offered valuable critiques of portions of this work as well. David Robinson of the *Journal of Historical Geography,* Cathy French of *Environmental Practice,* and Adam Rome of *Environmental History* funneled comments from anonymous reviewers to me, along with suggestions of their own, that greatly improved sections of this book. I would also like to thank them for permitting me to republish here portions of my work that were originally published in their journals. Lary Dilsaver, Fred Day, Andrew Hurley, Ari Kelman, and John Cumbler gave of their time to offer critical comments on draft chapters. I also want to thank the anonymous reviewers who provided insightful critiques that greatly improved the final product and George Roupe at LSU Press, who gave such careful attention to the manuscript.

Map making assistance came from Paul Schultze of Southwest Texas and from the LSU geoscience cartographic section, especially Clifford Duplechin, who crafted the final maps from my rough sketches, and Mary Lee Eggart.

Generous research support came from an LSU Regents Faculty Research Award during the summer of 2001 and is greatly appreciated. The Minerals Management Service sponsored a research project on environmental justice that has provided background for this work as well.

I prized the collegial atmosphere that my colleagues and students at Southwest Texas State University and Louisiana State University provided and the gentle nudges accompanied by critical observations that they offered. I am particularly indebted to Bill Davidson at LSU because he saw potential in my work and helped make the move back to Louisiana possible. Also, the students in my New Orleans seminar (2001) and my urban environments seminar (2003) contributed through their analyses of a variety of environmental topics.

To the staffs at the Hill Memorial Library at LSU, the LSU Cartographic Information Center (especially John Anderson who doggedly pursued any request I made for a special map), the University Archives and Louisiana Collection at the University of New Orleans, the Special Collections at Tulane University, the Municipal Archives at the New Orleans Public Library (who do the most with the least), the Historic New Orleans Collection, the Louisiana State Museum, and the Louisiana State Library, I offer a hearty thanks. Often working with less than generous budgets, these archivists and librarians are defending the historical record of New Orleans from oblivion and helping researchers like me find what we need to tell that city's story. Ultimately, their work will outlast any interpretation of the vital records they protect and preserve.

Public agencies whose personnel have more pressing responsibilities than assisting researchers need to be recognized as well. Ed Lyon of the Corps of Engineers offered frequent and valuable contacts and opened the door to the corps' many resources. His assistance is particularly appreciated. The Sewerage and Water Board of New Orleans, the Jefferson Parish Department of Public Works, the Jefferson Parish Floodplain Management Program, the New Orleans Department of Safety and Permits, the New Orleans Planning Commission, the Mayor's Office of Environmental Affairs, the New Orleans Department of Parks and Parkways, the Audubon Louisiana Nature Center, the Audubon Zoo, the Louisiana Department of Environmental Quality, the Louisiana Department of Health and Hospitals, the Louisiana Department of Transportation and Development, and the Louisiana Department of Wildlife and Fisheries all made records available or provided access to experts on topics addressed in this work. Federal agencies proved equally accommodating and included the Federal Emergency Management Agency, the National Park Service, the Fish and Wildlife Service, and the U.S. Environmental Protection Agency. Their contribution is immeasurable. Also, Wes Busby, a retired Sewerage and Water Board engineer, provided valuable insight into post–1950 drainage efforts.

To my New Orleans friends, who over the years offered shelter and sustenance along with suggestions on everything from obscure research topics to outstanding eateries, I am particularly grateful. These fine folks include Steve and Kandace Graves, Gary Talarchek, Doug and Marylou Mabile, Frank and Juanita Perkins, and Ed Kleppinger.

One of my earliest childhood memories was taking a huge silver bus across the seemingly endless span of the causeway that links New Orleans with the north shore of Lake Pontchartrain. It was, as I vaguely recall, a somewhat frightening experience, but the lure of the destination dispelled any fear and held me under a fascinating grip. Over the next fifteen years or so, I visited the Crescent City repeatedly and came to be enchanted with it even more. I must thank my parents, Tom and Jane Colten, for introducing me to this wonderful city and for giving me opportunities for that attachment to it to grow. And to my lovely wife Marge, whom I met and married in New Orleans, I am indebted for her steadfast support and readiness to visit the Crescent City.

ABBREVIATIONS

EPA .... Environmental Protection Agency

FEMA .... Federal Emergency Management Agency

FWPCA .... Federal Water Pollution Control Administration

NFIP .... National Flood Insurance Program

NPL .... National Priorities List

NPS .... National Park Service

PRP .... Potentially Responsible Party

SCC .... Stream Control Commission

USPHS .... U.S. Public Health Service

AN UNNATURAL METROPOLIS

THE CITY AND THE ENVIRONMENT

STROLLING THROUGH THE Vieux Carré, the historic French Quarter, or ambling beneath the live oaks in Audubon Park, one gets the impression that New Orleans is a city without relief. Only the massive levees that stand between the city and the river provide a discernible change in elevation. Across the lower Mississippi River delta, subtlety is the key to topography. While far from obvious, the lay of the land in New Orleans has been critical to the city's development. Slopes of a few inches per mile make a tremendous difference in this low-lying city. What little relief there is directs the flow of water, of which there is an abundance in southern Louisiana: precipitation averages nearly 60 inches a year, while the river carries about 600,000 cubic feet per second by the docks; the water table lies just below the land surface, and Lake Pontchartrain laps at the levees guarding the city's northern shore. Since a sizable portion of the city rests below sea level and collects whatever water is not pumped out, managing the surplus fluid is critical. With little topographic assistance, massive engineered water-control devices help drain the city and keep the river and lake water at bay, and they have become key to New Orleans's continued viability. Wresting the site from its watery excesses and the associated problems was, and remains, a central issue in this city's existence. Recent mayor Marc Morial criticized the city's founders for selecting a site with so many inherently expensive water management problems.[1] Keeping the city dry, or separating the human-made environment from its natural endowment, has been the perpetual battle for New Orleans.

At its founding, New Orleans was an unlikely city. Geographer Peirce Lewis went so far as to call it the "impossible but inevitable city."[2] Surrounded by swamps, with little solid footing, threatened by floods, the site impressed the French founders with its many locational liabilities and its questionable suitability as a colonial capital.[3] Ultimately convinced that the portage between the river and the lake via Bayou St. John was the best strategic location, French authorities began the task of planting a city on the less than hospitable terrain. Situation, according to Lewis, won out. That is, New Orleans's strategic position as the gateway to the Mississippi River valley bestowed upon it commercial advantages that outweighed any inherent site shortcomings. Overcoming those physical inadequacies is the struggle that the city still contends with.[4]

New Orleans's site makes it unique, although how the city dealt with environmental circumstances places it within larger technological and political frameworks. Thus the site's environmental characteristics have proved significant both on the level of local urban development and on a national scale. Through and through, New Orleans's physical geography is interlaced with its local history. While race and slavery were the burdens of southern history, the environment is the burden of New Orleans history. From the city's founding to twenty-first-century political battles, dealing with the inappropriate site imbues all aspects of urban life there. When the brothers Iberville and Bienville navigated up the Mississippi River in 1699, indigenous people introduced them to a well-worn pathway that served as a portage between the river and Lake Pontchartrain. The portage spanned the slightly higher natural levee, while Bayou St. John linked the better-drained ground with the lake (Fig. I.1). The natural levee has had a defining impact on the city in two key ways: as a swath of high ground, it influenced selection of the city's site, and through its effect on drainage, it influenced urbanization patterns.

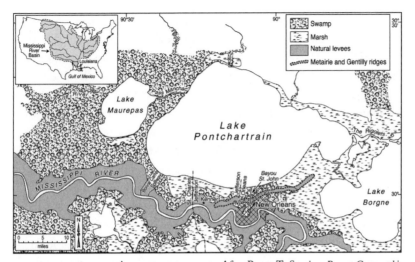

FIG. I.1. NEW ORLEANS'S LOCAL SETTING. After Roger T. Saucier, *Recent Geomorphic History of the Pontchartrain Basin, Louisiana* (Baton Rouge: Louisiana State University Press, 1963).

Large river systems like the Mississippi create the land adjacent to their courses. Over the last several millennia, the Mississippi River has been extending its delta into the Gulf of Mexico while building up the expansive alluvial floodplain, particularly south of Baton Rouge. Spring floods filled the waterway to overflowing. As the floods escaped the channel, the water slowed and the sediment that it carried settled out. The material deposited by the river built up the land mass adjacent to its channel—a process described in the eighteenth century by the historian Le Page du Pratz.[5] In the case of the Mississippi River, the initial deceleration of water caused coarser sands and silt to settle out closer to the river's edge. This created a pair of matching ridges parallel to the stream. Their cross section resembles a wedge. The riverside slopes discernibly into the waterway, while the land tapers off imperceptibly from the crest in the opposite direction for about two miles. At New Orleans, the peak of the natural levee rose about 12 feet above sea level.[6] It was on this high ground that Bienville had the city platted. Thus the land-building forces of the river created the very site upon which the settlement stood. The Place d'Armes, now known as Jackson Square, occupies that strategic location. Although subject to regular flooding, this relatively higher site was the place least susceptible to inundation and the first to emerge from abating floods.

The gentle slope away from the river descended gradually toward sea level at Lake Pontchartrain over a distance of about 1.5 miles. A relict natural levee, created by the Mississippi River when it followed a different course several thousand years ago, stands about 7 feet above sea level and runs from what are now the western suburbs eastward toward the Rigolets. Bayou St. John has cut through the ancient land form, creating remnants known as the Metairie and Gentilly ridges, which are about a mile wide at their broadest point and taper off to the east.[7] These modest ridges have been truly significant in shaping New Orleans. While water from the natural levee along the river's current location tends to drain toward the lakefront, the Metairie and Gentilly ridges stand as a barrier to this flow. River-made topography has created a "bowl." On three sides the natural levees that followed the river around its giant crescent made lips to this basin, and the Metairie Ridge closed it on the north side. Heavy rains and river flooding could fill this ill-drained area, creating a breeding ground for disease-carrying mosquitoes and an impediment to urban growth. Since the ridge was lower than the natural levee, high water found an outlet to the lake via Bayou St. John. This watercourse served as the critical link in the colonial-era portage by shortening the distance canoes had to be dragged across land. It was also a prominent feature in later transportation and drainage efforts, as were other bayous (which offered routes for colonial-era smugglers) and their natural levees (which provided solid footing for an invading British army). Artificial levees built on the crest of the river's natural levee beginning in the eighteenth century and, much later, along the lakefront have secured the city against regular flooding but accentuated the bowl-like features and make drainage a bigger challenge today than in the past. Intense thunderstorms and hurricane-spawned rain have replaced the river as the greatest threats to the city in a saucer.

Lakeward of the Metairie and Gentilly ridges was a low-lying area of cypress swamp that graded into a grassy marsh. Soils made of fine-grained river sediments and decaying plant material have accumulated from 5 to 20 feet in thickness.[8] While these soils have a tendency to subside under their own weight, regular rejuvenation of sediments by floodwaters and ample moisture in the ground kept these soils above sea level before urbanization. Initial settlement avoided these zones in favor of the more solid natural levees and the Metairie and Gentilly ridges. As the city grew, developers using massive drainage schemes and levees transformed these wetlands into suburbs. Much of the mayor's critical remarks about the founders' poor site selection related to problems encountered in draining and maintaining these former wetlands. None of New Orleans's site was above the level of river floods, and much of it barely deserved to be called land. With drainage and encirclement by levees, the peaty soils compressed, and without the regular delivery of fresh sediment by flooding, these areas have subsided. Much of New Orleans that was drained for residential development is now below sea level and continues to subside, further exacerbating the city's drainage problem. Manipulating the site to accommodate a great city has been and continues to be a centerpiece of the New Orleans story. The decline of New Orleans as a major American city has paralleled it physical subsidence.

In addition to the low-lying site, New Orleans faces an additional situational challenge. The very river that created the site is a monstrous entity that drains a vast portion of the interior United States. While other cities have occupied wetlands, few have the combination of poorly drained and flood-susceptible territory of New Orleans. Portions of Washington, D.C., occupied wetlands, but there was ample solid ground above the reach of the Potomac's worst floods. Chicago's founders platted their city on a wetland site, but the sluggish Chicago River did not drain the massive territory of the Mississippi. Unlike any other riverfront city, as New Orleans grew, it expanded not toward higher elevations but onto lower ground surrounded by levees. This circumstance was made even more critical by the city's being situated near the outfall of the continent's largest natural drainage system. Spring snow melts combined with frontal rainstorms throughout the Ohio and Missouri basins could induce river stages that exceeded the capacity of a municipally funded flood protection system. The continental scale of the river's drainage basin made flood control more than a local issue, and leaders have had to battle constantly to secure federal assistance to deal with the flood hazard.[9]

Situational interpretations present cities as part of larger global political and economic systems. William Cronon's magnificent *Nature's Metropolis*, for example, opened with the nineteenth-century boosters' proclamations that Chicago had natural advantages inherent in its location. Entrepreneurs translated those advantages into a domination over nature across vast agricultural and resource hinterlands.[10] While local businessmen proclaimed similar advantages for New Orleans, this account will steer away from large-scale political and economic concerns and focus instead on the *site* and human efforts to transform it into an urban place. After all, without a viable site, no gateway could have developed. This volume will explore the fundamental struggle to make a habitable city, to transform the flood-prone, ill-drained, mosquito-infested site into a metropolis. To use Matthew Gandy's term, it will examine "reworking nature."[11] Certainly, regional, national, and international markets and New Orleans's economic hinterland were vital elements in the city's development.[12] Additionally, external concepts of engineering, public health, urban planning, and resource management affected practices in the Crescent City, as did national environmental laws that intruded on the lower delta. This volume will examine how these external influences affected New Orleans's efforts to remake its site. Such mundane concerns as rainfall, spring floods, sewerage, garbage, insects, shade, and hurricanes have also been of fundamental significance in building the city. In reshaping the city to deal with a troublesome nature, there has been a continuous effort to squeeze obviously undesirable aspects of nature out of the setting. Lewis Mumford has suggested that cities displace nature, and Henry Lawrence has written that cities stand as the antithesis of nature.[13] Activity to transform New Orleans has reflected the urge to remove nature. New Orleans has so thoroughly reworked its original setting through forest removal and drainage that one could call it the "unnatural city"—although it never completely escaped nature. The city's efforts to manage nature, as well as global politics and economic influences, have shaped the city's internal geography and the resulting urban landscapes.

It is the historical geography of New Orleans that I want to explore here, the geographic evolution of the Crescent City. Obviously it is difficult to cut a city out from its setting while still claiming to examine its relationship to the larger environment. Therefore this account will focus on the city itself but also draw in adjacent suburban parishes and critical environments that have close connections with the city. Jefferson Parish, in particular, has absorbed much of the expansion of the central city. Lake Pontchartrain, an essential influence on the city, will be included, as will various tracts of swamp and marsh that became part of a late-twentieth-century effort to reclaim nature. Of course, the entire Mississippi River basin also plays a role. The territory treated here will be more than Orleans Parish, but less than the Isle of Orleans (bounded by Bayou Manchac, Lake Maurepas, and Lake Pontchartrain on the north; the Mississippi River on the south and west; and the Gulf of Mexico on the east).

The city comprises multiple components: streets and structures, people and businesses constitute the superficial urban expression. Geographers have considered the cultural significance of street patterns and the built environment.[14] They have analyzed the evolving pattern of commercial development, industrial location, and residential expansion.[15] Additionally, they have considered periods of urban expansion driven by advances in transportation systems.[16] But typically the central concern is with the human overlay on the site—the pattern of economic systems and infrastructure. Nonetheless, manipulation of the earth's surface is an essential precursor to the construction of roads and buildings. In addition, human modifications inevitably have both direct and indirect impacts on the environment. Urban heat islands stir up increased precipitation, paved surfaces and buildings divert rainfall into surface runoff, waste disposal sites contribute to groundwater contamination, and urban sprawl consumes open space, expanding the urban heat island. Further, the weight of buildings on top of alluvial soils causes subsidence, deterring some construction. It is these intimate interactions between human society and the urban setting that I hope to examine. And New Orleans, the unnatural metropolis, with its unlikely and inappropriate site, will provide the focus.

NATURE IN THE CITY

For many years geographers have sought to explain city-building as an economic process. In doing so, they largely excluded any mention of the environment. Models of urban growth presented urban sites as "isotropic plains" with no topographic or hydrologic irregularities. Land values decreased away from the city center, causing land uses to assume concentric rings of decreasing intensity. Residential patterns developed similar arrangements, with rings arranged by outwardly increasing income levels. The models acknowledged that a coastal or lakefront city would have only partial circles, but they dismissed the physical setting.[17]

The economic depictions could not account for the irregular distribution of clay pits or quarries essential for extracting raw materials used in city building. They did not factor in the expense of creating new land where there was none by dumping waste into the ocean, lakes, and rivers to build sites for urban expansion. They offered no consideration of amenities such as favorable winds, scenic vistas, or parks that distorted the concentric rings.

Furthermore, they ignored the spatial patterns of flood risks and noxious industrial emissions. Some assumed that such irregularities were deviations that did not alter the models' overall clarity. But in fact the deviations were fundamental parts of the urban pattern, and their particular arrangement distorted the models' regularity.

Economic explanations of urbanization, while powerful, deny some of the very real problems faced by city builders at the municipal, corporate, and individual level. In particular, they do not factor in the costs borne by the city and its private and corporate citizens to make a site suitable for economic development and, conversely, how they contend with urbanization's environmental impacts. How does a municipality gain control of its territory through its infrastructure—the roads and other public utilities—and preserve open space for parks? How do these efforts affect land values? How do cities regulate the placement of undesirable activities? How do manufacturers modify sites to make them viable to their trade? How do individual landowners contribute to a city's size and its vegetative cover? Certainly economic factors drive many site selection choices, but reworking property to suit other needs and desires sometimes defies neat land-rent models. The city that results from the interplay between actors on the urban stage and environmental considerations is highly complex.[18] Recognition of this fact led to more sophisticated models that suggested development occurred along major arteries, which in turn produced sectors rather than circles, and subsequent models that identified nucleated land uses were attuned to various transportation and economic influences. These models, like their predecessors, attempted to portray cities as they *were,* not how they *became.* In effect, they presented static cities and neglected the multiple stages and phases of urban evolution. They failed to consider how cities directed development through environmental modifications. While perhaps more attuned to reality, the second generation models also largely ignored how the physical features of the city dramatically altered the pace of growth or prompted certain land uses. By considering the temporal nature of urban growth, James Vance's urban realms model accommodated the physical geography of the city more than prior models.[19] But like others, it failed to incorporate land-use adjustments made by property owners in order to conform to environmental regulations.

A contrasting approach has been to look at the city as an ecological system. The emphasis of those who follow this tack is on urban air, land, and water quality, along with the survival of urban wildlife and forests.[20] Humans are considered invading species that disturb, disrupt, and often degrade vulnerable systems. Roads and buildings become "impermeable cover," not the urban fabric woven by decades of human endeavor. The human-environment approach focuses on the "transactions" between human society and the environment.[21] Humans cope with hazards or they exploit resources. In either scenario, human efforts to contend with the environment are the focus of this type of investigation. The resulting landscape is one of "risk surfaces," waste sinks, and zones of resource extraction.[22] While the human-environment approach places much greater emphasis on the human role in urban environments, like the ecological approach, it does not deal effectively with the broader topic of landscapes as spaces created and inhabited by people.

Environmental historians have begun the task of looking at cities as places where humans affect the environment. In the work of these historians, the environment is typically one actor in a complex cast. Much of their work has emphasized the infrastructure, which provides essential services such as water delivery and sewerage and garbage removal.[23] This fine scholarship brings to light important technological and political issues that influence environmental modification and, in many cases, emphasizes those aspects over the environmental relations society has with urban places. Historians have also begun the work of examining questions of environmental equity as a part of human-environmental interactions in cities.[24] The expanding emphasis on urban environments can also be found in multiauthor collections that portray the range of complex issues in urban environments.[25]

From a geographer's perspective the role of the environment is fundamental.[26] Gandy has argued for the essential role of nature in New York City's development, using the city's reach into its expansive watershed and the influence of Central Park on land values to demonstrate his point.[27] This viewpoint has been made evident in several contexts. Considering metropolitan-scale activity, geographers have noted the relationship between high-income neighborhoods and elevation and the relationship between natural resources extracted to build the city and waste disposal.[28] Public health issues have also shaped urban development. Shifting theories of medicine—from the environment as the source of illness to bacteriology—altered how urban authorities managed urban environments, and this in turn directed the social and economic patterns of the city.[29] In the twentieth century, the development of the basic infrastructure was a key force in shaping urban growth.[30] While geographic interpretations may emphasize the significance of human-environment interactions in molding land use or medical geographies, the fact that humans cannot operate outside of the environment is a cornerstone to their approach.

This volume will start and conclude with the environmental circumstances that city builders faced. Economics and politics certainly matter, but they will not be the central reference points. This work will also consider the human-environment transactions as key processes in shaping an elaborate lived-in urban landscape. I will structure the chapters chronologically, always considering how society's view of nature and its technical capabilities to manipulate and manage nature affected urbanization in each time period. *Nature,* of course, is a word fraught with complex meanings. If we think of nature as conditions untouched by humans, then there might be no corner of the globe that deserves the title "natural."[31] Even wilderness preserves are modified by their designation as "wilderness," to say nothing of the other types of historical and prehistoric modifications they have endured.[32] In cities, the most humanized landscapes, nature still exists—and not just in parks. Cold Canadian air masses sweep across the continent delivering clean air to urban areas, and snow melting in the Rocky Mountains sends water past the cities lining the Mississippi River. These natural systems, while not so obviously visible as a forest, still directly affect cities, and urbanized areas do little to disrupt these massive natural systems.

At the local level, Native Americans and colonial settlers had modified the site of New Orleans by 1803, when this account begins. Midden heaps had created viable settlement sites, and regular use of the well-worn portage between the river and Bayou St. John made the site strategic before Europeans first set foot on the natural levee.[33] The French and Spanish initiated the never-ending chore of levee building and digging drainage canals to the rear of the site.[34] They had begun the process of manipulating the non-human environment. Yet even at the local level, elements of nature persisted in the city. The combination of warm temperatures and moisture from the Gulf of Mexico resulted in frequent rain. Wetlands harbored disease-bearing insects. Gravity constantly pulled at the alluvial sediments underlying the city, causing a slow settling. The low-lying position of the city kept the water table near street level, affecting building and burial practices. Nature never fully disappeared from the city. Urban residents meagerly tried to resist the more obvious undesirable aspects of nature by manipulating the site.

Human effort to manage the environment has been a vitally important dimension in shaping New Orleans's landscape, and the landscape is the visible record of human transactions with the environment. The mighty levees encircling the city serve one fundamental purpose: flood protection, from both high river stages and hurricane-driven storm surges from the lake. The numerous canals that dissect the city bespeak the longstanding need for drainage. Shaded boulevards and lush parks reflect various programs that sought environmental solutions to social ills. Massive landfills and derelict incinerators testify to the gargantuan challenge posed by the city's refuse. Protected marshes and swamplands mark fundamental shifts in attitudes toward nature and the public policy adjustments that accompanied them. The landscape created by humans in New Orleans is the social response to concerns with environmental conditions.

People live in and constantly rework this landscape. Consequently the human dimension is also a fundamental part of this story. Access to amenities as basic as water and sewerage has not been even in this racially complex city. Questions of environmental equity have found answers that are sometimes unpleasant but nonetheless have played a part in shaping New Orleans's landscape. From recreational facilities to flood protection, environmental equity emerges as a concern. Whether a function of racism or white privilege,[35] the presence of landfills and toxic chemical manufacturers in African American neighborhoods is a fact of life in New Orleans. Additionally, suburbanization during the 1960s and 1970s fractured the urban area along racial lines and created different environmental concerns for suburbanites and city-center dwellers.

REMAKING NEW ORLEANS

At the outset, I will consider how society dealt with hazards presented by the environment. Nineteenth-century assessments and reassessments of conditions that threatened the city—namely, floods and miasmas—chronicle both the identification of hazards and the creation of plans to minimize them. Instituting a defense against floods and miasmas involves a selection of techniques within the available technologies and within the cost a society is willing to pay. It also requires a social commitment, in the form of policy at some level, to create a mechanism to finance, build, and maintain the bulwarks. Choices are shaped by what decision makers view as hazards at the time and the control options available. Concepts embraced by engineers and physicians directly influenced the choices made in nineteenth-century New Orleans. Notions of environmental health promoted forest removal and swamp drainage around the city; and expectations that a river confined between levees would scour its channel deeper encouraged the use of levees as the exclusive means to control floods.

Loss of environmental quality, or desired resources, gave rise to policy reformulations to manage the most dominant threats to desirable conditions. As geographers Jacque Emel and Elizabeth Brooks tell us, the diminishment of natural resources, in this case clean air and water, leads to policy adjustments.[36] In this country, policy typically proceeds from an unregulated, common-law approach in which individuals file suits to seek compensation for some damage to their personal property or government actions attempt to protect the public good. Once society recognizes a resource scarcity, it creates a specific statutory definition and administrative controls. In New Orleans, with increasing population and industry, clean air and water quickly became imperiled resources. The city took steps to define particular activities as nuisances, to regulate the location of industrial activity, to prescribe proper places for burial grounds, and to issue regulations regarding garbage and water services. In doing so, the municipal government took steps to preserve environmental quality within the scope of social expectations at the time. Specifying certain land uses as nuisances and regulating them had direct environmental consequences. Steps to provide urban amenities such as clean drinking water and parks also furthered the imposition of the urban will on nature. Where the city was unable to meet the expectations of providing a suitable environment, the social elite took flight from the city to their rural summer retreats.

Early-nineteenth-century projects to manage environmental conditions in New Orleans were piecemeal, fragmented efforts that did not even attempt to deal with the entire city. In the late nineteenth century, a fundamental shift in public health concepts based on the germ theory of disease along with an emerging engineering profession and political reform movements that sought to deal with problems on a citywide basis led to a new era of environmental transformation. Investment in new, costly infrastructure accomplished many of the objectives of failed prior attempts. In particular, new sewerage, drainage, and water systems delivered numerous improvements to the city as a whole. However, as historian Martin Melosi tells us, once a particular approach is chosen, "path dependence" results, and the infrastructure employed continues to be used beyond its functional obsolescence.[37] Thus choices made in the early twentieth century still confront public works officials in New Orleans today and contribute to the mayor's complaints about the city's site. Those choices not only influence current decisions but limit the options available to renew the old systems. Thus, in turn, environmental conditions are also affected in areas still served by the last century's infrastructure.

Extension of the urban infrastructure and environmental improvements under the principles of rational engineering should have been consistent across the cityscape. But in fact, racial and economic attitudes deflected the even extension of services. Inequities in environmental conditions resulted, and some remain, contributing to charges of environmental inequity.

Following World War II, urban residents participated in an unprecedented expansion of the nation's cities. Residents moving to the urban fringes brought with them desires for environmental amenities, and a coalescing ecological consciousness shaped their expectations. In search of bucolic settings and armed with new technologies, suburbanites contributed to a major overhaul of the urban environment. The physical expansion, accommodated by personal automobile transportation, altered the scale and form of the city, intruding on vast wetlands around New Orleans—many of which were unsuited to suburban construction techniques.

During the 1950s and 1960s, as metropolitan sprawl was in full swing, a shifting emphasis in public policy followed scientific and public concern with environmental quality—in the modern sense of the term. Within the city, demographic change produced new environmental relationships— some decidedly unfair to minority residents who were unable to escape undesirable conditions at landfills that became hazardous waste sites. The "hazardous" label attached a long-lasting stigma on places, unlike the older nuisance designation. That stigma radiated outward and affected entire neighborhoods, creating landscapes of tragedy.[38] In addition, the entire city faced revelations about its public water supply that recast drinking water from an occasionally foul-tasting liquid into a toxic brew. As part of a broader social questioning of the hubris of massive engineered solutions to environmental problems, Louisiana and New Orleans had to rethink the safety of consuming the effluent coming from cities and factories through-out the Mississippi basin. Policy and public actions responded to the threat posed by upstream industries by restricting what they could discharge and by seeking an alternate potable water supply.

Suburbanization itself contributed to a new set of environmental rela-tions. In Jefferson Parish and east New Orleans, drainage of former wetlands produced problems with subsidence and flooding. By hemming itself in with levees, the urban area became a giant catchment basin for heavy rains produced by summer storms or hurricanes. The city has continually struggled to deal with excess water since a spate of heavy rains began in the 1970s. De-pendence on structural flood protection methods has deterred the adoption of federally mandated land-use solutions.

New Orleans, after nearly three centuries of trying to exclude nature, now has rediscovered its environment—in the form of swamps and marshes. With rising federal efforts to preserve wetlands, local concerns with eroding coastal marshes, and heightened appreciation for untouched nature, several steps being taken in the New Orleans area demonstrate a desire to bring the swamp back into the city. A zoo exhibit devoted to local swamp life spurred local rediscovery of a vanished part of the local urban site. Subsequent cre-ation of both a national park unit and a wildlife refuge consisting of wet-lands within the urban territory exemplify this urge. In a more commercial vein, the growth of swamp tourism allows New Orleans to trade on its nat-ural history.

ENVIRONMENT AND GEOGRAPHY

While there is new interest in the environment surrounding New Orleans, nature still presents complex challenges at a more rudimentary level. The same conditions that inspired early drainage systems still exist and remain a focus of New Orleans's infrastructure development. Without huge invest-ments in drainage and pest control, the city would not exist as it does today. Furthermore, real concern exists about the threat of a hurricane pushing the contents of Lake Pontchartrain over the levees surrounding the city. The environmental context is rooted deep in the city's physical geography and history and is as critical today as it was three centuries ago. Indeed, human transactions with the environment have been as powerful an influence as any other factor in shaping the Crescent City's unique landscape. In New Orleans, and other cities, the environment matters. Without understanding the human response to nature's challenges, our understanding of urban growth is only fragmentary.

New Orleans, through massive environmental transformations along with fundamental shifts in public attitude toward nature, has been able to reverse the public perception of its local geography. Once viewed as an unhealthy place that local residents sought to flee in the summer, it now is an attraction for hordes of tourists. The nineteenth-century open sewers carried filth and disease, while the swamps generated miasmas that ravaged the unacclimated. Manipulation of nature altered these conditions and public perceptions of them. Summer heat and humidity may deter some visitors today, but the wide boulevards, that once were sewage ditches, and nearby moss-covered cypress swamps now appeal to visitors. The current geography of New Orleans has been thoroughly shaped by the city's long-term relationship with its environment.

CHAPTER 1

WATER HAZARDS

THE MISSISSIPPI RIVER surges around the sweeping crescent that gives New Orleans its nickname and into a sharp bend at the foot of Jackson Square. Even at low stage, the river's width is considerable in comparison with European waterways that were known to colonial explorers and settlers. When the river rises above its banks, its size becomes even more impressive. In the early eighteenth century, floodwaters could spread out over several miles on either side of the mighty stream, destroying spring crops and ruining homes. The floods of the lower Mississippi were destructive by shallow immersion, not due to a torrential current. A thin veneer of water could spread over the countryside, stand on the fields for several months, and drown young plants. Floodwaters also crept into houses, softening their foundations, transformed firm roadways into quagmires, and interrupted urban life for extended periods of time. French colonial leaders recognized these hazards, and they debated the viability of the site that became New Orleans before reluctantly deciding to plant the capital there.[1]

The geography of flood hazards is not the same in all locations, and the topography of New Orleans was, in many respects, the reverse of what settlers were accustomed to. Rather than a broad concave valley with safely elevated settlement sites on land that rose with greater distance from the waterway, the Mississippi delta was a nearly level surface, with subtle but significant topographic undulations. The river built the land with its frequent inundations, and thus New Orleans's original plan occupied a tract subject to regular flooding. The high ground was not set back from the river but consisted of only the relatively narrow natural levee. The crests of the high ground stood only about 12 feet above sea level. The *batture*, or actual river bank, dipped into the waterway, while the back side of the natural levee followed an invisibly gentle gradient in the other direction. Most of the city naturally drains away from the river. Less danger existed atop the elevated and better-drained natural levee (Fig. 1.1), where French settlers built New Orleans and where most of the city stood in 1800. Although subject to seasonal inundation, the ridge that paralleled the river was the last land to go under water and the first to emerge from receding floods. Indeed most flooding occurred when crevasses, or breaches in the natural levee and later the artificial levees, allowed water to break through the higher terrain and flow directly to the low ground farther from the river.

Areas to the rear, or away from the natural levees, remained under water longer and formed the cypress swamps draped with Spanish moss. These dark, foreboding wetlands harbored not only alligators and clouds of mosquitoes but the mysterious and dreaded miasmas. In the minds of nineteenth-century residents, the swamp and its pestilential emissions posed as much of a hazard as the river to those dwelling in New Orleans. Efforts to control flooding concurrently sought to eliminate the backswamps as a source of disease. William Darby's 1817 geography of Louisiana stated: "It must be observed, that there are two evils, arising from surplus water, to be remedied on the Mississippi; one, the incumbent waters in the river; the other the reflux from the swamps. It is in most instances very difficult to remove one inconvenience, without producing the opposite." [2] Floodwaters contributed to the moist conditions of the backswamp, and thus the two threats were thoroughly mixed. Efforts to control one, as Darby pointed out, often exacerbated the other.

Geographers portray the realm of human-environment interaction as a two-sided process. Relations with positive outcomes define *resources*, while negative results constitute *hazards*. The river and backswamps in and around

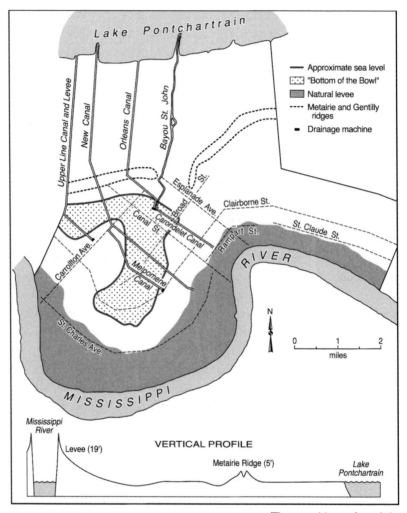

FIG. 1.1. TOPOGRAPHY OF NEW ORLEANS, CA. 1900. The natural levees formed the best-drained and highest ground, while the Metairie and Gentilly ridges provided secondary bands of high ground. The natural levee sloped from the river to a flood-prone area below sea level, riverward of the Metairie Ridge. From the narrow ridge, land sloped to sea level and Lake Pontchartrain.

nineteenth-century New Orleans represent both sides of this connection, and thus the human-environment perspective is useful for beginning our discussion. As resources, the river served as a vital communication link, and the swamps provided durable cypress timber. At the same time, the waterway and the wetlands posed undeniable hazards to lower river valley residents. This chapter will examine the hazards side of the human-environment relationship. Dealing with hazards involved appraising them, creating plans to contend with them, implementing these plans, and then maintaining the means used to defend against unwanted environmental conditions. Preparing for and responding to water hazards were powerful influences in shaping the largest city on the lower Mississippi. While flood and environmental disease were only two of many hazards, they were perhaps the most frequently discussed and also prompted the most sweeping transformations of New Orleans's environs. These manipulations were the measure of transactions between humans and nature.[3]

CONFINING THE RIVER

By 1800 the two prominent hazards at New Orleans had elicited significant human response. The French reaction to floods was to erect levees (from the French word *lever*, "to raise"), ridges of soil heaped up along the natural high ground to hold back high waters. In the urban setting, where the concentration of people and public buildings was greatest, the corporate sponsor, the Company of the Indies, initially took on the levee-building responsibility. In other words, the initial protection device was a public project and not financed by private landowners. By 1727 a bulwark 4 feet high stretched about a mile along the waterfront, on top of the natural levee. However, isolated stretches of levees did not keep high water from finding its way to the backswamps upstream or downstream from the protected territory. Since the natural levee sloped back from the river over 10 feet to the city's low point, high water that escaped the river upstream from the city could rise from the back side. Consequently New Orleans continued to endure backswamp flooding on a regular basis, and occasionally floods would crest the 4-foot mound along the waterfront. Company of the Indies officials understood the settlement's topographic situation and constructed a pair of levees perpendicular to the river that extended toward the backswamp. Another levee, along the current route of Rampart Street and roughly parallel with the riverfront bulwark, tied the levees together and completed the enclosure. This first levee system enclosed a mere forty-four square block area. Although it fended off most high water, the most formidable levee in the valley collapsed before the 1735 flood, and the city suffered extensive damage.[4] Despite such failures, efforts to protect the colonial capital remained a centralized function. Through the Spanish rule of the Louisiana colony, public funds underwrote the urban levee system's maintenance.[5] This underscores the obvious importance of the city to the colony and exhibits the public, as opposed to private, responsibility for shielding the urban population and property from floods. This practice set the city apart from the rural country-side in terms of both policy and protection.

Coordination with its expanding agricultural hinterland was necessary to effect a viable flood protection barrier for New Orleans. To guard the growing agricultural district and link rural levees with the urban bulwark, colonial laws enacted in 1728 and in 1743 required individual landowners to build levees—a type of labor requirement that did not exist in the city.[6] In effect, the second thrust of urban environmental change was the requirement that rural property owners build their own levees that would contribute to New Orleans's protection. The city's economic success depended on a thriving agricultural hinterland, and without adequate flood protection neither city nor hinterland could survive. The French long-lot, or arpent, survey system arranged individual holdings in narrow parcels of land stretching back some distance from the river and suited the private levee-building requirement well. Individual grants typically ranged from 2 to 8 arpents (384 to 1,536 feet) in width and were usually 40 arpents (7,680 feet) deep. Proprietors were thus responsible for constructing levees along their property's short axis. By dispensing grants in contiguous parcels, French authorities sought to encourage a continuous line of levees fronting the agricultural "coast," but this goal was never realized. Levee construction became a sizable investment for landowners and was only feasible for wealthy planters using slave labor. Consequently, most small landholders were unable to complete their protective structures. Although even wealthy planters may have been reluctant to make such a large investment, the threat of confiscation for failure to comply motivated most to participate—to some extent. When Spain took over the colony in 1768, the Spanish government seized on the precedent established by the French, continuing to encourage contiguous settlement and also requiring landowners to construct protective barriers against floods.[7]

Despite a sound policy, privately built structures were notoriously inconsistent in design and effectiveness, and floods continued to breach these ever-lengthening earthen embankments. Nonetheless, levees stretched along about 50 miles of riverfront above New Orleans by 1763.[8] The leveed

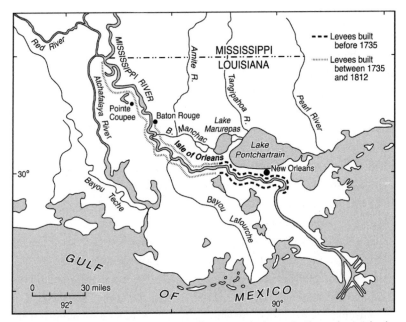

FIG. 1.2. LEVEE DEVELOPMENT TO 1812. Levees stretched several miles up the river by the mid-eighteenth century and nearly to the mouth of the Red River by the early 1800s. After Albert E. Cowdrey, *Land's End: A History of the New Orleans District, U.S. Army Corps of Engineers, and Its Lifelong Battle with the Lower Mississippi and Other Rivers Wending Their Way to Sea* (New Orleans: U.S. Army Corps of Engineers, 1977).

territory served as the productive agricultural base for the port of New Orleans, while the unprotected territory remained subject to inundation. When the new U.S. territory of Louisiana passed its first levee law in 1807, it assigned authority for maintaining levees to the parishes, which in turn held rural landowners accountable—perpetuating traditional landowner responsibility.[9] When Louisiana became a state in 1812, levees paralleled the Mississippi River from almost as far as the mouth of the Red River to below New Orleans on the west bank and from the bluff at Baton Rouge to below New Orleans on the east bank (Fig. 1.2).[10] But without an overarching design and in the absence of a central flood protection authority, levees continued to present a piecemeal barrier and offered only erratic effectiveness.

New Orleans, by contrast, continued to maintain its municipal levees after it became a U.S. possession. To fund this ongoing project, it taxed watercraft tied up along its waterfront. In 1805 the *Conseil de Ville* issued a resolution that read: "considering that the levees are being constantly damaged by the ships, lighters, boats, etc. that land and stay in the port of the city, and that it is quite justifiable to make them contribute to the expenses occasioned by the considerable damages they cause daily and whose repair has been, up to the public chest."[11]

This resolution replaced a preexisting anchorage assessment with a levee tax that set up a fee schedule and assigned an individual to collect the taxes. Owners of vessels weighing more than 100 tons paid up to $40, while owners of craft weighing less than 100 tons paid $12. Flatboats, keel boats, and rafts of timber were charged from $3 to $6 for the privilege of tying up alongside the city's levee. In 1819, the city collected over $12,000 for levee maintenance with this tax.[12] Thus the city passed a share of the cost of maintaining its desperately needed levees on to transient shippers while maintaining local control of construction and maintenance. Indeed, when the U.S. Congress questioned New Orleans's authority to collect a tax on what was considered federal property, the city council sent a strong resolution to Washington claiming that "it is an established fact that the Port of New Orleans would not exist, that the whole city would soon be submerged if the waters of the Mississippi were not confined by levees." It concluded with the assertion that "the existence of this tax is therefore indispensable for the maintenance of the Port of New Orleans."[13]

It was apparent by the early 1800s that levees, while essential, did not eliminate the flood hazard. One reason for their ineffectiveness was that levees displaced high water into unprotected territory. As New Orleans raised barriers along its waterfront, the need for levees outside the city increased. Flood protection in one location redirected risk to open floodplains elsewhere. By necessity, levee building proceeded up and down the river and along both banks. The priority of protecting the city propelled similar action in the countryside.

William Darby pointed out a second reason for the levees' limited effectiveness in his 1817 geography: "The confined body of water increased in height."[14] As the width of the floodplain available to the river was restricted, the same volume of water reached higher stages. In other words, the levees raised the flood level. As levee construction extended along more and more of the banks, the area open to high water decreased, further heightening the flood stages. Consequently, society on the lower river faced a continual struggle to raise the levees in order to offset the higher flood stages they created. The prevailing policy exacerbated the growing flooding problem and may have contributed to the massive flood of 1785, which inundated New Orleans and much of the lower valley.[15] By the early nineteenth century, the 4-foot levees fronting New Orleans had been raised to about 6 feet to compensate for the rising flood stages.[16] The city surveyor oversaw this effort and used chain-gang labor to maintain the protective barrier.[17] Levees remained the only realistic option. Under a policy that called for localized (city or individual plantation) flood protection, there could be no coordinated regional planning. Neither state nor federal governments were ready to step in at the time. Although people along the river understood the implications of levee building, no one had the wherewithal to do anything more than heap up a mound of dirt in between their property and the river and hope for the best.

Even as protective devices displaced some of the risk, the rising crests continued to threaten New Orleans. After a pair of urban inundations in the late Spanish occupation (1791 and 1799), sizable floods occurred in rapid succession during the early American period. High water in the lower valley threatened the piecemeal levee system in 1809, 1811, 1813, 1815, 1816, and 1817. During that spell of successive floods, the New Orleans city council passed an ordinance that made individual landowners responsible for building and maintaining levees within the "liberties" of New Orleans—or the urban fringe. Much like the territorial law of 1807, the municipal ordinance called on proprietors to construct levees at least one foot higher than the "highest swell." By doing so, it sought to enforce a more consistent level of protection and placed the cost on those living outside the more densely built-up urban territory. To ensure compliance, the ordinance empowered the mayor to have the work inspected and to order contractors to complete any unsatisfactory sections at the owner's expense.[18] This ordinance shifted a portion of the city's burden to those who lived within Orleans Parish but beyond the city limits. Like the territorial laws that applied to other parishes, it functioned to protect the city.

Despite great efforts to create impenetrable barriers, contemporary accounts highlight obvious failings of the antebellum levees. Henry Brackenridge, who visited the city in the early years of statehood, provided some of the most extensive descriptions of the levees as they existed at that time. He noted that landowners set them back from the river about 30 to 40 yards—seeking to prevent undercutting by the meandering river, while not sacrificing too much agricultural land. The preferred construction material was a stiff clay, which provided a more effective waterproof barrier. Once the 4- to 6-foot-high levees were in place, builders added sod to prevent erosion and cypress slabs to the inside to prevent leakage through the levees during high water. Drainage ditches had to be dug to move away any water that did seep through. Nonetheless, weaknesses existed, and Brackenridge pointed out crawfish holes as one serious problem.[19] Building levees entailed an enormous initial expense to landowners, but perhaps the greatest challenge was long-term maintenance. Erosion due to waves and current, slumping and subsidence of poorly built sections, and damage by wildlife made the chore of maintaining levees perpetual for both public and private builders.

Dispersing responsibilities to rural landowners did not keep the city dry, however. The 1816 flood broke through the levee at Carrollton, an upstream suburb, and inundated much of the New Orleans's rear quarters for nearly a month.[20] Writing about the variable quality of the levees, Edward Fenner confidently commented on the city-maintained section: "So firm and compact is the levee on the river bank before the city, that it is almost impossible for it to give way."[21] Weaker sections upriver, maintained by individuals, did fail, and water entered the city from the rear. Floodwaters rose three blocks into the French Quarter, as high as Dauphine Street, and reportedly inundated the lower parts of both the Marigny and St. Mary faubourgs, plus the Tremé, Gravier, and St. John neighborhoods. Apparently, the old enclosure levee had not been maintained, and private levee-building efforts gave urban residents a false sense of security from backswamp flooding. Fenner's report on the 1816 flood focused on the impact caused by water rising from the city's rear and stated that "inundation has driven many poor families from their homes; and should not those in affluent circumstances come to the aid of their less fortunate fellow citizens, great indeed, we fear, will be the distress of the latter, from poverty, famine, and perhaps pestilence."[22] Only by carving a channel through a shell embankment along the lakefront and permitting the trapped floodwater to flow into Lake Pontchartrain were citizens able to expel the floodwaters. After about a month, the city finally emerged from the standing water.[23] Planters suffered some losses due to levee failure, but the urban poor endured the most extensive privations due to the failure of private landowners to adequately protect the floodplain.

"Backdoor" floods prompted no fundamental change in the city's hazard management policy, and it was not long before the city's levees failed again.

In April 1823 high water on the Mississippi, augmented by extreme floods on the Red River, began to break through the agricultural levees upstream. Water remained high through July, and the saturated levees began to give way, producing extensive flooding throughout the rear, low-income sections of New Orleans.[24] Another massive flood, the greatest since the 1785 event, caused extensive damage throughout the valley in 1828. The crest reached 15.2 feet at the Carrollton gauge, threatening the city once again, although never breaking through.[25] Human barriers were flimsy protection from the mighty river's excesses, and weaknesses in the rural levees could work to New Orleans's advantage. If the levees broke on the opposite bank or sufficiently distant from the city, pressure on the New Orleans levees subsided. So although urban residents expected rural landowners to complete the flood barrier, weak links in that chain of protection were tolerated—in part because the city could not legally compel planters to do their bidding and because it was advantageous to the city.

During a period of relative flood security in New Orleans, political fragmentation within the city prompted the creation of three separate municipalities with one mayor. Beginning in 1836, each municipality had responsibility for maintaining its own levees, and the respective municipal surveyors tended the levees along the urbanized waterfront. Since the three municipalities differed greatly in terms of their tax base, levee maintenance was uneven.[26] In the midst of this flood hiatus, the politically influential planters and New Orleans politicians were able to defer some of the levee construction costs to the state. In the mid-1840s, Louisiana created an office of the state engineer, who was to oversee public works construction and maintenance for the state. In particular, his responsibilities included clearing snags from navigable streams and improving the levee system. The imperfect levee system inherited by this office extended from below New Orleans to near the Atchafalaya River. Despite the existence of this massive construction, the state engineers began to question the viability of a continuous wall of levees and to challenge the de facto levees-only policy.

In 1846, P. O. Hebert, the state engineer, cautioned that New Orleans and the entire lower river were in "imminent danger of inundation" annually:

Every day, levees are extended higher and higher up the river—natural outlets closed—and every day the danger to the city of New Orleans and to all the lower country is increased. Who can calculate the loss by an overflow to the city of New Orleans alone? Instead, therefore, of throwing suddenly a larger quantity of water into the Lower Mississippi and elevating its level by opening cut-offs above, we should, on the contrary, endeavor to reduce this level, already too high and too dangerous, by opening all the outlets of the river. We are every year confining this immense river closer and closer to its own bed—forgetting that it is fed by over 1500 streams—and regardless of a danger becoming every year more and more impending.[27]

The following year, the engineer reemphasized his main point: "For local and temporary purposes, levees will answer, but as forming a general and permanent system, they are defective." Indeed, Hebert maintained that "in addition to a great and constant expense, the gradual elevation of the bed of the river is the inevitable consequence of confining its turbulent water between levees. This operation of course increases the danger of inundation."[28] And yet neither New Orleans nor the rural planters were willing to give up levees in favor of outlets. Outlets would mean huge expenses for the state, and it would expose plantations along the bayous used as floodways to damaging inundations. Both these factors precluded support for Hebert's plan. In practice, the poor state of the existing levees created a constant pull for the state engineer to attend one minor disaster after another, particularly in politically powerful districts, and negated any effective development or implementation of an outlet plan. The next severe flood dramatically fulfilled the state engineer's prophesy of imminent danger.

Despite firm barriers along its waterfront, the urban center of the lower river remained subject to backdoor flooding, as the 1849 Sauvé Crevasse proved. After two months of rising water during the spring, upstream crevasses began breaking through the saturated levees and the river reclaimed much rural floodplain. In early April, a crevasse on the west bank let water loose over a massive area extending from 18 miles above New Orleans to 45 miles downstream. Water rose to about 3 feet in the backswamps and to lesser heights on the natural levees. Typically a breach on the west bank would lessen the pressure on the east bank levees. Nonetheless, softened levees combined with the exceptional volume of water to produce a second break on the east bank 17 miles above New Orleans—the notorious Sauvé Crevasse (Fig. 1.3). The Sauvé levee was weak because during the previous year the landowners had rebuilt a portion farther back from the river's edge.

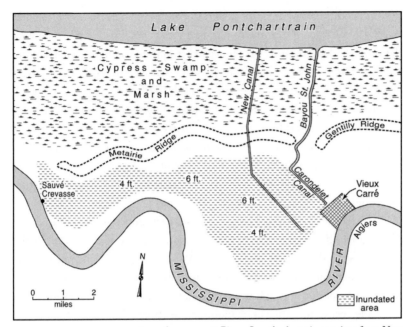

FIG. 1.3. FLOODED AREA, 1849. A crevasse at Pierre Sauvé's plantation upriver from New Orleans caused extensive urban flooding in 1849. Water flowed between the Metairie Ridge and the natural levee collecting in the "bottom of the bowl." The towpath along the Carondelet Canal served as a dam at the lower end of the flooded area. After George E. Waring, Jr., and George W. Cable, *History and Present Condition of New Orleans, Louisiana* (Washington: U.S. Department of the Interior, 1881).

Additionally, one expert thought it was too steep or had too narrow a base and therefore a less stable foundation. On May 3, this fragile link gave way, and within three hours there was a 30-foot-wide gap allowing water to pour over the floodplain. A natural spine of land that ran west to east across the floodplain, the Metairie Ridge, funneled the water directly into New Orleans's lowest portion (Fig. 1.3). Confined by the ridge to the north and the crescent-shaped natural levee on three sides, floodwater simply rose within this natural basin. Despite efforts to plug the gap, water continued to fill the bowl and reached Rampart Street (the rear of the French Quarter) by May 15 and continued rising into "the heart of the city" by the seventeenth. It proceeded an additional three blocks into the French Quarter by the end of the month, when it reached it peak. In the backswamp, water stood as high as 6 feet.[29]

Topography, in part, defined the social geography of New Orleans and, during floods, created inequity in terms of suffering. The highest ground at the Place d'Armes and in the wealthier districts remained above the inundation, but "the utmost distress prevailed among the poor" who lived in the lower sections that went under water first. Water surrounded over 200 square blocks of the city and about 2,000 tenements. This forced 12,000 residents, mostly poor, to vacate their homes or "live an aquatic life of much privation and suffering." [30] Most business and commerce ground to a halt, while older cemeteries were under water, displacing all burials to the new cemetery atop the Metairie Ridge. Overall, the most pronounced and prolonged suffering was concentrated in the low-income quarters, exacerbating preexisting inequities.

Initially the flood response concentrated on blocking the crevasse, but these futile efforts gave way to attempts to accelerate the drainage of the bowl between the natural levee and the Metairie Ridge. Workers tried cutting through the ridge to allow water to flow toward Lake Pontchartrain. Some water passed through these cuts, but excavating 2 to 4 feet for half a mile was costly, and officials abandoned the effort. Ultimately, the bulk of the water drained through existing outlets. Bayou St. John carried about one-third of the excess, while the New Canal handled the balance. The separate municipalities worked against each other in some cases, attempting to drain their high water onto the next community downstream. It was not until June 20 that a municipal engineer directed the closing of the crevasse, and with the water supply finally cut off, the city drained in a few days. Heavy rains that soon followed "washed off the terrible filth which for forty days had stood stagnant over street, yard, and tenement." While the city's levees held, its political fragmentation handicapped its response to the upstream levee break and exacerbated the flood's impact. [31]

While not disastrous in the sense of ripping houses off their foundations, the high water destroyed several bridges, interrupted business throughout the city, contributed to health problems, disrupted the lives of thousands, and caused extensive property damage throughout the city. Considering such consequences, city officials assessed future flood risks and concluded that the cost of erecting higher levees was worthwhile. Soon after the 1849 crevasse, the city once again raised its levee system. [32] In addition, the Second Municipality constructed a levee from the river to the Metairie Ridge to protect the rear of the city from a flood like the Sauvé Crevasse. Journalists, with questionable optimism, proclaimed that "a small sum of money,

28

judiciously expended on this work, will hem the city around with an impregnable barrier against the truant waters."[33] Indeed, the following year when water broke through the Sauvé levee again, the new traverse levee fended off backdoor flooding, adding to the false sense of security. By constructing the new levee, the city showed less confidence in the protection offered by plantation levees but still relied on rural owners to bear a portion of the flood protection costs. Within the city's politically fractured structure, piecemeal projects did not afford a consistent protective barrier for the entire urban territory.

A. D. Wooldridge, the new state engineer in 1850, questioned the total reliance on levees, saying, "I find myself forced to the conclusion that entire dependence on the leveeing system is not only unsafe for us, but I think will be destructive to those who shall come after us."[34] He criticized both the initial expense and the long-term costs required by repeated levee enlargements. From the 4-foot embankment in colonial New Orleans, the barrier system had risen to 15 feet in some places. The meandering river undercut levees on its outer banks, necessitating repairs and realignments. Wooldridge saw value in diverting some of the floods to the sea by way of outlets. He contended that both urban and rural dwellers had to recognize they had a "community of interest," although his was an urban perspective. Wooldridge also argued that the "dweller on the remote bayou" should be willing to "receive and convey" a portion of the floodwaters. Specifically, he suggested that the Atchafalaya River should be "the great natural drain of Southern Louisiana."[35]

Farmers and those in the swamps did not embrace the notion that they shared a community of interests with New Orleans residents. They did not subscribe to the concept that they should sacrifice their crops for the city's security. Wooldridge's suggestion began an ongoing debate over diverting floodwaters through the Atchafalaya Basin as a way to displace risks away from the city and plantations to a politically weak territory.[36] Wooldridge also argued that the best place for an outlet would be at the Bonnet Carré crevasse, about 35 miles upstream from New Orleans. This was the site of a naturally occurring crevasse and provided the shortest path between the river and Lake Pontchartrain.[37] Levees, nonetheless, remained the primary flood protection structure through the nineteenth century, although the preference for them did not mean the city sympathized with the bayou dwellers. They were merely the less costly of the two options, given the prior investment in them and the price of acquiring land for outlets. Levees were the status quo, and to modify the existing system would mean major manipulations of both public policy and the environment. Neither the city nor the state was up to that challenge.

The levee system had helped New Orleans become an exceptional city in the largely rural South by 1850. Its 116,000 citizens made it the fifth largest city in the country, far larger than its closest rival in Dixie. It had earned its entrepôt status by controlling the movement of cotton, rice, sugar, and other agricultural produce that flowed through its port. Consequently, its factors and bankers relied on the production of floodplain and upland farmers. This city was tied to its hinterland economically, and the problem of flooding created an equally important connection. Thus decisions to protect the agricultural holdings served the city as well as the countryside. When the federal government passed the Swamp Land Acts of 1849 and 1850, Louisiana was able to collect revenue from the sale of swamplands and apply it to levee improvements. In effect, this provided a federal subsidy for rural and urban residents alike.

An 1850 U.S. Senate report indicated that Louisiana had begun the process of selling former federal lands to improve its levee system. The fact that the federal government transferred the lands to the state reflected a realization that the federal government, and thus the country as a whole, stood to benefit from land reclamation on the lower Mississippi. The transfer also acknowledged, as New Orleans advocates had claimed for years, that the problem was much larger than Louisiana—it was as vast as the 1.2 million acres in the Mississippi River drainage basin. The first tracts alienated to private purchasers were those already protected by levees. The author of the Senate report noted that "the government has so far benefitted at the expense of the people of Louisiana, for none of these lands would have been disposed of had they not been reclaimed."[38] In effect, a levee system, built largely with private resources and erected initially to protect the primary city of the lower valley, benefitted the entire nation. This realization, pushed hard in later discussions about levee improvements, contributed to the gradual shift of rural levee financing from private, to state, and ultimately to the federal government.[39] Urban interests, of course, championed this transition since it reduced their financial burden.

On the eve of the Civil War, which left the levee system greatly deteriorated, New Orleans had protected itself with a feeble flood barrier built largely by slaves and convicts and paid for by taxes on shippers, mandated contributions from upstream planters, and the state. Although the city could not require outside interests to pay for its protection, its prominence in state politics and the obvious rural and urban benefits of levees ensured that others would share the cost of protecting the urban territory.

Floods continued to be a part of urban life in New Orleans during the nineteenth century, even as flood control shifted from local to federal responsibility. State programs, underwritten with federal assistance through the swamp lands sales, prevailed until 1879. During the interval from the Sauvé Crevasse in 1849 until the 1870s, water filled the city's streets on several occasions. In 1862, riverfront levees failed in several locations, and water ponded behind rail lines and flowed toward the city's rear districts. A local newspaper claimed that "there is not cause to fear any serious damage from the overflow spoken of unless the river rises much higher than it is at present."[40] Whether this calm response was to lull occupying Union forces into complacency or a reflection of the regularity of crevasses, the water disrupted urban life for several weeks. Again in 1871 water invaded the city. This time, a crevasse at Bonnet Carré allowed water to flow into Lake Pontchartrain and raised the lake level a couple of feet. Although the riverfront levees held, a rear barrier failed, and water rose in the urbanized territory.[41] Again in 1874, flooding occurred along the New Canal due to elevated lake levels caused by a crevasse at Bonnet Carré.[42] By the 1870s, the greater flood hazard had shifted to the lakefront. The city's riverfront defenses were firm, but weak levees upstream allowed floodwaters to fill Lake Pontchartrain, which then rose sufficiently to inundate low areas along the city's drainage outlets.

The post–Civil War floods had much more devastating effects on rural agricultural lands. High water in 1865, 1867, 1868, 1871, and 1874 delivered sequential blows to the valley. The rural levees, which suffered serious deterioration during the sectional conflict, were no match for these crests, and southern politicians clamored for federal assistance with the recurrent problem. Following the particularly severe 1874 flood, a federal board of engineers assessed available corrective options. Although recommending improvements, their report produced no action. In 1879, a second review of flood control options by army engineers concluded that a consistent levee system could be an aid to navigation. By citing navigational concerns as a device to garner greater national support for protecting riparian plantations, the engineers offered a package acceptable to Washington politicians. Subsequently, Congress created the Mississippi River Commission in 1879 to develop a federally designed levee system that was to provide flood control, although authorization of the program explicitly limited funding of the gargantuan project to navigational improvements.[43] Rural floods in 1881 (which also affected New Orleans) and again in 1882 compelled the commission to press its plans for a well-designed and consistent levee system along the lower river into action. Gradually they shored up the weak links and closed the outlets.

Nonetheless, another great flood in 1890 produced numerous crevasses in the agricultural hinterland.[44] During that event, New Orleans also suffered the highest water ever in the city's rear districts. An upstream crevasse again caused lake levels to rise, and stiff east winds piled water along New Orleans's lakefront. Water stood 2 feet deep in houses along the lakefront, roads and railroads disappeared beneath the pervasive flood, vast tracts adjacent to the Metairie Ridge became a lake, and the city's drainage canal spilled over into neighboring streets. The lake was so high that the city's drainage machines could not lift water from the drainage canals and had to be shut down till the water level subsided. Reporters pointed out that, once again, the city's poor suffered the most.[45] Although high water threatened the city with some regularity after 1890, the river never again breached the riverfront barrier. The levees had effectively made the lakefront the principal flood threat.

The city was not impregnable, although the Mississippi River Commission made notable strides in protecting the rural floodplains, and this offered New Orleans additional security. Most significant is the fact that Louisiana and other lower valley interests finally deflected the principal cost of levee building and maintenance to the federal government. The scale of the flooding problem was truly national, and New Orleans officials had made that point to federal authorities since territorial days. From the city's standpoint, the federal government had an obligation to build and maintain the massive bulwarks. With the creation of the Mississippi River Commission, the transfer of flood protection responsibilities was finally accomplished. However, the great flood hazard of the Mississippi River had not been eliminated; it was merely hidden behind a now federally maintained earthen curtain between the city and the waterway.[46]

DRAINING THE SWAMPS

Historian Anne Vileisis suggests that colonial settlers took advantage of swamps across the country—using some as pasture, others for rice production, and in Louisiana as a source for timber.[47] Although valued as resources, there was a prevailing view expressed in such literature as *Pilgrim's Progress,* that swamps were dangerous and evil places. Attaching such names as "dismal" to the Virginia–North Carolina wetland reflected this view. Setting aside the moral associations of swamps as treacherous places, there was another critical concern that caused settlers to be wary of wetlands—their function as an ostensible harbor for disease.

As early as 1720, Jean Baptiste Bernard de la Harpe, a prominent French explorer and respected chronicler of early conditions in Louisiana, criticized the selection of New Orleans's site owing to its unhealthy circumstances, among other reasons.[48] New Orleans's initial plat called for ditches encircling each block to provide drainage, and the early levee included a ditch to accelerate passage of any water that seeped through.[49] Spanish officials argued that vacant lots that collected water contributed to ill health by emitting "vapors that are pernicious to health" during the summer months.[50] Near the end of the colonial period, French settler and chronicler James Pitot commented on the "pestilential fever that manifests itself in a most violent way" during the late summer months, particularly among "strangers" (nonnatives). He claimed that clogged drains along with stagnant water contributed to this situation, which was aggravated by the lack of government action to reduce the "deficiencies of a swampland" and make the city a salubrious location.[51] He further contended that "Lower Louisiana is not an unhealthy place. Only in its city is centered the pollution that tears it down. . . . [S]urveys, landfills, and, of course, drainage, would generally provide in healthfulness of the area what other colonial countries freely provide under similar conditions."[52] Pitot's comments also reveal that part of the problem was the concentration of people in a city with wholly inadequate public works. This notion that health problems afflicted the city more than the countryside prevailed during the early nineteenth century. At the time New Orleans became an American city, however, the prevailing wisdom, or at least hope, was that although health hazards existed in the wetland, drainage could eliminate them.

Several aspects of the wetland site contributed to public health fears. Stagnant water and putrefying organic material found in both the swamps and in the city's lower sections were thought to generate effluvia or miasmas that contributed to diseases such as yellow fever. Swamp forests, in the minds of some, or the lack thereof to others, contributed as well. Shallow privies and outhouses, along with cemeteries, added their own foul air to the local atmosphere and posed additional problems. Finally, water supplies also were suspected as still another source of ill health. Depending on the authority, nineteenth-century New Orleans residents faced an assortment of hazards, and each had roots in the city's physical site. The common factor was the low-lying site, which produced a high water table and an ideal habitat for the cypress forest. It also inhibited downward percolation of rain and sewage, thus adding to an overabundance of standing water and decaying biological material. The bowl-like topography and minimal grade between the rear of the city and Lakes Pontchartrain and Borgne made it nearly impossible to drain off the excess moisture.

A medical view commonly expressed in the first half of the nineteenth century, drawing in part on Noah Webster's medical treatise, held that epidemic disease derived from environmental conditions. Webster had argued that places like Egypt's delta that were subject to annual inundations had to deal with disease outbreaks, and New Orleans certainly faced regular inundations.[53] Colonial historian Le Page du Pratz spoke of the process by which the river carried "a prodigious quantity of ooze, leaves, canes and trees," which, when the river escaped its banks, accumulated on its flanks. He described the land of the lower delta as aggrading, or building up slowly. As evidence of this gradual buildup, he noted that the numerous lakes on the riverside were "remains of the sea."[54] The protracted land-building process had not yet filled in the lakes and wetlands that surrounded the city, and the vegetable matter in the "ooze" contributed to the miasmas. Pitot reported that these "pools of stagnant and fetid water" produced unhealthy conditions.[55]

Early-nineteenth-century beliefs in environmental disease attributed ill-health to those water bodies. Geographer William Darby flatly claimed that "the stagnant state of water has ever been considered the fruitful source of disease." He added that "the deadly effluvia that imperceptibly arises from water in a stagnant state, must come from the putrefaction of animal and vegetable matter."[56] Climatic conditions prompted medical authorities to refine the notion that stagnant lakes alone caused the disease outbreaks. Jabez Heustis, a physician, noticed that disease was most prevalent in New Orleans during the late summer, particularly August. In 1817 he explained this condition by differences in seasonal precipitation and temperatures. During the spring and early summer rainy seasons, the ponds and lakes filled with fresh water, "rendering New Orleans healthy." The prevalence of sickness in late summer arose from the dessication of the lakes and the high temperatures that caused the vegetable material to decompose and release effluvia to the atmosphere.[57] A decade later, author Timothy Flint joined those who observed the massive number of fatalities due to the insalubrious site. He noted stagnant water as a contributing factor, but he also pointed out an old view that was taking on greater prominence, claiming that newcomers or "strangers" were more susceptible to disease. This view attempted to assign a social cause and thereby link recent "unacclimated" immigrants with spreading the deadly illness.[58] Public policy, however, did not drop environmental causation as the key source of pestilence.

Edward Fenner, a noted New Orleans medical authority, contributed to the ongoing discussion of stagnant water as a source of miasmas. He pointed out the large number of vacant lots that collected water during wet weather and released "deleterious effluvia."[59] In addition, he noted the ability of people to become acclimated to the local conditions and noxious emissions. The New Orleans Board of Health also cited standing water as hazardous: "of all the external causes affecting the salubrity of the city, probably moisture and filth are more instrumental than all others combined. . . . This liability to undue moisture arises from our being surrounded by swamps, large lakes and rivers in our neighborhood, but particularly the former."[60] Again in 1851, the eminent physician E. H. Barton reiterated the need to drain impounded water. Offering a more refined medical explanation, he claimed that stagnant water was the most favorable environment for the decomposition that produced miasmas. He also pointed out that the very canals used to drain the urban territory contributed to the problem by holding the offensive brew.[61] Trying to remedy a hazardous situation with open drains, the city actually worsened the conditions they sought to alleviate.

Conflicting views about forests' contribution to insalubrity existed. A thriving colonial cypress timber trade had reduced the forests around New Orleans by the 1750s.[62] With little forest remaining within the built-up sectors, Spanish authorities recommended planting forests, particularly around waste dumps and cemeteries. They argued that by shading decaying matter from the sun they would reduce putrefaction and prevent disease outbreaks. Furthermore, they claimed that trees would "intercept the said exhalations and vapors preserving the city from one and the other."[63] Apparently considerable forest remained toward the lakefront in the early nineteenth century. C. C. Robin observed between 1803 and 1805 that behind the city the forest had been cleared, but "further away a curtain of tall cypress trees blocks the horizon."[64] Additional descriptions mention limited forests along various bayous and the Mississippi River.[65] Estimates to construct a canal from the city to the lakefront in 1831 calculated that laborers would have had to remove some 3,500 trees, including many cypress, along the 6.5 mile canal pathway.[66] In 1839, the Louisiana legislature authorized the removal of the "woods which at present nearly cover the entire space between lake Pontchartrain and the city [New Orleans]" in order to allow lake breezes to reach the city free of "exhalations" from the swamp.[67] The local board of health claimed that forest removal in the vicinity of the city would, when combined with drainage, make the area much drier and healthier. These reports indicate that cypress forests remained around New Orleans and that medical opinion saw forested wetlands as health risks.[68] E. H. Barton challenged this view, in part. He claimed that trees should be planted to absorb noxious gases and moderate heat, which induced decay of organic matter in stagnant water.[69] His support of trees was limited to public parks and principal streets, while he encouraged their removal at the city's fringes.[70] The city's municipalities followed this advice and planted trees along the principal thoroughfares.[71] Nonetheless, by the 1860s lumbermen had yet to clear the entire cypress forest surrounding New Orleans, and the threat remained (Fig. 1.4).[72]

The concern with epidemic diseases in New Orleans was not unfounded even though the causation might have been misunderstood at the time. The first outbreak of yellow fever, the most pervasive bacterial threat to the city, occurred in 1796, followed by a second in 1799. A more devastating flare-up took some five hundred lives in 1803. By the 1820s the "saffron scourge" appeared every summer, and it reached epidemic proportions in 1822 and 1824. With increasing numbers of recent immigrants who had no immunity to the illness, the death tolls rose, and according to medical historian John Duffy, municipal authorities showed relatively little concern for the city's population, particularly recent immigrants. After several ill-fated attempts to organize a local health board to respond to epidemics, the city suffered its most severe yellow fever epidemic in 1853. An estimated 10,000 people died out of a total population of about 150,000, but that number is made more dramatic by the fact that about half the city fled at the epidemic's outset. All told, physicians treated about 30,000 to 40,000 cases of the fever that summer.[73] Such were the realities of the disease hazard. Although the disease was attributed to effluvia from the swamps and stagnant bodies of water around the city, it was in fact mosquitoes, which bred in the wetlands and standing

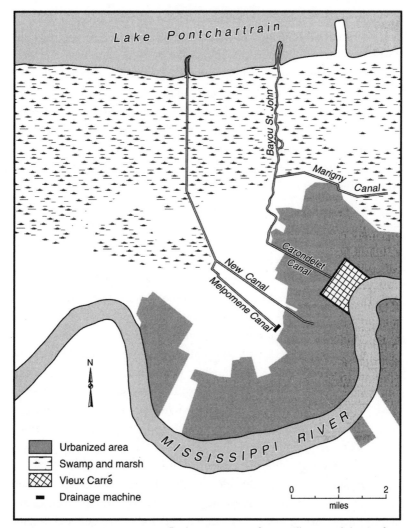

FIG. 1.4. NEW ORLEANS IN 1863. In the 1860s cypress forests still separated the city from the lakefront. Three canals offered some drainage for New Orleans, and drainage machines or pumps helped lift water from the low ground and out of the city. After Gen. Nathan P. Banks, "Approaches to New Orleans, 1863." Courtesy The Historic New Orleans Collection, Museum/ Research Center, Accession No. 1974.25.18.122.

water, that delivered the fatal virus. Concern about standing water was not ill-placed; it merely focused on the habitat and not the disease vector. Co-incidentally, a common medical belief held that mosquitoes were valuable warnings of the disease since they thrived in settings where "unwholesome exhalations" prevailed.[74]

Outbreaks often and most severely afflicted the city's poorer quarters—those districts either along the waterfront where imported cases first appeared or closest to the wetlands behind the city (the same areas that were also subject to flooding). The limited range of mosquitoes concentrated the outbreaks to relatively small territories—in the places of the disease's initial introduction, particularly along the waterfront and secondarily to the rear of the city. Medical authorities assigned the filth commonly found in immigrant neighborhoods as a contributing factor. This made the problem particularly urban. In the eyes of contemporary physicians, population density, which was greatest in the low-income quarters, and its associated problems made the city more susceptible to the generation of effluvia and the transmission of disease. Contributing to the situation were the many shallow privies, most of which extended only about four feet into the ground.[75] Into those shallow cavities New Orleans residents deposited some 5,633 tons of fecal material and 43,000 tons of urine annually. Although laws required the removal of night soil to the river, health authorities still feared that the "putrefactive fermentation" of this waste contaminated the atmosphere.[76] This was undoubtedly most severe in neighborhoods where residents could not afford regular night-soil service. In addition, the open drains, which carried surface runoff and sewage, presented an intolerable nuisance. The lack of current made drainage canals particularly offensive in summer months. Food wastes dumped on the river bank and the numerous aboveground cemeteries also attracted the attention of authorities as sources of unhealthy emissions.[77] The greater the population density in the already soggy site, the more voluminous the filth that created hazardous conditions.

There was one obvious, though difficult, solution—drainage. It was not enough to keep river floods from the city; additional measures were essential to rid the city of water that accumulated after every rain and became particularly problematic during high river stages. The initial plat of New Orleans included drains along each block of the Vieux Carré, and the Spanish commenced digging a canal that linked the rear of the city to Bayou St. John. This artificial waterway functioned primarily as a transportation link with Lake Pontchartrain but also as a sluice for runoff and sewerage when lake levels allowed movement in that direction. Completed in about 1796 and named after the Spanish governor who authorized its construction, the Carondelet Canal improved drainage in the Vieux Carré (Fig. 1.4),[78] but the gentle grade between its headlands and the lake made it only marginally effective for the city's lower districts. By 1810, local observers claimed that the canal had "become an unwholesome morass, from which pestilential emanations are continually evaporating," and that boats "plough through mud at the bottom, and large bubbles of poisonous gas are seen rising and exploding at the surface."[79] North winds could waft these offensive emissions toward the city and reverse the canal's flow. Flooding along the headwaters of the canal during prolonged periods of northerly winds completely negated its effectiveness. To revitalize the canal, the municipal government granted rights to a private company to enlarge and clean it. The job was completed by 1817, but the improvements were short lived, and indeed, the modifications did little to relieve the problem.[80] The restored canal's larger volume simply meant it could hold more sewage and create a greater menace.

Despite the physical obstacles to efficient water movement, drainage remained the most attractive and feasible solution. Even President Thomas Jefferson offered advice. In a letter to local resident M. du Plantier he recommended that a ditch 3 feet deep could drain an area subdivided into lots; proceeds from the sale of the lots could be used to underwrite the excavation of the ditch and construction of protective levees.[81] Though lacking in engineering adequacy, Jefferson's recommendation that drainage be linked with real estate development was a model attempted in subsequent years. Timothy Flint noted some successful drainage efforts in 1818 (the enlargement of the Carondelet Canal) and encouraged the city to continue them. "Tracts of swamp about the town are draining, or filling up," he wrote in 1828, "and this work, constantly pursued, will, probably, contribute more to the salubrity of the city, than all other efforts to this end united."[82]

A series of marginally successful efforts punctuated the drainage program of the early 1800s. Three canals dug through the ridges by 1830 drained separate sections of the city. The Melpomene Canal offered an outlet for the uptown American district in 1825, the Poydras Canal followed the path of the current street by the same name (later replaced by the New Canal in the 1840s), and the Marigny Canal offered minimal drainage to the lower faubourgs (Fig. 1.4). Neither individually nor jointly did the canals remedy the problem. The absence of gradient was a chief obstacle, and without sufficient current the large ditches became open-air septic troughs[83] and permitted wind-driven water from Lake Pontchartrain to back up into the city. Water from the lake inundated areas within several blocks of the Mississippi in 1831, 1837, 1844, and 1846.[84] Typically these events occurred during the winter months and were unlikely to contribute to conditions that favored the spread of epidemic diseases. If hurricane driven, however, they could coincide with summer heat. Once again, efforts to alleviate one problem contributed to another.

By the 1830s, steps to provide more effective drainage were underway. Unable to shoulder the financial burden, the city, as often occurred in public works projects, allowed entrepreneurs to fashion its infrastructure. In 1831 the state legislature chartered the New Orleans Canal and Banking Company and made it responsible for building a second major canal from Poydras Street to Lake Pontchartrain. This construction was to improve navigation to the heart of the city, while offering the side benefit of drainage. Real estate speculation ran rampant in areas that it would drain. The canal and banking company made huge profits when it subdivided and sold lots in suburban Carrollton in 1832–33, reflecting both the growing city's need for additional space and its desperate need for drainage. Following the financial panic of 1837, the company collapsed and turned the completed "New Canal" over to the state.[85] The New Canal extended from the rear of the American section of the downtown area (Fig. 1.4) through the lowest portion of New Orleans to Lake Pontchartrain, and it attracted considerable attention. Visitors to the city liked to take carriage rides to the lakefront along its shell road, built on the spoil from the canal excavation. The embankment that served as the roadway also provided a levee that stretched from the rear of the city to the lakefront, offering some hope of protection from upstream crevasses. Despite obvious commercial success, the lowest portions of the city enjoyed little benefit from this huge ditch because, once again, the subtle topography of New Orleans inhibited current. Furthermore, the raised roadway stood between much of the lowest ground and the drainage canal— obstructing any flow from the city's natural basin. As demonstrated by the Sauvé Crevasse of 1849, the roadway/levee also provided ineffective flood protection.

Seeking improvements it simply could not afford, the city convinced state lawmakers to pass legislation in 1835 initiating an effort to drain "off the stagnant waters which accumulate on the low and marshy grounds" in the city's rear. The legislation created a private company, the New Orleans Draining Company, to execute the improvements. To finance the project, the city and state committed to purchase stock in the enterprise. In theory, the company would profit by selling the lands it drained.[86] Due in part to the economic panic of 1837, this speculative venture failed to put an effective drainage system in place and the city remained at the mercy of the surrounding wetlands.[87]

Despite the new canals, an 1840 report called for further improvement. It charged that the various drainage efforts to that time had been piecemeal and without an overarching design. Political subdivision of the city into three separately governed municipalities in 1836 fractured effective public works projects and prevented adequate coordination, even where it was obviously necessary. Without coordination, the three municipalities undertook assorted drainage and filling projects that sometimes offset one another. This problem was further aggravated by inconsistency from administration to administration and a chronically strained city treasury.[88] Consequently, the separate drainage projects remained largely ineffective after any substantial rainfall. George Dunbar, the state engineer and author of the 1840 report, argued for a more coordinated system that employed steam engines to supplement the meager pull of gravity.[89] By 1849, Edward Fenner reported that substantial progress had been made. He noted that the territory within two miles of the city had been "pretty thoroughly drained" and large tracts of valuable land reclaimed. Drainage machines, or large waterwheels (Fig. 1.5), were in place to force water from the two principal canals into Bayou St. John and the lake.[90] A special report on fevers released in 1850 claimed that the ground between the city and Metairie Ridge had been well drained, "causing an extensive swamp to be dried up by the rays of the sun."

FIG. 1.5. DRAINAGE MACHINE, CA. 1860. Steam-driven waterwheels lifted excess water from low areas of the city into the drainage canals flowing into Lake Pontchartrain. Courtesy Tulane University Special Collections, New Orleans Municipal Papers, MS Collection 16, Public Works folder.

This, it suggested, had produced a "beneficial influence upon the health of the city."[91] But such optimism was premature.

The great yellow fever outbreak of 1853 soon followed with its devastating toll on human life. This tragedy prompted Louisiana's leaders to take another look at solutions to New Orleans's drainage problems. Local leaders had long denied public health problems, using their fiction to justify a lax response to the excess water problem.[92] The urban elite, with long family histories in the region, were better acclimated and less susceptible to the yellow fever onslaughts. By contrast, the immigrant community, the Irish in particular, labored in digging the new canals and were most susceptible to mosquito bites as they extended the drainage system into the backswamps. E. H. Barton estimated that more than 200 of every 1,000 Irish in New Orleans died during the 1853 epidemic.[93] In part because of the relative immunity of long-term residents and high fatalities among the laboring poor, urban leaders were less vigorous than their counterparts in other major cities to seek out and put into place remedies to the drainage dilemma. The outbreak of 1853 left them facing an undeniable reality with severe economic ramifications. Their denials that New Orleans was unhealthy sought to prevent the diversion of commerce to other ports.[94] Local leaders, however, were unable to suppress or distort the severity of reports about the 1853 epidemic. National recognition of this event threatened the economy, and leaders grudgingly acknowledged that concrete remedies were essential. E. H. Barton's report in 1854 argued for better drainage and the filling of low lots. Spurred into action, the state legislature authorized an investigation that also pointed out the need to improve drainage, specifically in the area between the city and the lakefront.[95] The report claimed that public health had improved in countries such as England that had implemented drainage projects. Although the report called for getting rid of surface waters, converting swamps to meadows, and removing forests to improve ventilation, no fundamental changes ensued.[96] Once again inadequate resources hampered the city's response.

In a follow-up report to the state legislature, Lewis de Russy prepared an estimate for draining the swamps between the city and Lake Pontchartrain. His novel plan emphasized not drainage but filling the low area—mimicking the process of sedimentation that had been terminated by levees. His concept called for a series of parallel levees from the river to the lakefront, where a perpendicular levee would link the bulwarks extending toward the lake, creating enclosed basins. He recommended diverting floodwater into these basins, where sediment would settle out and, over the course of several years, gradually raise the land level.[97] The de Russ scheme exposed a serious flaw in the levee system—it eliminated the regular delivery of sediments, which reduced flood risks and could actually aid in drainage efforts by raising the land level. The legislators, as might have been expected, preferred the more expeditious system of drainage machines, and de Russy's plan suffered the fate of other discarded recommendations.

As the legislature searched for a solution, New Orleans's common council called on its municipal surveyor, Louis Pile, to report on the feasibility of draining the swamps behind the city. Expressing obvious frustration with the council for ignoring previous reports that had been "unhappily filed without action in the city archives" and charging that the state's survey was a waste of public funds, he offered a plan following the Dutch solution. Referring to the "Hollanders" as the fathers of drainage, he advocated dividing the swamps into four polders—areas surrounded by ring levees with pumps to remove the water. In addition, he argued that existing canals needed to be enlarged and new draining machines, with weirs to block reverse flow of lake water, situated near the Metairie Ridge. These improvements would prevent flooding from the lake and would allow the machines to move water from the inhabited sections into the lake more expeditiously. This work, he estimated, would cost the city $1.3 million.[98] Like so many previous plans, the city was unable to fund Pile's recommendation. Despite repeated efforts and numerous critical reports about the city's drainage, New Orleans remained plagued with a host of problems associated with excessive water in 1860.

During the first half of the nineteenth century, residents with means took flight from the summer pestilence and avoided the most serious epidemics. The selection of rural retreats emphasized the notion that pestilence was a byproduct not just of the swamps but of filth associated with crowded urban living. New Orleans's elite had begun their search for refuge outside the city by the 1820s. Timothy Flint observed in that decade that the threat of disease "compels the rich to fly" to hotels and homes in places like Madisonville on the north shore of Lake Pontchartrain. He also described the coastal resorts east of New Orleans as attracting summer residents seeking healthful breezes from the Gulf of Mexico.[99] Benjamin Latrobe likewise noted that those who could afford to ventured to Bay St. Louis, Mississippi, or similar resorts between July and October, emphasizing the rural-urban distinction by noting that "bilious fevers are the common disorder, and the wealthy fly to the country." [100] Prevailing medical opinion held that residents of urban areas breathed impure air, while those in rural territories enjoyed air diluted and purified by the sun. Such a prescription obviously drove the annual exodus from New Orleans. But arguments for better drainage began to point out that solutions had to apply to those who had to live in the city for twelve months a year and not just those "who can take the 'wings of the morning and fly to the outermost part of the earth.'" [101] Drainage, along with the removal of forests to enhance lake breezes through the city remained the favored options, but delivering them was costly and beyond the city's financial capabilities.

Throughout the early nineteenth century, the city had been unable to pass the costs of drainage on to others as it had the levee building expense. The one attempt to have the state subscribe to bonds for the draining company failed to transfer the expenses or to drain the city. A combination of ineffective leadership and fiscal inadequacies, along with the considerable technological and financial challenges posed by the problem, allowed the costs of poor drainage to fall on the city's citizenry. This cost weighed disproportionately on the poor in the form of huge death tolls during the frequent yellow fever outbreaks. Wealthy citizens paid for inadequate drainage through the expense of taking refuge in the country.

Preparing for and responding to hazards are fundamental social activities. Writers on environmental hazards suggest that society first appraises a hazard and then develops plans to adjust to hazardous events, which it then may or may not adopt in full or in part. The dual threats of high water and environmental disease in New Orleans inspired different appraisals, plans, and responses, with contrasting results. Indeed, steps taken to remedy one problem often exacerbated the other. The scale of the hazards, which were continental in scope, were beyond the control of a single municipality. When the city could disperse the costs to a larger group it was fairly successful in implementing adjustments, but when it had to bear the full costs it failed to put effective adjustments into place, at least by 1860.

The appraisal and adjustment process for floods involved observations of prior flood stages, based on flood marks on trees. Colonial policy called for a public response to protect the city itself with a set of levees sufficiently high to keep out the highest known flood. As floods entered from the rear of the city, policy adjustments required rural landowners to construct levees that would aid urban flood protection. By the time of the Louisiana Purchase, the city had effectively transferred a portion of the costs to plantation owners. The municipality continued to maintain the levees at the urban core, although shippers subsidized this effort. Later, the state took on a portion of the expense, and ultimately the federal government subsidized levee building with the Swamp Lands Acts of 1849 and 1850 and later through the Mississippi River Commission. Although the flood protection system was imperfect and rural crevasses continued to damage the city, the structures erected along the urban riverfront proved remarkably effective after about 1865. A policy that called for continual monitoring and maintenance and required that levees be raised to the most recent high stage offered both a means to keep the levees in good condition and a flexible standard. This environmental transaction worked to the advantage of urban dwellers.

Drainage presented a far less manageable problem. The high water table, stagnant lakes, and decaying organic material represented a public health threat—an indirect hazard—particularly to the poor. The city sought to eliminate the disease hazard by draining the low-lying districts in and around the municipalities. Due in part to a fragmented municipal government, financial constraints, and limited technological capabilities, moving water from the soggy city remained a vexing problem through the mid-nineteenth century. Initial attempts to drain the city relied simply on gravity to propel water from the built-up portions of New Orleans to the lake. With inadequate gradient, this approach was hopeless, despite the construction of several canals by 1840. The addition of pumps, or draining machines, yielded better results, but poor coordination among the three municipalities and inadequate maintenance of the drainage systems rendered the overall effort ineffective. The city had turned to private developers and the state to help underwrite the drainage effort, but ineffectual management of the private projects produced little public health benefit. As long as the urban elite could escape the summer pestilence, there was little compulsion to fulfill the various costly and complex drainage plans.

The management of water hazards in New Orleans, and throughout the lower delta, is a tale of sharp contrasts. While far from perfect, the levee system was remarkably successful in New Orleans. It protected the city and, to a lesser extent, a large portion of its economic hinterland. Tied together by the ribbon of levees, the city and the plantations blockaded the threat of high water. As that task became more expensive, they were able to defer some of the costs and maintain their economic well-being. By contrast, an expanding city faced increasing costs as it pushed back away from the better drained natural levee into the swampy mire behind New Orleans. Colonial governments endowed the American city with a single ineffective drainage canal. Even when supplemented by additional outlets and pumps, the canal system remained useless as a means to drain the swamps and eliminate disease threats. Unable to secure effective outside finances for a drainage system, the city still faced much the same problem in 1860 as it had in 1800.

CHAPTER 2

REMAKING THE ENVIRONMENT

NEW ORLEANS MEDICAL authority Edward Barton concluded that environmental factors—namely prolonged warm temperatures combined with moist and filthy conditions—caused the monstrous 1853 yellow fever epidemic. In his recapitulation of the calamitous circumstances, the environment as hazard loomed large. Yet the map that accompanies his report labels troublesome places as *nuisances*—a term that was distinct from "hazard." Hazard commonly referred to exposure to dangers. Nuisances, a legal as well as a public health term, were related to *activity* that produced some offensive or undesirable outcome that could infringe on the enjoyment of one's property or, in Barton's terms, produce illness. If society desired to relieve the nuisance, it could regulate the activity—either prohibiting it, modifying it to be less offensive, or forcing it to relocate. Indeed, Barton spoke of the epidemic's causes as "removable." He recognized the disease as a symptom of activities that could be altered, thereby eliminating environmental conditions that threatened public health. Society, in Barton's view, had the power to manipulate the environment to the extent that it could mitigate the nuisances wreaking havoc on New Orleans.[1]

Beliefs in environmental causation, such as those Barton and his contemporaries subscribed to, influenced public policy during the late nineteenth century.[2] They compelled public organizations to take numerous steps, often ineffective, to eradicate unwanted conditions. As population density increased and human activity diminished desirable environments, the city council and the Louisiana legislature stepped up the regulation of nuisance-causing practices. This progression is found in municipal ordinances and state acts that shaped the resulting urban landscapes. The regulatory revisions reflect a typical progression from common to statutory law in an effort to deal with threatened resources. This legal evolution helps to explain the means used to overcome environmental problems.[3] As in other situations where a desired resource became scarce, society took specific actions to protect it. In the case of disappearing tolerable environments in New Orleans, steps to regulate nuisance conditions—sewage, garbage, cemeteries, and offensive industries—shaped the urban landscape. What in effect was early environmental policy, therefore, must be considered as a powerful force in creating the Crescent City's landscape.

Environmental manipulation did not stop with the removal of unwanted conditions. As a counterpoint to nuisance elimination, the city also strove to create bucolic settings that would have a beneficial effect on citizens. Planting trees along boulevards and creating parks represented a social effort to create a landscape that would improve public health and also shape a better society.[4] By the early twentieth century, New Orleans was making strides, albeit faltering ones, toward remolding the environment to suit its desires— in terms of both eliminating nuisances and creating amenities.

NUISANCE LANDSCAPES

Barton's nuisance map included a host of activities seen by mid-nineteenth-century medical science as contributing to public health problems. The "terrene" conditions he identified included the recently dredged canals intended to remove municipal effluent, excavations along the river bank, filth in the streets and gutters, cemeteries, slaughterhouses and other offensive industries, and dense tenements.[5] The full range of nuisances may at first appear somewhat scattered throughout the city, but upon closer inspection, one can

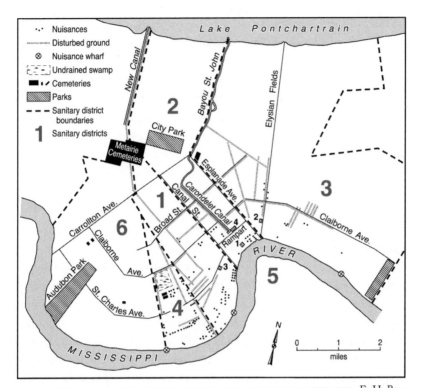

FIG. 2.1. NUISANCES, CEMETERIES, PARKS, AND SANITARY DISTRICTS. E. H. Barton mapped nuisances in New Orleans (drainage canals, cemeteries, and offensive industries) following the 1853 yellow fever epidemic. Cemeteries and parks are shown here as they existed in the 1880s. Small cemeteries remained scattered throughout the city in the 1880s, but large cemeteries along the high ground of the Metairie Ridge had become the principal burial places. The city's older parks (as numbered here) included (1) Jackson Square, (2) Washington Square, (3) Lafayette Square, and (4) Congo Square. Audubon and City parks were developed by the city in the late nineteenth century. After Barton, "Report upon the Sanitary Condition of New Orleans," in City Council of New Orleans, *Report of the Sanitary Commission of New Orleans on the Yellow Fever Epidemic of 1853* (New Orleans: Picayune, 1854), and Waring and Cable, *History and Present Condition of New Orleans,* 1881.

see that offensive industries clustered near the waterfront upstream from the Vieux Carré, while the canals, cemeteries, and tenements created an arc behind the commercial district (Fig. 2.1). These activities did not severely impede real estate development by taking up desirable property, but they represented two infringements on other resources. The term *nuisance* is traditionally used to refer to something that limits property owners' enjoyment

49

of their property.[6] In this sense, nuisance's long-standing association with common law is apparent. The eminent English legal commentator Blackstone defined nuisance as "a species of offences against the public order and economical regimen of the state; being either the doing of a thing to the annoyance of the King's subjects, or the neglecting to do a thing which the common good requires."[7] By the late nineteenth century, dictionaries defined *nuisance* as an activity that "unlawfully annoys or incommodes, or causes damages or inconveniences."[8] In situations where such conditions occurred, individuals could file suit against neighbors to obtain a legal remedy. Although Louisiana followed French civil law, nuisance suits were part of the legal practice there as well.[9]

While the activities Barton inventoried had impacts on neighboring landowners, they also presented a second type of offense, that of public nuisance. By generating harmful airborne, and therefore mobile, effluvia, specific sites could affect the surrounding citizenry and thereby threaten public health, which in the nineteenth century was an assault on commerce as well. Rapid urbanization during the late antebellum period—a population that more than doubled between 1840 and 1860—and ineffective delivery of public services produced what were possibly New Orleans's most abysmal environmental conditions at the time of the 1853 epidemic. Tolerable environments were extremely limited resources. Encircled by river and swamp, the city had little space to expand, and this meant that few individuals in New Orleans's burgeoning population were far removed from nuisances. Barton's cartographic snapshot suggests a shortage of healthful environments. Throughout the balance of the nineteenth century and into the twentieth century, city and public health officials struggled to restore acceptable conditions using various legal tools. Public nuisance suits were an option, but one seldom utilized. City officials favored nuisance regulations that outlawed certain businesses and public health ordinances that provided specific requirements for particular activities. As elsewhere, removing unwanted activities reshaped the urban landscape.[10]

The struggle with sewage was high on the municipal agenda. Even after the terrors of the 1853 epidemic, sporadic attempts to clean the filth-laden canals proved ineffective. The city surveyor was responsible for maintaining these open ditches and occasionally contracted workers to reexcavate the canals. His specifications called for the workers to dig out the accumulated sewage and organic waste and toss it several feet back from the canal. The apparent objective was to restore the canal's full capacity, but medical officials considered disturbed soil a source of effluvia and not a remedy to the nuisance.[11] So in effect, the dredging merely repositioned the nuisance from the canal's bed to its banks. Furthermore, the low-gradient canals soon refilled with filthy sediments. Eventually, the city received assistance from the federal government—albeit as an unwanted invader.

The first effective urban cleansing took place during New Orleans's occupation by the Union army (1862–1865). After his troops took control of the city, General Benjamin F. Butler found conditions deplorable and soon learned of the supposed environmental causes of the 1853 yellow fever epidemic. He also discovered that southerners were actually waiting for nature to unleash another outbreak among the unacclimated Yankee troops, hoping that it would loosen the northerners' hold on their city. Butler took on the public health issue as a military cause—to hold the city, he had to protect the health of his soldiers. Indeed, this was essential to maintain their morale in the face of constant reminders of the disease threat whispered to the troops by resentful residents. The Union general embarked on a vigorous effort to cleanse the septic drainage canals and to flush the gutters and streets. This, he believed, would remove the source of effluvia. He also established an effective quarantine station on the Mississippi River to block entry of infected individuals. Jointly these two projects kept yellow fever from running rampant during the Civil War.[12]

The Union occupation, however, was short lived, and Reconstruction did not bode well for either the economy or public works in New Orleans. Just a few years after the northern soldiers left, New Orleans engineers commented that "our present system of surface and open ditch draining keeps all the objectionable matter, which is allowed to find an outlet at all, exposed to open view in the most densely populated parts of the city, where the whole atmosphere becomes impregnated and polluted with effluvia."[13] Among the numerous nuisances prevalent in New Orleans, sewerage remained particularly vexing. Inadequate gradient made gravity-powered transport impractical, and increasing population density in a narrow urbanized territory exacerbated the problem.[14] The municipal water supply and garbage also posed perennial problems, as did nuisance-causing industries and mosquitoes. At this time, such environmental problems were largely municipal concerns, and the financially strapped city sought private-sector assistance in most situations.[15]

To deal with sewage, postbellum New Orleans relied on a combined privy and *vidangeur* system. Individual households installed outdoor privy vaults and when they reached capacity, private contractors, known locally as *vidangeurs*, would empty the contents and transport the waste to the municipal nuisance wharfs for disposal in the city's ultimate sink, the Mississippi River. Ideally, this arrangement would minimize both nuisance conditions and public health problems by relocating the waste to the city's massive diluting machine. But in practice, poor privy maintenance, particularly in low-income neighborhoods, along with the high watertable rendered the system ineffective. In order to minimize the release of effluvia into the local atmosphere and thereby restore salubrious conditions, the city enacted an ordinance that provided specifications for privy construction and waste removal. Article 543 of the 1857 General Ordinances required all privies to be at least 3 feet deep, with the uppermost 1 foot built of brick laid in cement, and set back at least 3 feet from a public street. This design did nothing to prevent the downward movement of liquid effluent into the soil, however. The ordinance also specified that when the contents rose to within 1 foot of the surface, the user was to have the privy emptied and the "feculent matter" transported to the river.[16] The street commissioner had the authority to compel occupants to clean their privies or even have the city pay for the job. Despite such authority, the city only cleaned four privies each year in 1859 and 1860. Fearing inadequate enforcement, the state legislature created a corps of "sanitary inspectors" in 1866. The Reconstruction-era city was unable to pay for their services, and by 1870 medical authorities wrote with disgust that sanitary policing was not working and that "innumerable privies are all underground with floating contents close to the surface."[17] Regulations exceeded the city's ability to enforce them.

Inadequacies of this system were all too apparent, and it came under vigorous criticism as a result of the 1878 yellow fever epidemic. The worst "yellow jack" outbreak since 1853 ravaged the city and locations throughout the Mississippi River valley. More than four thousand deaths due to the fever represented nearly half of New Orleans's mortality total that year.[18] Worse yet in the minds of New Orleans business leaders, it produced an unprecedented interruption in the city's commerce. While privies cannot be condemned for directly causing yellow fever, their input to the soil raised the already high watertable, thereby contributing to standing water on private lots, in municipal gutters, and drainage canals. The presence of sewage, according to contemporary sanitation theory, vitiated the air and contributed to disease. In reality, this surface water provided breeding places for disease-carrying mosquitoes. Although insects were not known at the time to be vectors, health authorities considered puddles containing putrefying material to be nuisances and therefore contributing factors. In describing conditions in the city's First District, sanitary inspector Joseph Holt noted the association between privies and surface water: "streets and premises are subject to overflowing during every heavy fall of rain, and the contents of vaults and cess-pools are at such times spread over the surface of the earth to be acted upon by the sun."[19] In the Third District, another report noted, the privies "frequently overflow, thereby causing the contents oftentimes to be carried upon sidewalks and into gutters, and creating a stench that is extremely offensive, to say nothing of the dangerous and often deadly effects to human life in densely populated portions of our city."[20] The fact that there were approximately 44,000 privies in the city, many in desperate need of repairs, was not lost on local officials.[21]

Joseph Holt addressed his colleagues at the New Orleans Medical and Surgical Association meeting in 1879 on the privy system's evils. He proclaimed that finding a remedy to the "cess-vault" system was the most important sanitary issue facing the city. To drive home the point, he calculated that the city's 190,000 people were producing over 100,000 tons of excrement annually. According to his estimates, the vidangeurs removed approximately 2,000 tons a year, leaving some 98,000 tons to seep into the soil or overflow into the streets and putrefy in the canals. Holt lamented: "Imagine the quantity of human excrement, undergoing slowly the lowest and most offensive form of putrefactive fermentation, and escaping from the sinks of 26,500 habitations, partly by overflow into yards, gutters, and under the houses; partly by evaporation into the atmosphere, but chiefly by soakage into the earth, and from every direction poisoning the air."[22] This comment emphasized the link between soil contamination and pollution of the atmosphere, which pushed sewage to the forefront as a citywide nuisance issue. Elsewhere Holt commented on the privies' contribution to the soil that "it may be properly stated that the people have a huge privy in common, and that the inhabitants of New Orleans live upon a dung heap." The poor, many living in the lowest and most crowded portions of the city, obviously faced a greater threat than those who occupied the high ground on the flanks of the natural levee. The Second, Third, and Fourth districts each had an average of more than one privy per premises, reflecting the dense population in those neighborhoods. Furthermore, both the Third and Fourth districts had "defective" privies at rates (17 and 23 percent respectively) well above the urban average (12 percent). To remedy the situation, Holt advocated the complete replacement of privies with water closets and the establishment of a municipal sewerage system. As a less expensive option, he suggested completely lined vaults.[23]

Shortly before the 1878 fever outbreak, the city had enacted new ordinances and regulations to relieve some threats to salubrious environments. Indeed, it had already taken action in accord with Holt's recommendation. An 1877 ordinance required that any new privy built in the city could extend only two feet into the soil, had to have a watertight bottom, and could not drain to the yard or a street. This measure attempted to prevent sewage from escaping either into the groundwater or surface drainage. Before emptying, users had to deodorize the privy contents to prevent it from releasing harmful odors while in transit. Furthermore, the occupants of the premises had to obtain a permit for the Board of Health to empty the privy.[24] As under previous ordinances, the contents were to be transported in secure containers to the river. Through the new ordinance, the city sought to eliminate sewage's ability to foul the soil and the air. To compel compliance, it imposed monetary fines on violators. Older, faulty privies continued to exist, but city officials hoped to reduce the overall nuisance of human wastes through more stringent regulations—and thereby restore salubrious environments.

While this regulatory approach had little impact, due to the city's inability to enforce regulations, more extensive efforts followed the epidemic. In 1879 local citizens, frustrated with efforts by commercial interests to block public health reform, mobilized to supplement the municipal effort with voluntary programs.[25] Plans for additional improvements moved along two fronts: flushing the open gutters and canals and construction of a sewerage system. Immediately prior to the epidemic, the municipal budget allocated no funds for drainage or street cleaning. Considering this fiscal crisis, local physicians and business leaders formed the Auxiliary Sanitary Association to initiate private-sector-based sanitation. Within the association, the flushing committee sought to improve the existing drainage system. Street drainage in the late 1870s comprised practices imposed by older regulations. From the colonial period, property owners had to maintain ditches in front of their land to facilitate drainage. Gradually, the city replaced the easily clogged

FIG. 2.2. STREET DRAINAGE. Small gutters lined both sides of New Orleans's streets to collect and transport runoff. They often became clogged with refuse and human waste and presented a persistent nuisance. St. Ann and Charters Street looking away from the river, 1901. Cornelius Durkee Photograph Collection, no. 9. Courtesy New Orleans Public Library.

earthen ditches with wood-lined curbs and gutters, but this improved surface drainage system was still hard to maintain (Fig. 2.2). Beginning in 1802, water from the river was used to flush the streets, at least during high stage. When the first municipal water system became operational in 1819, steam pumps enabled year-round flushing of a small portion of the city. Yet poor maintenance rendered this system largely inoperable by 1844.[26] After the 1853 epidemic, work on a new water delivery system began. This development enabled the city to open hydrants that would drain the streets running perpendicular to the river—only these routes had any gradient to facilitate washing. The flushing committee in 1879 sought to provide similar service to the cross streets, but the limited distribution of the water supply system undercut success on this front. To deal with the canals, the committee employed a "mud scourer" to remove the accumulations and also oversaw a systematic cleaning of all the open ditches.[27]

Throughout the implementation of the flushing program, the sanitary association advocated a sewerage system, and ultimately its members convinced the city to give the option serious consideration. In 1880 a municipal committee visited the newly completed Memphis sewerage system, but the inspection yielded no tangible results in the Crescent City.[28] In the absence of adequate funds, it took more than a decade for a citywide effort to take shape. In the meantime, several businesses constructed their own sewers to the river. Among those installing private service were the hospitals, larger hotels, and several manufacturers such as the sugar refineries and a brewery.[29] Households, with no other viable options, continued to use privies and *vidangeurs*. As with the flushing effort, it took the action of private citizens to organize a sewerage service. In 1894, Joseph Holt, the indefatigable advocate of sewers and by this time president of the newly chartered New Orleans Sewerage Company, offered the inaugural address at the opening of this private venture. He waxed poetic on the prospect of removing the filthy conditions using new sewer lines and a pump-driven system to discharge the city's effluent to the river.[30] Despite great expectations, the company went into receivership a few years later after accomplishing little more than completing engineering plans.[31] Ultimately, it fell to the city to implement a municipal sewerage system as part of a threefold sanitation program to improve drainage, remove sewage, and deliver water that began taking shape after 1900 (discussed in the following chapter). Thus, at the close of the nineteenth century New Orleans residents still lived, in the words of Holt, on a giant "dung heap" inadequately drained by several open canals emitting effluvia to a common resource, the atmosphere. Some sewage flowed into Lake Pontchartrain, and *vidangeurs* dumped a small portion into the river.

The economic costs of this filth eventually inspired a civic response. When property values along the drainage canals depreciated due to the offensive odors, civic leaders claimed that proper drainage would restore them.[32] Arguing for improved drainage, S. S. Herrick, a local physician, calculated that malaria alone cost the city nearly $300,000 a year—based on the cost of attending victims, the diversion of time from more productive activities, loss of life (at $1,000 per victim), and funerals. He calculated that pulmonary consumption added another $900,000 to the social cost of disease. By constructing a viable subsoil drainage system, he argued, these two maladies would significantly decline, saving the city over half a million dollars annually. Calculating the cost of adequate drainage at $1.75 million, he concluded the system would pay for itself in just over three years.[33] Greater yet were the disruptions to regional commerce caused by serious disease outbreaks. In a letter to the mayor, Joseph Jones, president of the state Board of Health, stated that a single yellow fever epidemic cost the city $15 million. Over the course of thirty years, the combined costs of yellow fever, malaria, and other fevers soared to $118 million. He estimated that the city could carry out its sanitary affairs (inspections and disinfection) for about $16,000 annually.[34] Adding to the paltry expense of municipal sanitation services the estimated costs of underground drainage ($1.75 million) and improved canals ($2.375 million),[35] officials could easily see that improvements were substantially less expensive than one yellow fever outbreak. At the same time, however, critics charged that over $13 million had been poured into street and drainage improvements over a thirty-four-year span with little impact.[36] Certainly by the 1880s, New Orleans and state officials acknowledged the serious cost of filth and disease, but summoning the resources to remedy the problem remained an elusive goal. Not only were tolerable environments in short supply, the financial resources to combat them were insufficient as well.[37]

Garbage was a second critical concern in the battle to restore and maintain healthful environments. Barton complained of conditions along the batture in 1853, the "exposure of the naked bank of the river for about six miles, many parts of it made a common receptacle of, and reeking with garbage and filth of all kinds, exposed to the sun and rain, without a single police officer, to prevent its being made a common deposit for these nuisances."[38] Granted, the river would wash away foul accumulations each spring, but the problem lay with dumping during the summer heat when there were few flood waters to cleanse the batture. The riverfront was not the only problem area, however. The city was growing away from the river, and many platted lots still had no structures on them. Residents took it upon themselves to dump garbage and other waste on these low-lying lots in order to raise them out of the mire. Barton characterized these vacant lots, particularly in the Fourth District, "as being a receptacle for, and exposing filth of all kinds."[39] In effect, the city had two unofficial zones of discard—the batture and the rear of the city, although the river was the sole officially sanctioned sink.

The city had regulations to deal with filth and garbage, but enforcing them was another matter. As early as 1819, the New Orleans's city council sought a geographic solution to garbage. It institutionalized a series of locations where the *vidangeurs* and garbage transporters could deliver their loads for transfer to the river. The city built several docks—designated "nuisance wharfs"—and maintained a fleet of boats to export the offending wastes downstream. Ordinances declared that it would be unlawful "to deposit in any part of the city, except the nuisance wharf, any manner of nuisance, manure, filth, offals or foetid matter of what nature soever." A subsequent code specified that it was illegal to "fill up or partly fill up any lot with manure or other offensive or deleterious matter."[40] The 1870 health ordinance added further authority to the nuisance regulations. It stipulated, "All persons are forbidden and are prohibited from allowing, keeping, throwing, dropping or depositing any ordure, excrement, offal, filth, manure, foul and offensive matter, stagnant, corrupt or putrid water, or any shells, hay, straw, kitchen stuff, paper cloth or any substance of any kind which may be offensive to the smell or injurious to health in any yard, lot, room or building, or any banquette [sidewalk], street, alley, wharf, levee, or any public place."[41] Progressively public health requirements sought to be more inclusive of both the types of materials discarded and the range of environmental settings used as dumps. They also specified that citizens were to place ordinary refuse on the curb in suitable containers daily to be hauled off by the offal carts.[42] Not only was the city providing nuisance wharfs where garbage could be dumped, but it outlined the means and provided the service to see that this was done.

Despite regulations and good civic intentions, illegal garbage dumping remained a problem. A state sanitary inspector in 1874 reported that along the batture there were "nearly thirty holes or cavities, some containing stagnant water constantly, others dry part of the time. Many of them are made dumping places for street scrapings, kitchen offal, stable manure, and whatever filth people choose to deposit."[43] According to the inspector, local authorities allowed this situation to exist despite pressure from the state officials to clean up the area. Following the 1878 epidemic, Joseph Holt castigated city officials for their mismanagement of garbage in his district. He characterized their actions as "[a]bsolute negligence on the part of the authorities and their employees; direct aggravation of existing evils in the dumping of garbage into the streets and filling of lots from the dumping grounds" and decried "the fact that no provision had ever been made for properly cleaning the district by sanitary engineering."[44] Likewise in the Fifth District, the sanitary inspector called for the city to provide a nuisance boat for that district because "the ground used as a place of deposit of all kinds of garbage is a disgrace to any community, and a constant source of annoyance to every one living near it."[45] With inadequate enforcement of ordinances and lapses in municipal services due to inadequate finances, the city failed to alleviate the festering problem.

The city continued to use the nuisance wharfs as transfer points for garbage headed to the Mississippi River through the 1880s, although there were breakdowns and interruptions to regular service—at which times refuse merely accumulated. An 1882 ordinance prohibited dumping directly into the river from its bank. In addition, the state legislature stepped in and mandated that boats operating from the nuisance wharves had to navigate to the lower limits of the city and dump the offal, garbage, and night soil into the middle of the river.[46] Both these regulatory efforts indicate that the outlawed actions were problems. Due to numerous inadequacies in the nuisance wharves, the city sought an improved system by the 1890s. An ordinance passed in 1893 called for a private-sector solution—once again city officials hoped a corporation could solve a problem the city could not. A private contractor would collect garbage and refuse and transport it to a plant site approved by the city council, where waste would be incinerated or reduced "into merchantable products"—namely fertilizer. Turning to technological solutions, the city chose to divert the waste from the convenient sink, while offering a financial reward for entrepreneurial effort. The New Orleans Chemical and Fertilizer Company submitted the accepted bid. Thinking that it had found a scientific and sanitary solution, the city ordered the sale of its garbage fleet and demolition of the nuisance wharves in 1894.[47] The state Board of Health hailed New Orleans's garbage plant as "the largest and most complete of its kind" in the country.[48]

Apparently, the state's and the city's optimism was premature. To permit the conversion of garbage to grease or fertilizer, the contractor severely restricted the type of garbage it would haul. New city regulations allowed residents to place "slops, offal, garbage, and dead animals"—organic material —in watertight containers. The public found that this early form of recycling required too much sorting and objected to the new restrictions on what they could discard. Opposition to the sorting, coupled with delays in completing the new plant, resulted in the accumulation of huge garbage heaps throughout the city, and this inflamed public opinion. To prevent a terrible situation from getting worse, the city resumed refuse collection and river disposal, although this was not the final solution. The New Orleans Chemical and Fertilizer Company sued the city, claiming the municipal government was stealing its raw materials, and the courts agreed that the company had exclusive rights to the garbage. Despite its court victory, the faulty start handicapped the company and it went into receivership by 1897. Consequently, the city had to resume operation of its garbage facilities.[49] In spite of grand plans to produce revenue from garbage, the city spent more on the new system than the old and still had not resolved the garbage issue by the end of the century. The river and batture remained garbage sinks along with the low lots and the swamps at the rear of the city.[50]

Finding and developing a suitable water supply was another of this low-lying city's environmental challenges. Although water was abundant—from the river, ample precipitation, and high water table—delivery to houses in a potable form was another matter. Although provision of water is obviously not a nuisance activity, it merits consideration here as a typical community resource that cities sought to protect through regulations. Additionally, nuisance activity could threaten the water supply. Yet in New Orleans municipal ordinances did little to protect this resource. Instead authorities sought to manipulate the means of collection and transport so that citizens could safely consume the essential fluid. In the early 1800s, vendors sold water hauled from the river as the initial supply. After straining through cheesecloth, charcoal, or other filters, it was drinkable. Seeking a more efficient way to supply water, the city authorized a private effort to develop a water delivery system in 1810. This effort produced a limited cypress-pipe system and a small reservoir supplied by hand-pumped river water that was ineffectual. In 1811 the city approved a contract with Benjamin Latrobe to construct a more effective water delivery system. Over the course of several years, Latrobe struggled to get the enterprise operational. Finally, in 1819 he installed a steam pump to lift water from the river through a limited series of wooden pipes. Although it never served the entire city, Latrobe's New Orleans Water Works operated from the 1820s to 1840.[51] At that time, a second company took over the inadequate system until the city resumed control in 1869. Only a few thousand households had connections in the early years of Reconstruction, and in 1879 fewer than 10 percent of residences received river water through the delivery system.[52]

Unlike other cities where residents tapped groundwater, most New Orleanians eschewed subterranean water from colonial times. Nonetheless, some households resorted to wells, and bakeries actually favored the ammonia-tainted water for making bread. Following the city's takeover of the waterworks in 1869, the commissioner ordered a groundwater study. It reported that shallow wells yielded water that was unfit for drinking, washing, or cooking. The author pointed out that without an effective sewage system, the shallow groundwater would contain large amounts of deleterious matter that would not only cause bodily harm but could give rise to fatal diseases. Leaving no uncertainty, the report stated that "in thickly populated places, the well waters become so impregnated as to render the water absolutely poisonous." The report went so far as to claim that "graveyard water" was purer than New Orleans groundwater.[53] Nonetheless, groundwater remained an inexpensive option for many residents. In 1879 some 6,261 households—or about 16 percent—still depended on well water. A few families in the oldest section of town, which also had the most connections to the water system, still used well water. In the less affluent Sixth District, the inspector reported that there were 840 wells—"the wholesomeness and purity of whose contents are not above suspicion"—and not a single hydrant.[54] By 1894 the number of wells had fallen to 1,290.[55] For the poorest residents, however, drinking a fluid likened to "graveyard water" remained an overwhelming likelihood.

Given the groundwater conditions, most residents relied on cypress cisterns that collected rainwater from their roofs (Fig. 2.3). There was some concern about the safety of consuming this water too, however. Barton observed in his 1854 assessment of the yellow fever epidemic that rainwater collected from urban rooftops contained the filth and soot that accumulated there, plus "the gaseous impurities with which the air is impregnated." He argued that New Orleans residents should filter cistern water through charcoal to remove the foreign substances. Yet he also championed a city-owned water works that could supply pure drinking water to all homes.[56] Nonetheless, in 1872 about 78 percent of the households had cisterns.[57] There was little change by the time of the 1878 yellow fever epidemic, when over 75 percent of the 39,000 households in New Orleans still used cisterns. According to Joseph Holt, the cistern system raised concerns abut quantity as well as quality. Low-income families with small storage capacity faced water shortages during extended dry spells and sometimes resorted to drinking the filthy gutter water.[58]

To protect water consumers and to make the water resources more ac-

FIG. 2.3. FRENCH QUARTER CISTERN. Many residences relied on rainfall collected in cisterns for drinking water. Unidentified courtyard in the French Quarter, ca. 1900. C. Milo Williams Photograph Collection, no. 11. Courtesy New Orleans Public Library.

cessible, the state and city took several steps. After a series of hearings, the state enacted legislation that would move the slaughterhouses situated above the water intakes to a downstream site. Although it took several years to pass the act, graphic testimony to the legislators made clear the fact that entrails and other refuse from the cattle sheds and slaughterhouses mingled with the water supply.[59] Although some argued that dilution made river water safe, the city took a step in concert with the state's effort in 1869 by prohibiting the dumping of offal, refuse, or other injurious matter above the water intake.[60] The city also reclaimed the waterworks that year with the intent of rehabilitating and extending the system that had been neglected during the war. It announced plans to offer free drinking hydrants so that all citizens could have water as they moved about the city. Yet the system the city took over was barely functional, and it had precious few resources to invest in a major renovation. Most fire plugs were unserviceable, and all pipes needed replacement.[61] Even if protecting and rehabilitating the waterworks was effective, these steps only protected a quarter of the city's households. To assist the remaining three quarters, an 1870 regulation called for all cisterns to have a capacity of at least 1800 gallons and required an annual cleaning, although enforcement was lax.[62]

The postbellum city was unable to make the expensive yet necessary improvements to the water delivery system. In 1876, for example, still only half the fire hydrants were operational; the pumps were able to move only half the water they were designed to handle; the reservoir was half full of sediment; and some of the elite neighborhoods were still without connections— to say nothing of the poorer quarters.[63] Regulatory action had again fallen short of the desired outcome, and thus the city was unable to impose its will upon the environment. Amid lingering concerns about the inadequacies of both water supplies, the city once again transferred the waterworks back to a private corporation to institute quality improvements and expand the system's reach.[64]

The city turned its operation over to the New Orleans Water Works in 1879 on the condition that it deliver an adequate clear water supply. First among the difficulties facing the water company were the reservoirs. The two basins it inherited from the city were clogged with sediment. Even after standing in the basins, the water that arrived in households was still "heavily charged with sediment."[65] The company quickly repaired the reservoirs and laid seven miles of new pipe during its first few years, but delivery of clear water remained an elusive goal. To uphold its chartered obligations, the company continually investigated the possibility of installing a filtration system. Yet as long as it delivered turbid water, the company faced an eroding customer base and was unable to fulfill its promise. The city regularly encouraged the corporation officials to complete their improvements and even passed ordinances to abate unauthorized use of the company's water for flushing streets. The state also stepped in and passed legislation requiring its inspectors to issue fines for houses that did not have either a connection to the water supply or cistern capacity of 200 gallons per room.[66] Despite this governmental support, only 4,914 households out of over 11,000 private residences with connections paid for water delivery in 1883. Those who declined the service complained that water quality was not worth the expense.[67] Unable to expand its modest customer base, the company was never able to accumulate adequate financial resources to meet its primary obligation.

Seeking a way to satisfy the demand for clean water, other than by filtration, led the water company to consider bringing in water from north of Lake Pontchartrain, tapping the freshwater rivers that drain the Florida Parishes. Unlike cities such as New York and Philadelphia that could buy rural watersheds, build reservoirs, and allow water to flow through pipes by gravitational pull to their citizens,[68] New Orleans was on the high ground, occupying the narrow crest, albeit a low one, between the turbid Mississippi River and the brackish Lake Pontchartrain. There simply was not a sufficient drainage basin to yield a satisfactory supply from the bayous that drained the natural levee, nor was there adequate relief to build a reservoir. Use of Bayou St. John as a surface drain for sewage stymied further consideration of that waterway as a drinking water source. Several rivers north of Lake Pontchartrain, the Tangipahoa, Tickfaw, Tchefuncte, and Bogue Falaya, were the closest watercourses with suitable flow. An engineering report concluded that the Bogue Falaya had sufficient discharge and was of excellent quality to meet the city's needs for some years to come. Tapping this river would require not only building a reservoir, but pumping the water a substantial distance around the lake's perimeter. In the 1880s, this notion was rejected out of hand by the financially strapped water company.[69]

By the end of the nineteenth century, the waterworks company, still unable to deliver a satisfactory filtration system, was faltering.[70] Repeated complaints about inadequate water to fight fires, turbid tap water, inequitable rates, and large users building their own delivery systems exposed the company's shortcomings. To forestall the loss of industrial customers, the company filed suit against the city and private industries claiming it had sole right to deliver water.[71] It won this battle. To boost demand, it also started a campaign to raise doubts about the safety of drinking water from its major competitor—cisterns. In its annual report, the company claimed that cisterns were a "menace" to its revenues but pointed out that the domestic storage tank had "grown steadily in its unpopularity, and is now condemned by the more intelligent of our people, and by the members of the present and preceding Boards of Health. It has proved not only objectionable as to its character, but unreliable as to quantity."[72] While apparently hoping to turn public opinion against cistern water and gaining official sanction against it, the company pressed forward with its filtration plant installation.[73]

Cistern water had enjoyed a decent, if not excellent, reputation until the water company began discrediting it in the late nineteenth century. Although cisterns collected foreign material washed from roofs, devices were available to divert the initial runoff during a rain storm and accept only water that flowed across a rinsed surface. Furthermore, the fact that individual households could manage their own water supply stymied the spread of certain diseases. For example, the disconnected household water supplies helped prevent the spread of typhoid via a municipal water system. Storing water aboveground rather than relying on groundwater also discouraged epidemics of waterborne diseases. Nonetheless, by the end of the nineteenth century, concerns about cistern water had surfaced. In addition to the quantity issue addressed by city ordinance, health authorities began questioning the quality of water that remained in the cisterns for extended periods of time. They were concerned that the sediment in the tank contributed to disease. In 1900 the state Board of Health noted that as households drew water from nearly empty cisterns, disease rates increased. They attributed this to biological decomposition of organic sludge at the bottom of the cistern. Indeed, the state board claimed that each month-long drought claimed more than a hundred lives due to this condition.[74] Official approval of cistern water had evaporated.

Although public confidence in rainwater had eroded, the waterworks was unable to fulfill its legal responsibility to supply clear water—leaving the public with no viable options. Using technology developed for rivers with much less sediment, the water company installed a trial filtration project that produced a still defective product. Given the waterworks' perennial inability to deliver a satisfactory supply and other problems with the extent of service and rates, the state legislature initiated an investigation in 1898. The legislature concluded the waterworks supplied only about one-fifth of the built-up area with water that required further filtration and boiling once it arrived in homes, and it charged inequitable prices for this faulty product.[75] On the heels of this investigation, the city finally approved a bond issue calling for a city-managed water, drainage, and sewerage system, that eventually ended the sporadic and ineffective efforts of privately operated municipal utilities (see Chapter 3).

The various efforts to protect the vital public drinking water resource and regulate its use had marginal beneficial effects. Increasing the required cistern capacity did not solve the drought problem, and assigning the waterworks company the responsibility to deliver clear water failed as well. Furthermore, even within the severely circumscribed portion of the city served by waterlines, only a small number of residents could afford the commercial water. Therefore, despite an abundance of water, by the end of the nineteenth century the city was unable to provide its citizens with a satisfactory drinking water supply. Regulating the environment to eliminate the water resource shortage had failed. Groundwater, rainwater, and river water remained potential threats to the citizenry.

Cemeteries were another critical part of New Orleans's nuisance landscapes. Barton noted that the six cemeteries (Fig. 2.1), which received over seven thousand bodies during the 1853 epidemic, were "an important aid in corrupting the air."[76] Like garbage regulations, the public policy to control burial ground nuisances segregated the activity from the population. This meant sequestering the cemeteries as much as local topography would allow. Initially this involved moving them to the rear of the city—the zone of discard. Later, cemetery locations shifted to the high ground on the Metairie Ridge to take their place away from the main population concentration. Placing them at the urban fringe was a geographic solution. Regulation of burial practices, long a topic of rumor and speculation in New Orleans, offered a technical rather than spatial separation of interments.

According to prevailing medical opinion in the late eighteenth and early nineteenth centuries, decaying corpses contributed to the harmful effluvia that threatened cities like New Orleans. During a 1788 fever outbreak, immediately following a disastrous fire, officials moved the cemetery from "the last block" (between Burgundy, St. Peter, Toulouse, and Rampart streets), to an area beyond the original grid—what is now referred to as St. Louis No. 1. They feared that grave diggers would expose decaying corpses, thereby releasing foul smells and emissions that would cause further illness.[77] Moving burials still farther out, the city selected a second municipal cemetery (St. Louis No. 2) nearly half a mile from the city limits in 1823. Following the cholera outbreak in 1832, when over six thousand died and heaps of decaying bodies littered the streets awaiting burial, the city council enacted new ordinances to control the burial nuisance. In 1833 the city authorized another municipal cemetery on what was then known as the Leprous Road and outlawed underground burials at the old Catholic cemetery. This law permitted families to continue using the old burial grounds, but only if they erected aboveground tombs. An 1835 ordinance prohibited underground burial at all cemeteries within the city limits, although it permitted aboveground tombs. It also required all persons dying in the city limits to be buried at a planned cemetery on Bayou St. John—well beyond the city boundaries. Neither of these ordinance-mandated burial grounds ever materialized, but the ordinances reflected an urge to move cemeteries farther and farther from the core population and to discourage underground interments. When the city created the St. Louis No. 3 in 1854, it occupied a site near Bayou St. John on the flanks of the Metairie Ridge.[78] Each displacement of the municipal cemetery shifted this nuisance farther outward, even though the city subsequently encroached on the new locations. In recommending the removal of the Girod Cemetery (a Protestant facility), a health inspector summarized the basic thinking in 1871: "Cemeteries should not be in the heart of cities, but at some distance from them. This general principle is generally well observed every where in the infancy of cities, but as they grow they extend irregularly in surface, and localities formerly outside may after a time be embraced within their limits and occupy central locations. Due regard to health require[s] that they should be removed."[79] As they did in many other cities, cemeteries shifted outward, at least to an extent, in New Orleans.[80]

By mid-century, several cemeteries occupied property where Canal Street intersected the Metairie Ridge (Fig. 2.1). The Cypress Grove, St. Patrick's, and Charity Hospital cemeteries all occupied this topographically higher ground by 1850. Use of this location enabled deeper burials (up to 7 feet), which was believed to reduce "emanations from the putrefying corpses" that caused disease. Deeper interment and new city ordinances that called for more secure burial vaults combined to minimize supposed exhalations from the burial sites.[81] Other cemeteries followed, and by 1888 the state Board of Health reported that the Metairie Ridge cemetery cluster consisted of "some fifteen cemeteries, forming quite an extensive city of the dead remote from those districts which are thickly populated by the living." At that time, of the thirty-six cemeteries throughout New Orleans, thirty-one still practiced underground burial, although the majority employed both vault and subterranean interment. To control the nuisance associated with tombs, regulations eventually prohibited their reopening for a year after the burial of a person who died of natural causes or two years following the interment of those who succumbed to a contagious disease.[82] These regulations expressed a belief that diseased corpses presented a longer-term nuisance than others and that the nuisance was merely temporary. This circumstance allowed the common reuse of vaults. Furthermore, the nuisance was inherent in the body, not the location. Thus cemeteries as nuisance sites constituted a threat only through the activity and not as a result of the site's inherent properties.

Despite attempts to regulate the nuisances, burial practices continued to produce undesirable conditions. Joseph Holt recounted deplorable conditions near the potter's field (Locust and Freret streets). The city allowed shallow underground burial at the potter's field, which in some situations resulted in coffins being placed only a few inches below grade. Neighbors offered shrill opposition to this situation. During the summer months, a "stench from human bodies invaded their homes" and the atmosphere was "heavy with exhalations of the dead." During the 1878 epidemic, sextons heaped putrefying dead on the ground while they awaited interment. During such times, hogs reportedly invaded the cemetery and feasted on the rotting carcasses.[83] This gruesome situation was in sharp contrast with the glistening white marble tombs of families who could afford the cost of a legal burial in the cemeteries. While municipal regulations forced most cemeteries to the edge of the built-up area, or required the use of suitably constructed aboveground tombs, the city itself used a potter's field within the urban limits and rejected a request to relocate this burial ground beyond the municipal boundaries. Furthermore, the city buried the dead contrary to the requirements it imposed on other cemeteries, thereby maintaining a serious nuisance. Once again municipal finances negated the city's ability to achieve the intent of its own regulations.

Following the rapid creation of numerous facilities on the Metairie Ridge at mid-century, New Orleans cemetery land use remained fairly fixed during the final quarter of the century. The use and reuse of tombs precluded constant expansion, and the soggy terrain discouraged it as well. So even as the city grew during the late nineteenth century, there were few major new cemeteries. Reliance on aboveground tombs, which permitted suitable decay of corpses and therefore elimination of their nuisance properties, apparently satisfied public health officials and the citizenry, and there was little regulatory effort on the part of the city during the final decades of the 1800s.

Manufacturers constituted the other principal nuisance in the nineteenth century. Barton cited the soap and tallow chandleries, slaughterhouses, and livery stables as the main industrial sources of "polluting exhalations."[84] As it did with garbage and cemeteries, the city sought to regulate the placement of these and other offending trades to locations beyond the city limits. For preexisting operations, a permit and inspection system evolved.

The city council enacted an ordinance restricting the establishment or continuation of certain nuisance industries in 1855. Specifically, this action mandated that operators of soap factories, tanneries, bone black factories, and slaughterhouses obtain permission from the common council. Furthermore, additional articles stated that slaughterhouses could not release blood or other wastes to the streets or open lots or even emit an offensive odor. Police were to make weekly inspections and could levy fines for offenses.[85] By 1867, the public health regulations added more restrictions. The nuisance laws prohibited soap makers from storing tallow or grease in a state of putrefaction. It also gave the mayor authority to have the city physician inspect any manufacturing plant that "exhales fetid or offensive odors or vapors." If the physician determined the vapors would "impair the salubrity" of the neighborhood, he had the authority to halt operations until conditions were improved. Violators who refused to modify their practices to comply with the order were subject to fines.[86]

Given the city's enforcement history, it should come as no surprise that the post–Civil War population found industrial nuisances beyond its tolerance level—particularly those emanating from the many slaughterhouses. Several stock-landing sheds and slaughterhouses clustered along the waterway in the upriver community of Jefferson. These operators dumped solid and liquid wastes and even carcasses of diseased animals into the river.[87] A public health officer charged that "[t]he amount of filth thrown into the river above the source from which the city is supplied with water, and coming from the slaughterhouses is incredible. Barrels filled with entrails, liver, blood, urine, dung, and other refuse, portions in an advanced stage of decomposition, are constantly being thrown into the river but a short distance from the banks, poisoning the air with offensive smells and necessarily contaminating the water near the banks for miles."[88] Despite opposition from influential New Orleans citizens, the state legislature finally passed a sanitary act in 1869 requiring the consolidation of all slaughterhouse activity on the west bank in Algiers. The legislative position sought to remove the nuisance conditions from within the densely settled areas of the city and also move the activity below the city water intakes—again a strategy of geographic isolation. This was an approach that had proven successful in France and in cities on the eastern seaboard.[89]

Local butchers challenged the legislation on the grounds that they could not slaughter livestock in their small shops scattered throughout town.[90] The law, they claimed, denied them use of their property, even though it allowed them to continue their trade in the consolidated slaughterhouse. In what became a landmark constitutional case, the courts ultimately upheld the right of the slaughterhouse owners to build and operate a single facility as long as it permitted use by individual butchers. The decision upheld the right of the state to use police power in securing public health objectives.[91] The original location, however, was rejected in favor of a location just downstream from the city limits on the east bank. When constructed, the new facilities offered much greater sanitary protection with watertight floors to prevent blood and other fluids from seeping into the soil where it could release effluvia. The walls received a coating of black varnish to keep them from absorbing blood, and pipes supplied wash-water for the entire facility. By 1880, public health authorities had proclaimed the operation a vast improvement over previous conditions.[92]

The consolidated slaughterhouse's success contrasts with other persistent nuisance industries. Detailed maps from the 1880s depict numerous soap works, foundries, and stables in the industrial district upstream from Canal Street.[93] Stables and foundries also continued to operate in the Vieux Carré. An 1887 ordinance imposed some restrictions on nuisance-causing industries. It mandated that those with furnaces erect chimneys at least 20 feet tall to prevent cinders and soot from falling on neighboring properties. The city nonetheless granted many exemptions for industries including foundries, stables, and slaughterhouses within the city limits.[94] Despite persistent concern with nuisances and ongoing regulatory efforts, the city had not eliminated offensive industries by the end of the nineteenth century.

Nuisance landscapes lingered in the Crescent City. Soggy soil contained far more than just earth material. Overflowing privies and open sewage canals released a horrific odor that earned New Orleans the reputation of the death hole of Dixie. Inadequate garbage disposal relied on two zones of discard—the great river (and all too frequently its banks) and the swampy ground to the rear of the city. Under pressure from a growing population, most cemeteries shifted outward to the higher ground of the Metairie Ridge, where aboveground vault entombment reduced the nuisances associated with burial. Yet the city continued to employ shallow underground burial at its potter's field in the midst of residential neighborhoods. Although the city attempted to force certain nuisance-causing industries out of the city, it permitted many preexisting firms to continue their operations. As long as the city relied on geographic isolation of nuisances, it would reencounter the activities it exiled. And by grandfathering in activities that predated laws, it offset the benefits of isolation. Enforcement of regulations was lax or absent in the financially strapped city as well. Consequently, the countless nuisance-related laws did not eliminate undesirable conditions by the end of the nineteenth century. The grand effort to restore tolerable environments produced only marginal gains.

CREATING AMENABLE SPACES

As the city struggled to expel undesirable activity, it also worked to create amenable spaces—to counteract nuisances with "nature" and to uplift its citizens with bucolic parks. This approach fundamentally differed from regulating nuisances. It was also unlike modern open-space planning that preserves undeveloped green territory in urban areas. New Orleans's effort to establish amenity spaces sought not to preserve but to establish naturalistic parks for the first time, and pristine or undeveloped spaces were not the intent. Overall, this effort sought to impart a humanized face on the landscape. Additionally, each phase had distinctly different purposes and created particular landscapes. During the second half of the nineteenth century, the focus was on large urban parks, yet the platting of plazas and planting of street trees prefaced the larger-scale undertakings.

Each of the three municipalities had an open square in the early 1800s: Jackson Square in the Vieux Carré, Lafayette Square in the American Sector, and Washington Square in Faubourg Marigny. Jackson Square, originally the Place d'Armes, was a component of the original city plan surveyed in 1721. Maintained throughout the colonial period as a parade ground for military and other public ceremonies and a central plaza during the Spanish period. Early maps show walkways through the plaza and trees planted around the perimeter. In 1812, the city passed an ordinance to install brick walkways in the Place d'Armes and to surround the square with a cypress balustrade.[95] The city renamed the plaza after the hero of the Battle of New Orleans in 1850, when it also installed a statue of the general-president. It also planted new trees as part of the park's redevelopment.[96] So commemorated, the square remained a key landmark in the French Quarter. In 1829, a comparable square was established in the Faubourg Marigny (the first downstream suburb) and was named after the country's first president, George Washington. Three rows of oaks were planted at the time of its creation, and a cast-iron fence was built around its perimeter in 1853.[97] Gravier Square, later renamed after the French hero General Lafayette, was part of the original 1788 plan for the upstream Faubourg St. Marie.[98] As it had done at the other parks, the city installed formal diagonal walkways, planted shade trees, and erected an iron fence. Congo Square, situated just outside the original Vieux Carré, had its origins as a market where slaves sold produce and as a place where African Americans congregated to perform traditional dances on Sundays. It functioned as a lively social gathering place for the community's African Americans and particularly for the Tremé neighborhood. Although it never received any formal landscaping until 1845, it was an important part of the city's set of plazas.[99] These parks harken to the European tradition of municipal plazas. Their delineation in the urban landscape was not as market spaces or commons as found in towns in New England, nor private residential squares. Rather they were specialized public places set aside for social and ceremonial purposes and to promote the health of residents.

New Orleans also embraced the notion of tree-lined boulevards and planted trees along major thoroughfares during the second decade of the nineteenth century.[100] One result was that the three main boulevards enclosing the French Quarter had shade trees growing by 1813, and bird's-eye views from the 1850s show that the trees had matured to provide ample shade by mid-century. Benjamin Norman described them in 1845: "Shrubbery, and other ornaments, are in progress, and they already begin to assume a beauty that does much credit to the city authorities."[101] Tree-lined boulevards drew on European traditions, and although not unique to New Orleans, they became a characteristic feature of its landscape.[102] The initial purpose of these tree-lined spaces was to help cleanse the urban air and to provide shade from the near-tropical heat. Barton had offered the opinion that trees would absorb the noxious gases and improve the city's salubrity.[103] Thus the early efforts to establish a sylvan landscape had direct links to preserving public health, to creating spaces in the city that would obviate deleterious conditions produced by the ubiquitous nuisances. The tree-lined boulevard, more than the small plazas, were accessible to all citizens who traveled the major thoroughfares.

The initial effort to create a grand city park also found its rationale in concerns for creating a salubrious setting for city dwellers. When the city acquired over 100 acres of land from the estate of John McDonough on the Metairie Ridge in 1854, Mayor Waterman proclaimed that the site would become "a place of great resort for our population, and when improved, as it should be, it will be without a doubt a most popular resort for all that portion of inhabitants who do not leave the city during the summer months as well as the citizens in general."[104] In the tradition of the picturesque park movement, the city installed a few benches before the Civil War. The unpleasant interlude deferred investment in the park, and the minimal improvements fell into disrepair as local dairies allowed their livestock to graze on the grounds. In 1872 the city commissioned New York landscape architects Bogart and Cutler to design a picturesque park, although no action was taken on their design.[105]

Audubon Park, originally known as Upper City Park, owes its birth to picturesque park planning impulses as well. In 1870 the state authorized a special tax in New Orleans to transform the former plantation site into a municipal park. Largely conceived as a tool for real estate speculation during the turbulent Reconstruction, the New Orleans Park Commission acquired land adjacent to the upstream suburb of Carrollton. Speculators apparently fleeced the commission and left it with property but no funds to improve the unkept grounds. By the early 1880s, the city struck a deal to lease a right-of-way to a railroad company through the park along its batture and use the income for improvements. However, virtually no action was taken to carve a park from the former plantation grounds before 1884.[106]

The decision to host a major international exposition in New Orleans sparked new interest in the site. Once selected as the location for the World's Industrial and Cotton Centennial Exposition, investors and government bodies pumped money into making improvements to the park grounds in 1884. This included a drainage system and the construction of a central exposition hall, a government building, and a horticulture hall. Barely ready on opening day, the exposition proved to be a disappointment, and attendance fell far short of the optimistic projections.[107] Nonetheless, the expo-

FIG. 2.4. CITY PARK, CA. 1900. City Park was one of two picturesque parks developed in late-nineteenth-century New Orleans. Harry D. Johnson Photograph Collection. Courtesy New Orleans Public Library.

sition helped transform a raw site into a destination for recreation and left one permanent building that became the core of a subsequent park-making project.

Both City and Audubon parks witnessed major development projects during the 1890s. The intent for parks during this time went beyond creating spaces that would rejuvenate foul air or permit contemplative strolls whereby visitors could escape from the artificial city into "nature" (Fig. 2.4). Embracing Progressive Era notions of civic responsibility for the urban masses, park planners sought to create parks that would both offer healthful settings for recreation and provide a refining moral influence for their users. Drawing on ideas of park proponents in San Francisco and Buffalo, the New Orleans officials stressed the need to create a healthful and relaxing setting that would keep its citizens away from base forms of entertainment available elsewhere in the city.[108] Advocates proclaimed large parks would "provide for the dwellers of cities convenient opportunity to enjoy beautiful natural scenery and to obtain occasional relief from the nervous strain due to the excessive artificiality of city life."[109]

To promote such developments in New Orleans, the state legislature created park improvement associations for both City and Audubon parks. Each developed plans for its respective tract. The Audubon Park Improvement Association hired the Olmsted firm in 1897 to design its park and began a piecemeal installation of the plans prepared by John Charles Olmsted, nephew of Frederick. The Olmsted vision included a series of meandering lagoons near the park boundaries, backed by vegetation. Within the park were to be formal gardens, walkways, and various recreational facilities. Work on City Park began with fencing out the cows, laying out shell-covered walkways, planting trees and flowering plants, and dredging the old Metairie Bayou to create a scenic lagoon. Each park association struggled to secure adequate funds to carry out its mission during the early 1890s, but eventually city appropriations made budgeting improvements somewhat more dependable.[110]

By the end of the century, with financial assistance from the city, both parks could claim to offer the bucolic and uplifting setting the associations sought to create. Spreading over several hundred acres, the two parks inserted scenic grounds into the urban fabric that offered relief from New Orleans's numerous nuisances. These larger parks may not have shaped the behavior of the general population—indeed, some doubted the public was even interested in them initially—but they did offset the less desirable influences of sewage, cemeteries, and industry. In doing so, they reflected a very deliberate effort to insert "nature" in the city, to fashion a landscape that would not just deflect the offensive odors of garbage dumps and stinking factories but manipulate the behavior of the city's residents in a positive way. In this respect, they stand as an effort of the urban elite to shape the character of the urban masses.

New Orleans did not suffer from the excessive population density of cities with multistory tenements. At the turn of the century, it retained a low profile. Nonetheless, it had true urban density due largely to the narrow band of natural levee where it was feasible to build structures and lay out transportation corridors. This confining circumstance kept the 287,000 residents in close proximity to the pervasive nuisances. Massive open canals transected the city, laden with sewage and other filth; they infused the atmosphere with effluvia that the gentle Gulf winds could hardly carry away. Garbage along the waterfront and at the rear of the city enveloped working-class citizens who lived nearby in an inescapable stench. Objectionable industries, armed with special permits, persisted in the city as well. Despite a series of regulations that stepped up the restrictions on undesirable activity, nuisances dominated the urban landscape in 1900. Delivery of a palatable and safe water supply remained an unattained goal. The city authorities, along with the state legislature, recognized the various problems and re-wrote ordinances to target particular problems. Yet a financially strapped city found enforcement difficult, and this left legal solutions moot. When the city turned to private-sector operators to run its public utilities, it found them no more effective. Specific ordinances had less influence on the common resource than their drafters intended.

New Orleans also took measures to offset nuisances in the urban environment. By installing plazas, planting tree-lined boulevards, and establishing picturesque parks, local authorities sought environmental solutions to public health problems. By the turn of the century, the Progressive Era reforms strived to push the influence of parks beyond the mere rejuvenation of local environments to uplift the citizenry as well. This effort established two major urban parks in New Orleans and set aside two large tracts as "anti-nuisance" zones.

CHAPTER 3

INEQUITY AND THE ENVIRONMENT

BASIN STREET TAKES its name from a turning basin at the upper end of the Carondelet Canal that linked nineteenth-century New Orleans with Bayou St. John and Lake Pontchartrain (Fig. 3.1). Although the basin represented the canal's headwaters, a mere five feet of fall aided flow toward sea level. Adjacent to the turning basin, African Americans had created Congo Square, a site noted for their social activity from the colonial era into the mid-nineteenth century. By contrast, land near the river front was about 10 feet higher. There stood the splendid St. Louis Cathedral facing the civic plaza, Jackson Square. The two prominent social spaces for African and European American citizens exemplify the subtle topographic and racial segregation in the Crescent City. With greater means and power, the white population occupied the better-drained sections of the city, while blacks typically inhabited the swampy "rear" districts.[1] Jackson Square was a showplace, and Congo Square, while never grand, deteriorated during Reconstruction.[2] Environmental inequity was inherent in these contrasting landscapes.[3] This chapter will examine early-twentieth-century environmental management projects that sought to alter local hydrology and topography and consequently also reworked local racial geography.[4]

After years of delivering ineffective drainage, sewerage, and water service, New Orleans embarked on a massive and, for the first time, coordinated public works program at the turn of the twentieth century. This project took place concurrently with similar Progressive Era urban redevelopment projects throughout the country.[5] In the South, it also coincided with the rise of Jim Crow racist politics. A Progressive Era engineering project, in theory, should have been color-blind. To install a viable system, it was essential that the canals, sewers, water mains, and pumping stations reach all corners of the city. The politics of exclusion, however, had the potential to undermine an ideally equitable design.

By lowering the water table, the New Orleans drainage system opened new areas for settlement and created an opportunity to revamp the city's racial geography. Indeed, new highly efficient pumps installed in 1917 have been identified as *the* agent for racial segregation in New Orleans.[6] However, public policy, more than infrastructure, imposed limits on residential options. Sewer mains, the system's second component, gradually and somewhat selectively followed the drainage network to all sections of the city, although gaps in the service suggest temporary inequities. Drinking water, the third element of this public works overhaul, also delivered inequitable service — at least for a while. A fourth, separate aspect of environmental development during this period was a parkway system. As an outgrowth of City Beautiful planning impulses, a municipal commission embarked on an early-twentieth-century project to plant trees along New Orleans's many boulevards — some of which were formerly open drainage canals that had been buried as part of the public works project. Inequities influenced this effort in the white-run community as well. What can these Progressive Era projects tell us about environmental equity? How did drainage, sewerage, water, and parkways contribute to the process of segregation? Are there obvious or subtle deviations from the plan that reveal early-twentieth-century environmental inequities? Despite a fundamental engineering mandate to create a citywide system, did the construction sequence favor certain districts at the expense of others? Or did public works prompt shifts in residential patterns? Most importantly, how deeply rooted are current environmental equity patterns in historical practices?

This chapter will invert the normal environmental equity inquiry. Rather than demonstrating the presence of undesirable land use proximate to the minority population, it will examine inequity in the design or creation of desirable environmental modifications. By identifying gaps in the system, it can more clearly document a linkage between public projects and neighborhood populations and thereby identify inequities.

ENVIRONMENTAL EQUITY

Jim Crow policies deliberately forced inequities on the African American population in the South after Reconstruction and found expression in voting restrictions, access to public facilities, and other areas of life. As discriminatory practices gained strength in the South, Progressive Era reforms were also under way. Cities measured their progress by the development of systematic urban services, such as sewerage and water.[7] These systems, by design, had to serve entire urban areas; to exclude one area would be inefficient engineering and could handicap the overall system. Yet as C. Vann Woodard observed, there was a fundamental conflict between Jim Crowism and progressivism: "The blind spot of the Southern progressive record . . . was the Negro, for the whole movement in the South coincided paradoxically with the crest of the wave of racism."[8] Although Progressive Era programs sought a type of environmental determinism, improving people by improving their environment, the exclusion of southern blacks illustrates an obvious choice not to elevate this group. New Orleans offers a grand panorama of this paradoxical struggle.

Late-nineteenth- and early-twentieth-century policy makers in southern cities did not allocate public utilities with an eye toward environmental equity as we understand the concept today.[9] Long before concerns emerged about landfills and hazardous waste sites, nuisance and insanitary conditions comprised undesirable environments. Extension of sewers and waterlines to affluent neighborhoods reflected the first nineteenth-century efforts to remedy environmental disamenities, and undeniable inequities existed in those programs.[10] Progressive Era engineering called for citywide systems that minimized inefficiencies. New Orleans's poorly drained setting called for a much more thorough environmental redevelopment than most other cities and hence unquestionably demanded a citywide system. Drainage made places within the city limits habitable for the first time, improving the quality of life for all citizens. How well drainage, sewerage, and waterlines truly served a neighborhood reflected the municipal officials' adherence to progressive engineering tenets. Clearly, tree planting was also an environmental amenity that had geographic properties and could expose favorable treatment of one group or another. Lapses or delays in service delivery, on the other hand, indicate deliberate efforts to deny neighborhoods an environmental amenity.[11] The racial composition of neighborhoods without services (both before and some time after) provides an indication of race-based environmental inequities. To understand how this condition came to be, it is essential to trace the process of both service extension and neighborhood demographic change—since neither was static during the early twentieth century.

Racial geography in the urban South always exhibited some degree of segregation, particularly sequestering blacks into less-desirable quarters. The most common form of African American residential cluster was a bottomlands settlement near the city boundary.[12] Poor drainage, flimsy housing, and inadequate public services characterized such neighborhoods.[13] Indeed, insanitary conditions became associated with the occupants of these areas rather than their physical situation.[14] It was in these neighborhoods and at the fringes of the central business area that rural migrants sought new urban homes during the early twentieth century. As the century progressed, inner-city concentrations became more common. New Orleans's racial geography, although somewhat unique, eventually followed many of these patterns.

It was typical in southern cities for early public works projects to bypass African American neighborhoods. In Birmingham, financing the sewerage system by special assessments made that service unattainable to low-income blacks, despite pleas by health officials in the second decade of the twentieth century to eliminate the health menace posed by the dense concentration of privies in the "quarters."[15] Atlanta's public works extension into black neighborhoods in that decade followed a decision to publicly finance sanitation facilities when concerns about the health of the white residents, who might be afflicted with disease emanating from African American neighborhoods, came to the fore.[16] Such was the conflict inherent in Progressive Era public works engineering in the South. Denial of services to one segment of the population could cause the entire city to suffer. Only with this recognition were cities willing to fund public sanitation projects throughout black neighborhoods.

Emergent Jim Crow politics stood in the way of Progressive Era reform by rigidly institutionalizing white superiority in the South and requiring segregation in most public settings.[17] This derailed the dreams of many blacks to achieve even a small measure of equality after attaining their freedom. Among the most obvious areas of segregation or unequal access were restrictions on housing access. Municipal ordinances and later deed covenants specifically excluded blacks from designated sectors in New Orleans and many other cities.[18] These policy tools played an exceptionally important role in the Crescent City's evolving racial geography between 1910 and 1940.

The complete picture of New Orleans's racial geography requires a review of both the engineering works and the policies that contributed to its evolution during the early twentieth century. Although New Orleans was noted as having a low degree of residential segregation during the antebellum period, neighborhoods dominated by a single racial group emerged during the height of Jim Crow and Progressive Era reforms.[19] Certainly segregation existed to some degree in New Orleans before 1865, and African Americans had less access to most public facilities than whites. There was some limited racial mixing in taverns, gambling houses, and bordellos, but there were both formal and informal restrictions against integrated activities, and they remained after the war.[20] During Union occupation of the city, the streetcar companies attempted to replace the segregated interiors of their vehicles with separate cars for white and black riders. This inspired protests by the African American population and ultimately led to a reversal of the separate-cars policy in 1867.[21] Thus there were antisegregationist victories for African Americans during Reconstruction in New Orleans. Yet census figures indicate that there were wards that exhibited higher than average black residential concentrations by 1890.[22] Thus when Progressive Era engineering and Jim Crow policies began their transformation of the urban South, there were definable African American neighborhoods in New Orleans. At least two processes contributed to full-blown segregation: (1) systematic reengineering of urban public works and (2) methodical deprivation of equal treatment to one racial group. The question at hand is: was one an agent of the other? Geographically selective public works installation into an already segregated city could offer decisive evidence of inequities. Residential adjustments following the construction would suggest forces other than just the public works system. By 1940, when the New Orleans public works system was largely in place, African Americans' clustering had become very pronounced.[23] What was the relationship between the two processes?

DRAINAGE AND NEIGHBORHOODS

Residential segregation was a part of New Orleans's racial geography, although it was less obvious citywide in the colonial and antebellum periods because most slaves lived on the same property as their owners. But New Orleans had a sizable free black population with greater flexibility in residential choices. During the early American period, the French and American districts—centering on the Canal Street business district—had horseshoe-shaped fringes of African American residences partly encircling them. Toward the rear, or low area, were truck and dairy farms. By 1850, European immigrants had displaced most of the black population in the American sector and pushed them toward the "back of town," or poorly drained areas.[24]

During the nineteenth century, several drainage companies constructed canals flowing into Lake Pontchartrain to augment the sluggish Bayou St. John and enhance the movement of water toward the lake. Several rudimentary pumps aided natural flow toward the lake, but the pre-1890 system was unable to keep pace with the average 60 inches of annual rain, let alone major downpours. These private enterprises alleviated water-laden conditions in some areas, but they were far from adequate to lower the overall water table behind the natural levees. Indeed, the drainage canals, with little natural flow, became "beds of garbage and excrement, fit only to generate fever and breed mosquitos."[25] According to the Louisiana Board of Health only the Carrollton section deserved favorable comments about its drainage. Situated near the upper end of the crescent, the Carrollton area is on a slight rise formed by crevasses. New Orleans residents considered this area a healthful location, and it was a place they resorted to for summer entertainment. Many African Americans lived in this suburban area, which had a black population of over 50 percent (nearly double the concentration found in other districts). The state characterized the main business district and the Vieux Carré as poorly drained and subject to flooding following rain. Likewise the downstream neighborhoods were locations of "great nuisance" and the "greatest sanitary evil" due to ineffective drainage, and they had only 25 percent black residents. Even the fashionable Garden District had a large number of low lots and "defective drainage" in the neighborhood's rear. A narrow portion of the adjoining upstream district, which straddled the edge of the edge of the "bowl," also received critical comments in terms of periodic flooding.[26] This portrait, on the eve of the great drainage overhaul, reveals the relationship of topography to drainage and the perception that poor drainage was a scourge to all residents' health. It also shows both upper- and lower-class citizens endured undesirable conditions, although the poor had less ability to select a better residential locale and could not escape the city during the summer. At the end of the nineteenth century, water service only reached very limited areas. Mains from the old private and municipal systems extended across the Vieux Carré, the commercial district, and upstream as far as Felicity Street. This service was oriented directly toward white neighborhoods. The only sewer lines were private ones installed by businesses or public institutions. Public works remained inaccessible to many residents, including blacks and recent immigrants.

PUBLIC WORKS PLAN

After decades of piecemeal drainage projects seeking "to benefit small disconnected sections" of town, the New Orleans Common Council appointed an engineering committee in 1893 to develop a systematic plan for relieving soggy conditions. It received a mandate to control surface runoff, lower groundwater levels, and develop a separate sewage system. The city council expressed concern that many areas of the city were unoccupied because "they are practically swamps" and therefore were impediments to urban growth and prosperity. Furthermore, these swampy tracts contributed to "unsanitary conditions," likewise frustrating economic growth. In response to these dual concerns, the engineers proposed that "a drainage project should therefore be extended to all [emphasis added] territory which is now, or will be, built up in a reasonable time, and it should effect the removal of rain and ground water from the same, so that the whole area can be made and kept thoroughly dry."[27] Sanitary improvements, even in areas occupied by blacks, would serve the entire city by reducing disease threats and thereby enhancing economic opportunities.

At the time, the built-up area was much smaller than the territory within the city limits (Fig. 3.1). There was a residential and commercial enclave at

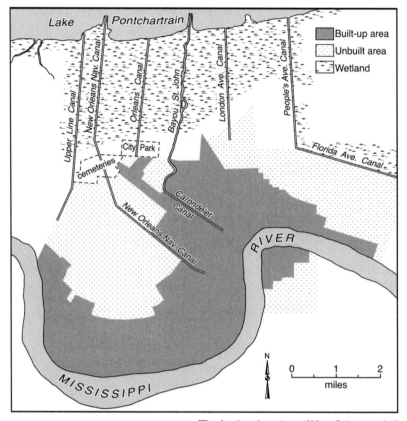

FIG. 3.1. URBANIZED TERRITORY, 1900. The developed portions of New Orleans pushed back from the natural levee into the low ground by 1900. After New Orleans Sewerage and Water Board, *Fifth Semi-Annual Report* (New Orleans: 1902).

the river bend known as Carrollton. Moving downstream, below Audubon Park, the site of the 1884 exposition, development existed atop the natural levee. Streetcar lines had encouraged development along the main arteries extending uptown. Closer to the central business district, the settlement pattern resembled a triangle, with its base on the French Quarter and it apex near the headwaters of Bayou St. John. Parallel drainage canals enabled urban land uses to extend lakeward behind the business district. Encircling the business district and lakeward of the main thoroughfares that followed the sweeping bend of the crescent, dairy farms and other rural land uses that could contend with marshy soils predominated.[28]

The public works program finally approved in 1899 sought to utilize the

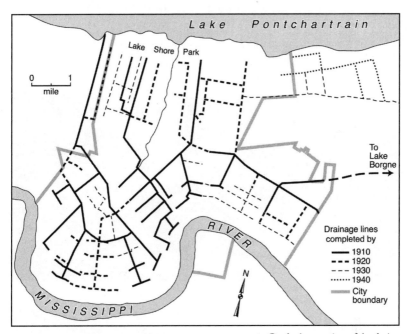

FIG. 3.2. DRAINAGE SYSTEM EXPANSION, 1900–1940. Gradual expansion of the drainage system eventually provided service to most of the city's built-up area by 1940. After New Orleans Sewerage and Water Board semiannual reports, 1900–1940.

power of gravity as much as possible to remove water. This meant that by enlarging the older canals and adding new drainage courses, the revitalized system would move water away from the natural levee along the river, through low areas, toward their ultimate outlets. Two viable discharge points existed: Lake Pontchartrain to the north, where the existing piecemeal system released its flow, and Lake Borgne, a shallow tidal bay east of the city (Fig. 3.2). Fearing pollution of Lake Pontchartrain near the lakefront entertainment district, the planners called for canals and pumps to intercept water flowing through the old drainage system and transport it eastward into a new channel that emptied into the Lake Borgne wetlands (Fig. 3.3a). Following major downpours, when the runoff would be highly diluted, the system would send excess water into Lake Pontchartrain via the preexisting canals. The authors proclaimed that "the proposed plan thus provides for thorough drainage of *every* [emphasis added] part of the city."[29] Evident in such a statement was the obvious desire to implement a complete system, based on rational engineering principles. After all, if the drainage

FIG. 3.3. DRAINAGE SYSTEM FEATURES. TOP: Early-twentieth-century canals built by the Sewerage and Water Board greatly improved the city's drainage. New Orleans Sewerage and Water Board, *Thirteenth Semi-Annual Report* (New Orleans: 1906). BOTTOM: Pumps lifted water from low areas and, as shown here, discharged into canals that flowed into Lake Pontchartrain or Lake Borgne. New Orleans Sewerage and Water Board, *Eighth Semi-Annual Report* (New Orleans: 1903).

component excluded one segment of the city, unhealthy conditions would persist, denying economic opportunities and offsetting the plan's desired benefits.

The lack of gradient posed a substantial challenge to the engineers. Although the slope along the back side of the natural levee was sufficient to move water into the main canal, the gentle gradient toward the lake offered little head. Along the 7-mile length of the main canal, the fall was only 2 feet, and at times Lake Borgne's tide and storm-influenced level could be higher than the canal's, thereby requiring pumps to move the water away from the city and weirs to prevent it from flowing back in (Fig. 3.3b). To handle excess storm runoff, the pumps would divert a portion of the flow to relief canals equipped with their own auxiliary pumps, to push the water through the ridges towards Lake Pontchartrain—planners expected that the highly diluted sewage carried by storm runoff would not create unpleasant conditions. Despite the grand scheme, however, excessive rain could overwhelm the system and cause localized flooding in the low areas, and thus the system designed to drain the entire city left the lowest areas vulnerable to inundation following exceptional rainfalls.[30]

The plan could not be implemented in its entirety due to fiscal constraints, at least not immediately, so the engineers set priorities, recommending that the initial effort focus on the main business district.[31] They argued that this section, because of "the concentration of improved properties, paved streets and business houses, and of its central position in reference to the most densely inhabited area of the city, is now more urgently in need of improved drainage than other localities."[32] Yet the New Orleans Navigation Canal (or New Basin Canal) and the Carondelet Canal, which terminated at Basin Street, bordered this district and already provided some drainage benefits that were unavailable to the rest of the city. The rear of the business district was low and largely unsettled (an indication of poor drainage), and the board's map also suggested that the rear uptown area had incomplete drainage and thin settlement, as did the downstream suburbs. The planners, by calling for drainage improvements in the central business district, were serving the business elite, but the residential population of this section was more than 30 percent African American—above the city average (Fig. 3.4). At its outset, at least, the plan did not deny service to some black neighborhoods.

The system's second component handled sewage. George Earl, super-

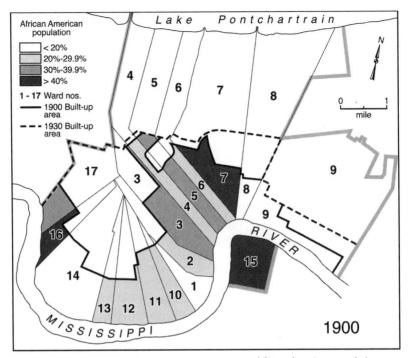

FIG. 3.4. AFRICAN AMERICAN POPULATION, 1900. African American population concentrated in the Seventh, Fifteenth, and Sixteenth wards in 1900. Source: U.S. Census.

intendent of the Sewerage and Water Board, described the horrendous conditions on the eve of construction:

> When, however, water closets are connected either to these vaults or to cesspools sunk deeper into an already saturated soil, then trouble begins and constant emptying at considerable cost discourages the owner, who finally constructs shallow drains near the surface, into the surrounding soil, or in a more direct, though unlawful, way allows overflow into an open gutter. . . . All kitchen, laundry, bath and other liquid household wastes go direct to surface gutters through flat and shallow alley gutters or pipe lines, and are what render the New Orleans gutter the reproach it is, which only a sewerage system can relieve.[33]

In order to use the Mississippi River's diluting power, the sewerage plan called for installing pumps that would lift domestic effluent through enclosed pipes up the natural levee and into the river downstream from the city. At the outset of the sewerage system's construction, the old open drainage canals handled much of the sewage, either directly or by way of seepage from vaults. In discussions about the new system, officials reasoned that separate drainage and sewer lines could be installed more expeditiously and thereby benefit the existing built-up area in less time.[34] There were obvious benefits seen in the combined effect of the surface drainage and subterranean sewer lines. Of central importance in the sewerage plan was the seemingly unlimited ability of the Mississippi River to assimilate and dilute household effluent while transporting it away from the city.

The limited water distribution system inherited from the several nineteenth-century efforts served a very small territory. Its mains passed through the Vieux Carré and throughout the American Sector—the suburb immediately upstream from Canal Street. One line also passed through the fashionable Garden District into the elite residential district uptown. This territory was largely white.

Municipal authorities, following a prevalent French practice, had initiated tree planting along major thoroughfares during the eighteenth century, and this continued into the 1800s.[35] Seen as a means to cleanse the atmosphere, trees lined the streets bordering the Vieux Carré. By the mid-nineteenth century, shaded boulevards were a trademark of New Orleans. Esplanade and St. Charles avenues, along with other uptown boulevards, passed beneath canopies of live oak branches, while more modest trees lined such streets as Canal.[36] Municipal efforts continued to expand the boulevards lined by broad live oaks as the nineteenth century progressed.[37] One of the most celebrated boulevards, Esplanade Avenue, was a major artery through the neighborhood occupied by Creoles of color. Other routes with ample shade predominately served white neighborhoods. Nonetheless, since major thoroughfares were public routes, white and black, rich and poor, could enjoy the shade. Neighborhood residents, however, did benefit most directly. A vigorous protest by St. Charles Avenue residents over tree cutting to accommodate streetcars in the 1890s reveals the importance of this municipal amenity.[38]

SYSTEM CONSTRUCTION AND SEGREGATION

1900–1910

The first public works construction phase introduced improved drainage to the high-value business district and all surrounding residential areas—

regardless of race. One main drainage canal, with several feeders, drained the Basin Street district into the new outfall canal that emptied into Lake Borgne. Another, unconnected series of canals drained the upstream business area, the Garden District, and the low ground near the center of the crescent. The initial drainage effort encompassed two wards with higher than average African American populations. By all appearances, drainage construction up to 1910 followed basic engineering principles: address the city's high-value sections, provide attachments for the low areas, and install the initial arteries for a comprehensive system. An optimistic annual report in 1910 noted that heavy rains caused flooding in areas not yet served by the system but touted "there was no flooding in any portion of the city where the drainage canals and drain pipes have been completed."[39] Drainage service covered some 22,000 acres at the time.

Officials attributed a dramatic decline in malaria deaths to the elimination of soil moisture and mosquito breeding sites. According to the Sewerage and Water Board, improved drainage drove the malaria death rate down from 104 to 8 per 100,000 between 1900 and 1912. Yet the death rate among the black population remained much higher than for whites, suggesting a lingering disparity between services offered to the two racial groups.[40] Malaria and typhoid both claimed more black victims per capita in 1907.[41] In keeping with prevailing medical views, public health authorities blamed this situation on African Americans. "Improvement in the colored death rate has been retarded by reckless and improvident ways of the race and their utter disregard for all hygienic and sanitary laws," one report claimed.[42] Despite this racist assignment of fault, the health benefits of the improved drainage system were most pronounced, at least initially, among white residents. Many other factors, such as access to health care and diet, undoubtedly contributed to higher mortality rates among blacks and obscured the precise impact of drainage improvements.

A more obvious service gap appeared in the sewerage system. Up to 1910, installation was sporadic and concentrated in built-up areas "where the property holders have petitioned for the laying of the sewers, pledging to connect with the same within six months after they are laid." Connections to the sewerage system required a deposit of either $25 or $50 and thereby limited access to property owners with the resources to pay the fee. Only 9,036 premises out of more than 40,000 had connections by 1910.[43] Poverty, regardless of race, impeded acquisition of sewer connections.

An early assessment of the water system declared that the city needed to install over 390 miles of waterlines to serve 275,000 people. While this total was less than that projected for other major cities, the lower population density in New Orleans translated into higher installation costs per household.[44] Using the rationale of efficiency, system planners temporarily excluded the most sparsely settled areas. While it avoided fringe locations, the first construction phase (1906) brought water service to largely white uptown neighborhoods.[45] In the next few years, service reached most built-up areas, including several neighborhoods with black populations, such as the area behind the business district and the Garden District. By 1910 there were 513 miles of mains, above the initial projection, delivering service to 20,680 households. The only obvious gap by this time was the area at the bottom of the bowl and the area behind the downstream neighborhoods — where sizable numbers of African Americans and recent European immigrants lived.[46]

The city council created the Parking Commission in 1909 and assigned it the responsibility "to plant, maintain, protect, and care for trees, shrubs, and other plants in all the public highways of this city."[47] Although it did not commence planting for several years, the new commission declared that "there must be no distinction between the rich and poor quarters, for all are entitled to and must have the best." Ultimately, they sought a balance between barren streetscapes and tree canopies that were so thick that they would promote dampness and inhibit ventilation. They proclaimed this could be achieved best with native flora.[48] At the commission's inception, the shaded boulevards placed under its authority were the same that existed in 1900 — including major thoroughfares such as St. Charles, Esplanade, Claiborne, Canal, and Rampart. Although white residents lived along most of these streets, Esplanade, Rampart, and St. Roche passed through African American and Creole of color neighborhoods (Fig. 3.5).

Between 1900 and 1910 some slight population adjustments occurred. In the Seventh, Eleventh, and Sixteenth wards, black populations topped the 30 percent level, indicating higher concentrations than the citywide average (Figs. 3.4 and 3.6). The Seventh Ward was a triangle of land downstream from the French Quarter, situated near the emerging "main street" for the African American community — and bordered Esplanade Avenue's shaded boulevard. The Eleventh and Sixteenth Wards were uptown sections that stretched from the well-drained natural levee toward the low ground. Both

FIG. 3.5. TREES PLANTED ON ST. ROCHE AVENUE, 1901. Tree planting along boulevards penetrated all neighborhoods. Cornelius Durkee Photograph Collection, no. 28. Courtesy New Orleans Public Library.

were adjacent to commercial sectors and higher-value residential areas. Ab-
solute population increases in black populations in these wards reflected a
residential expansion into some of the formerly swampy areas improved to
the point of habitability by the new drainage system.[49]

1910–1920

The drainage system reached more corners of the built-up area between
1910 and 1920 (Fig. 3.2), but it was inadequate to handle large downpours.
In May 1912, 4.5 to 6 inches of rain left much of the low area near Broad
Street (in the bowl) inundated due to the pumps' inability to keep up with
the downpour.[50] To address this shortcoming, the Sewerage and Water
Board installed its much-heralded Wood screw pumps in 1917. The new lift-
ing devices, which had greater capacity and enabled speedier rainwater removal than those used previously, substantially lowered the water table. This
affected the newly served territories and particularly the lowest areas within
the bowl. Operation of the new pumps more than doubled the system's ca-

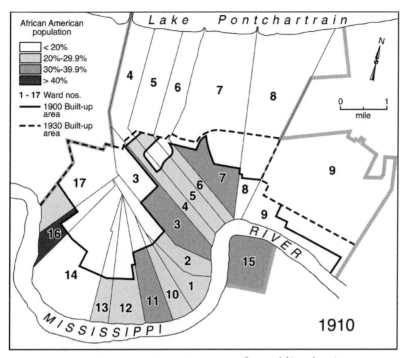

FIG. 3.6. AFRICAN AMERICAN POPULATION, 1910. In 1910 African American concentrations appear to decline slightly with some shift uptown. Source: U.S. Census.

pacity from 3.2 to 7 billion gallons per day.[51] Despite the new pumps' benefits, heavy rain and budget shortages hindered progress and forced a near cessation of construction and maintenance between 1916 and 1919. Nevertheless, by 1919 the Sewerage and Water Board claimed that the system was draining nearly all the built-up areas, and as a result, death rates per 100,000 from typhoid had dropped from 38 during the decade 1900 to 1909 to 13 in 1919 and to 7.5 by 1920.[52] Blacks still succumbed to typhoid at a higher rate. In 1915, the local board of health reported a typhoid death rate of 20 per 100,000 for whites and 31 per for blacks.[53] While the area served by the drainage system increased from about 22,000 acres in 1914 to 30,000 in 1925, progress was not consistent across the urban territory. Notable were ill-drained pockets within the lowest area uptown and in a section of the downstream neighborhoods populated primarily by European immigrants.

With only 20 percent of residences having sewer system connections by 1910 and privies still posing a serious health threat, the Sewerage and Water

Board reassessed its connection fees. After securing new funding from municipal improvement bonds, the board removed the sewerage connection fee in 1911. This dramatically increased the pace of connections, but the board desired to accelerate the pace further, lamenting that less than a third of households had service. As one report stated, "A great sanitary benefit to the city at large is thus being operated at a heavy cost in proportion to the number of premises served, for it costs no more to serve twice as many premises as it does those now connected, and the disgusting nuisance of overflowing cess-pools and household wastes being discharged into the gutters, and manufacturing wastes being discharged into the canals, continues."[54] To alleviate these conditions, the board resolved in 1911 that homeowners would face a fine if they did not accept connections and close their cesspools and privies. In 1912 the board dispatched teams to install connections at its own expense, and the success of the program became obvious. The 1912 annual report indicated nearly three-quarters of all premises had connections to the sewerage system, and without the restrictive fee it had become more equitable in its distribution.[55] By 1917, about 70 percent of all premises had sewerage service, and by 1920 the figure climbed to 94 percent.[56] The Sewerage and Water Board's continued efforts to provide service increased the size of the sewerage system to a total of 508 miles and 53,000 connections.[57] Undoubtedly some houses without indoor plumbing remained unserved, particularly in black neighborhoods, but engineering and public health principles guided the more comprehensive expansion.

Between 1910 and 1920, the Sewerage and Water Board slowed the pace of water main installations focused on establishing universal domestic connections—which it paid for. Premises with water service jumped from about 46,000 in 1912 to over 56,000 by 1920. Indeed, the board proclaimed that it had achieved 97 percent coverage for its water service. However, some inequities persisted in the water delivery system. Although some of the backswamp neighborhoods had secured water service by 1920, there remained a sizable service gap in the bottom of the bowl.[58]

As might be expected in the Jim Crow–era South, sanitary conditions for black and white populations remained highly skewed. For New Orleans residents, the typhoid death rate per 100,000 in 1918 was 18.1 for whites and 30.1 for blacks, although officials suspected serious underreporting for the latter group. A major health survey in 1919 concluded the highest death rate existed in Wards One, Two, and Three, which had sizable black popu-

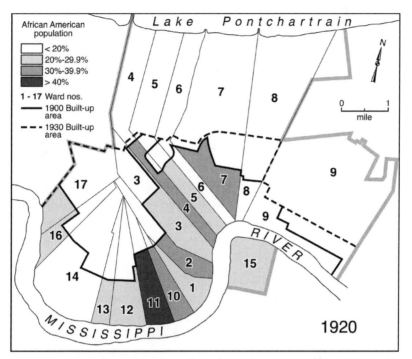

FIG. 3.7. AFRICAN AMERICAN POPULATION, 1920. In 1920 Wards Ten and Eleven display an emerging African American population concentration. Most would have lived away from the river. Source: U.S. Census.

lations.[59] Lingering shortcomings in the drainage and sewer system, combined with several other factors, contributed to the high mortality rate. Four wards stand out in the 1920 census with above-average black concentrations: the Second Ward, behind the business district; the Tenth and Eleventh wards, on the lake side of the 1900 built-up area; and the Seventh Ward, below the French Quarter (Fig. 3.7). The black population percentage of both the Second and Tenth wards moved above the citywide average, and the Eleventh Ward topped 40 percent. The extension of drainage lines (Fig. 3.2) to the lowest portions of these wards (albeit only marginally effective following any heavy rain) opened them to black residential development, and population increases reflect occupation of the rear or low areas. White residential and commercial land uses dominated the higher, riverward sections.

After public pronouncements that parkways would be offered to all neighborhoods, the Parking Commission failed to reach its objectives. In 1915, tree removal along Esplanade Avenue sparked vigorous protest from

Creoles of color who lived along the fashionable boulevard and from their neighbors in the largely African American Seventh Ward. Again in 1920, the commission embarked on a project to remove unsightly or rotting trees on Esplanade Avenue. Without consulting residents, the commission had municipal workers cut down "scores" of elm and oak trees. Arguing that some of the historic trees had been planted by the city's founder, Jean-Baptiste Le Moyne de Bienville, residents confronted the commission and demanded that the work be halted. After a brief controversy, a hastily formed tree-protection association secured a promise from the mayor that tree removal would cease, that the Parking Commission would replace trees that had been cut, and that damaged trees would be trimmed to encourage regrowth. Thus incursions on the shaded boulevards that traversed the city's elite Creole and African American neighborhoods were short lived and made only a negligible dent in the greenery.[60]

Public works were not the only factor in African Americans' and other low-income residents' plight. The wards' lakeward segments had higher population densities as a result of the city's peculiar radial street pattern, which created many small, wedged-shaped lots in the rear districts. Many of these diminutive lots remained unoccupied in the early 1920s, while larger ones had multiple residential structures. The street pattern and small lot sizes made such neighborhoods undesirable for the more mobile whites, leaving them to blacks with inadequate financial resources to make other choices. Crowding and poverty in these emerging black neighborhoods along with some residual reliance on privies and continued periodic flooding after heavy rains obviously contributed to poor public health.

1920–1930

The drainage system was extended to few new sections of the city during the 1920s (Fig. 3.2). Having excavated and connected the main canals in the first two decades of the century, the Sewerage and Water Board then focused on enlarging and lining the existing canals, installing subsurface drainage, pursuing street paving efforts, and keeping up general maintenance. Deficiencies remained in the system, however. The canals and pumps were up to the test of a 7-inch rainfall in February 1927, but a record downpour of 14 inches on April 15 overwhelmed the system. One generator powering the pumps burned out, reducing the system's capacity by 40 percent. This caused severe flooding in the city's low areas for periods up to 48 hours.[61] There was also high water along Claiborne Avenue and in Mid-City—both sections with large black populations. Charges of inadequate drainage followed these extreme events.[62] In response, the Sewerage and Water Board installed new drainage lines in one of the lower neighborhoods that had been leapfrogged in previous decades and was a largely white neighborhood at this time.[63] Additionally, a portion of the area within the bowl also finally received drainage service. Thus by 1930 the drainage system was providing service to the bulk of the built-up area, with little remaining evidence of neighborhood neglect. This is not to say racism had disappeared, but the lack of drainage in low-income and predominantly black neighborhoods had.

Although the Sewerage and Water Board sought to install a comprehensive system to serve the entire city, the most apparent gaps appeared in the sewerage system. In 1923, the board claimed that 92 percent of the city's population had sewer line access, but the unconnected territory was still equal in size to the entire area already served. Areas lacking sewers, most of which were sparsely settled, had an insufficient tax base to underwrite service extension. Officials wanted to encourage full residential and commercial development of the areas already served before expanding the system. Yet even within the older built-up districts, there were conspicuous unserved areas. In particular, the newly drained marsh on the lake side of the natural ridges and some of the backswamp neighborhoods had not received adequate sewer service, nor had a small but pronounced area in the lowest portion of the city where the black population was on the rise (Fig. 3.8). Over eighteen hundred houses were "unsewered," meaning they still relied on the soil or surface drains to handle domestic wastes.[64] This is the same section that had small lot sizes, poor drainage, higher population density, and adjacent industrial activity. Corresponding to poor sanitary services, public health statistics portrayed a troubling situation for African Americans. In 1926, the state Department of Health reported a typhoid death rate for blacks of 42 per 100,000, while the white rate had dropped to 13.[65] Although death rates by ward are unavailable, the racial differences are obvious at the metropolitan level. The lapse in sewer service to this low-lying, largely African American district suggests that a Jim Crow mentality perhaps continued to prevent full engineering efficiency.

In its assessment of water service, the Sewerage and Water Board expressed dismay at the rapid suburban growth in the early 1920s, particularly toward the lakefront. Between 1920 and 1923, the number of houses without

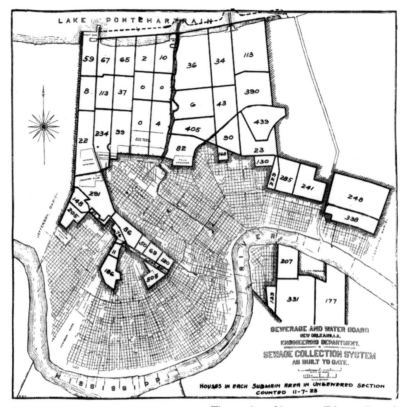

FIG. 3.8. AREAS WITHOUT SEWERS, 1923. The number of "unsewered" houses "in each submain area" is shown, indicating a notable delay in service delivery in the "bottom of the bowl" and in the lower neighborhoods behind the Ninth Ward. Lakefront housing was new construction, and the city had not been able to supply this newly developed section with sewers. New Orleans Sewerage and Water Board, *Forty-Eighth Semi-Annual Report* (New Orleans: 1923).

service increased, despite continuing installation efforts. New home construction simply outpaced installation.[66] Neighborhoods on the newly drained ground lakeward of the Metairie and Gentilly ridges experienced the greatest residential growth. An aggressive expansion effort to serve the new neighborhoods enabled the board to claim it was once again serving 97 percent of all households by 1927, with the total number of connections standing at 77,790. Another notable achievement of this decade was the extension of water service to much of the bottom of the bowl, a prelude to providing sewers to this area.[67] Once houses had municipal water, sewerage service was essential to handle the increased domestic waste volume.

The nearly complete absence of blacks in the newly drained territory on the lake side of the ridges stems from an explicitly prejudicial real estate system.[68] The New Orleans City Council passed an ordinance in 1924 that effectively separated white and black residential neighborhoods. Based on a 1912 state act that authorized the city to withhold building permits for blacks in white neighborhoods and a 1924 act that prohibited blacks from establishing residence (rental or purchase) in a white community, the ordinance formalized existing racial settlement patterns and largely determined for developers which racial group they could sell to.[69] When challenged, the state supreme court initially upheld the ordinance in 1926 for lack of a specific complaint.[70] Although the ordinance was ultimately overturned by the U.S. Supreme Court in 1927, property deeds that restricted racial integration in new neighborhoods soon provided another means to achieve the same ends.[71] Beginning in the 1920s, developers in the recently drained lakefront neighborhoods employed deed covenants to exclude blacks. The New Orleans Swamp Land Reclamation Company sold a sizable parcel of land to an individual developer and stipulated that no houses valued at less than $3,000 could be built in the neighborhood. It also specified that "no lots are to be sold to negroes or colored people."[72] Andrew Stafford, the developer, included the following restriction in his deeds when he resold the land as individual lots: "No person not of the Caucasian race shall be permitted to reside or congregate in any structure erected on said property, or any part thereof. This restriction shall not apply to domestic servants living on their master's premises."[73] Stafford's restrictions applied both to owners and renters. The deed covenants in New Orleans obstructed sale of selected properties to blacks into the 1940s, while economic restrictions also contributed to class boundaries.[74] Drainage certainly opened new neighborhoods, but restrictive real estate practices closed them to specific groups. The builders and realtors sought more affluent white buyers and developed neighborhoods for them. Although there were post–World War II developments for African Americans in the lakefront area, they were small compared to the extensive tracts reserved for whites.[75]

The public works program was not without inequities. Delayed sewer connections reflected a lower-priority status for black and other low-income neighborhoods on the Sewerage and Water Board's work schedule. Service delivery to African Americans progressed at a moderate rate during the 1920s, in part due to efforts to keep up with an expanding city. In 1920, the Sewerage and Water Board claimed that 94 percent of the city's premises had links to its sewer system. Although crews continued to expand the system, the percentage of connected premises fell to 93 by 1923. It remained at that level through 1927 although there were over 715 miles of sewer mains in place and 68,784 total connections.[76] By 1932 the number of connections had risen to 75,271.[77] The Sewerage and Water Board kept pace with new construction but accomplished little more during the 1920s.

That same decade, the renamed Parks and Parkway Commission (formerly the Parking Commission) worked within a revised financial framework that altered its original intent to provide all neighborhoods with shade trees. Special assessments became the means to pay for shade trees, and only neighborhoods that voted to pay for trees received new plantings. This limited the expansion to upper-income neighborhoods.[78] Although existing tree-lined boulevards continued to offer shade, expansion of the parkways was limited to more affluent areas.

More pronounced residential segregation appears by the time of the 1930 census (Fig. 3.9). Three uptown wards had African-American population concentrations above the city average—indeed, the Second and Eleventh wards had more than 50 percent black residents, with about 40 percent in the Tenth. By this time, greater white concentrations appear in the Fourteenth Ward uptown and the neighborhoods below the French Quarter (Eighth and Ninth wards)—each had more than 80 percent white residents. Despite apparent sewer system links, the Ninth Ward remained poorly served according to frequent complaints filed with the city council by local residents.[79] Most newly opened neighborhoods in the lakeward development were almost exclusively white. Yet the low ground (the bottom of the bowl), near the point of convergence of the streets that radiated outward toward the sweeping bend of the river, were becoming predominantly black neighborhoods. Industrial and transportation land uses occupied large portions of this area as well.

1930–1940

After a near cessation of expansion and improvement during the first half of the 1930s, the Sewerage and Water Board used WPA funds to press ahead with the drainage system. Federal assistance underwrote street paving and subsurface drainage installation in the "outlying districts."[80] Requests for

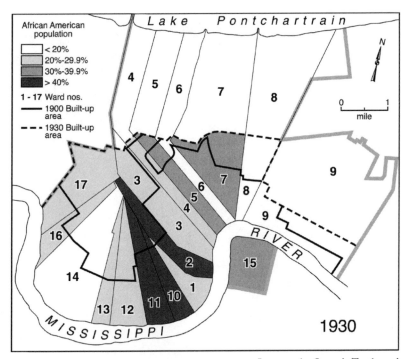

FIG. 3.9. AFRICAN AMERICAN POPULATION, 1930. In 1930, the Second, Tenth, and Eleventh wards had African American concentrations well above the city average, and the rear of these wards overlapped with unsewered tracts. Source: U.S. Census.

new drainage lines came from developers on the lake side of the ridges. WPA funds also helped connect homes to the sewage and water supply systems.[81] Construction in the city's northeast segment during the second half of the 1930s was the largest territorial expansion since the second decade of the century. Even with the added territory, the Sewerage and Water Board reported in the early 1940s that the system functioned admirably even with rains in excess of three inches.[82]

Sewerage service expanded minimally during the 1930s. Connections rose to only 79,735 by the end of 1939 and 80,678 by 1940. The heaviest demand for sewerage service came from the lakefront area.[83] Federal relief funds assisted in service extension to these new neighborhoods. By this time, most older neighborhoods had access to the sewer system. The water system experienced similar expansion during the 1930s and mainly grew into the new lakefront developments. A total of 88,424 homes had service by 1940.[84]

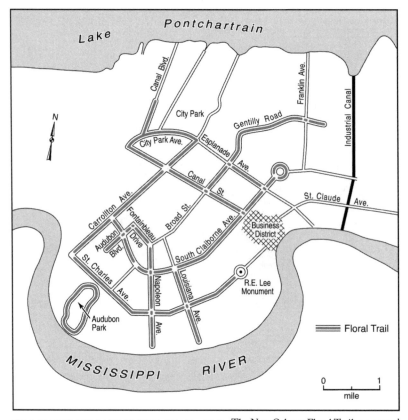

FIG. 3.10. NEW ORLEANS FLORAL TRAIL, 1949. The New Orleans Floral Trail penetrated all neighborhoods but avoided the Louisiana Avenue–Broad Street area in one of the lowest sections. Additional shaded boulevards were not included in the designated trail. After Parkway Commission of New Orleans, *Fortieth Anniversary Report, 1900–1949* (New Orleans: 1949), following p. 19.

Residents in the racially mixed, low-income Ninth Ward regularly complained that despite the presence of public works, service was ineffective.[85]

The Parks and Parkways Commission's major initiative during the 1930s exposed inequities in its activities. The commission created the floral trail, a series of parkways planted with decorative flowers, that followed several major streets. Most passed through largely white neighborhoods, and only the Claiborne Avenue segment passed through a predominately African American neighborhood (Figs. 3.10 and 3.11).[86]

FIG. 3.11. AERIAL VIEW OF CLAIBORNE AVENUE, 1949. When mature, live oaks provided extensive shade along major boulevards. Aerial Photographs Collection. Courtesy New Orleans Public Library.

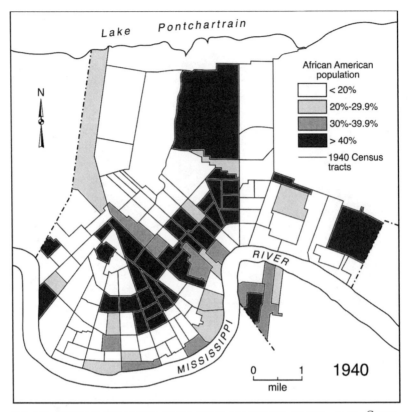

FIG. 3.12. AFRICAN AMERICAN POPULATION BY CENSUS TRACT, 1940. Census-tract-level reporting in 1940 depicts the relative immobility of African Americans and their clustering in low-lying districts. Source: U. S. Census.

Tract information became available for the first time with the census of 1940, revealing the city's racial geography at a finer resolution. These data indicate large concentrations of African Americans in the easternmost tract and in many of the low-lying sections lakeward of the central business district and St. Charles Avenue (Fig. 3.12). African American population concentrations remained high in the inner-city tracts. The black population percentage in the bottom of the bowl remained near or above 50 percent. A pair of western clusters showed a slightly higher-than-average African American population, split between a cluster near the river and a second in the lower, lakeward tract. An area immediately downstream from the French Quarter was well above the citywide average of 30 percent. Conversely, a large area that included a newly developed section of the lakefront area near City Park had 84 percent white population. The other areas with white population concentrations well above the average were tracts that straddled Audubon Park and a downstream neighborhood that housed a largely working-class and immigrant population.[87]

Congo Square's function as a social center for blacks declined in the nineteenth century, but the principal African American population concentration was adjacent to it in 1900. By 1930 African Americans had expanded into the low area within the bowl, making it a major residential neighborhood for the first time. The New Orleans drainage system contributed to this and other population shifts by lowering the water table and improving public health. While the initial system design called for equal service throughout the city, and ultimately the Sewerage and Water Board achieved this objective, there were race- and class-related inequities in the course of construction. From the outset, however, design and construction encompassed African American neighborhoods—a function of rational engineering principles overcoming racist tendencies of Jim Crow politics. Indeed, the first phase of construction included drainage services to a black neighborhood on the fringe of the central business district. Between 1910 and 1930 the drainage works permitted further development in the low areas uptown, where important African-American neighborhoods evolved. Sewerage connection fees proved exclusionary for low-income families, which included many blacks and recent immigrants, but the Sewerage and Water Board dropped the fees and made connections mandatory in 1911. Initial construction of the water system excluded fringe neighborhoods, which were largely black and low income, but soon extended to most areas. These steps obliterated any inequities, at least in design and policy. Progressive Era sanitation principles, and concern among white planners that poor sanitation conditions in black neighborhoods imperiled residents' health citywide, overrode overt racist tendencies in the public works landscape, although this is not to say they erased racist attitudes.

Despite plans to systematically drain the city, gaps in the system became apparent in the 1920s. A 1923 assessment of the sewerage system exposed a sizable neighborhood without sewer mains. This area lacking service was a low-lying, largely African American and industrial district. Additionally, serious flooding caused by intense rainfall left much of the sector under water for up to 48 hours in 1927. Thus both sewerage and drainage were either unavailable or ineffective in this low district. Water service also came late to this area. Public appeals for remedies ultimately led to improvements by the 1930s, when federal funds provided valuable assistance. A downstream neighborhood with a predominately white working-class population endured similar delayed service delivery, demonstrating that environmental inequities were not based solely on race. The drainage and sewerage system eventually reached citywide distribution with little apparent race or class bias. This does not mean the city achieved environmental equity, but it indicates that rational engineering was prevailing over racism in terms of public works. The city's parkways, however, took on a more race- or class-based distribution as the century progressed. As the city imposed special assessments for tree planting, more affluent, largely white neighborhoods benefitted.

Racial segregation proceeded during the twentieth century's first three decades. The first population realignment in response to drainage was the expansion of blacks into low-lying areas to the rear of the city. Drainage also spurred residential expansion toward the lakefront, but city ordinances and, later, deed restrictions were the primary agents of residential segregation there. Vast tracts of lakefront property drained after 1920 became entirely new subdivisions, and ordinances and racially restrictive deeds effectively closed them to African Americans. While these ordinances and restrictions may not have been the root cause of segregation, they legally sanctioned it and obstructed desegregation.

Low sections such as Basin Street and the area within the bowl stand out as black neighborhoods by 1940. This pattern resulted from a process that occurred in conjunction with, but not as the sole consequence of, the public works extension. In a time of overt and legally sanctioned racism, segregation accelerated. But neither the drainage nor sewerage systems were the exclusive causes. Although pockets of inequities existed in the installation of these systems in the 1920s, the Sewerage and Water Board tried to construct a citywide system. Thus the entire city ultimately received comparable service. At the same time, institutionalized segregation policies embedded in the real estate system were instrumental in shaping New Orleans's racial geography, although other factors such as economics and urban morphology played important roles. Despite the influence of racism, the public works program followed Progressive Era engineering principles; Jim Crow, however, emerged through overt real estate policies and neighborhood-based financing of urban amenities. Although the improved drainage system opened new areas to black residences, at the same time it contributed to segregation, reflecting established patterns of turning low-value land associated with environmental problems over to minority populations. The development of lakefront property also required expansion of the drainage system, and this improvement contributed to segregation in the higher-valued area restricted to whites.

CHAPTER 4

ENVIRONMENT COMES TO THE FORE

A GARBAGE DUMP becomes a sanitary landfill and then a hazardous waste site. A turbid river becomes a foul sewer and then a toxic sink. These are two examples of environmental transformations that occurred during the post–World War II period in New Orleans. They represent both a fundamental shift in public concern and official designations. Garbage dumps could be, and often were, nuisances—a legal term that could be invoked to protect private property rights. When objectionable odors wafted from a dump to a neighbor's land, courts could rule the conditions infringed on the owner's enjoyment of the property. Although for much of the twentieth century nuisance law was the key mechanism for protecting the common resource of the environment, its roots rested in private property law. After 1945, many shortcomings of relying on private property laws to protect the larger environment became all too obvious. In addition, an environmental ethic rose to prominence in social concern and public law. This environmental ethic resituated clean air and water as common resources, not private property.[1] With this change, the government, not individuals, became the watchdogs. New laws specified how garbage had to be handled to protect a shared environment, and engineer-designed sanitary landfills replaced garbage dumps. In a similar process, society redefined its conception of rivers. Traditionally, riparian property owners had rights and responsibilities under common law that limited how they could use adjacent waterways. Central to these rights was free access to navigable waterways and reasonable use of rivers to transport wastes. Post–1970 federal legislation redefined the Mississippi River as a municipal water supply, with far more protections than provided under old state laws.

Through the enactment of laws to protect land, air, and water, the federal government usurped local responsibility and also redefined environmental conditions.[2] No longer did government agencies merely offer public services (garbage removal and water supplies); they now engaged in protecting the environment. This was a much broader responsibility. Ecological concepts viewed the environment as a complex system of air, water, land, plants, and animals. Disruptions to one part could affect another, but human intervention based on ecological science, it was believed, could offset that harm. An environmental protection posture assumed that natural systems were susceptible to human degradation and that society had a fundamental obligation to protect them using available ecological knowledge. As part of this shift, bacteria became secondary to toxins as the contaminants of concern. Using new technologies to track what had been undetectable, environmental protection agencies began to monitor minute concentrations of toxic substances in the air and water and on the land. Laws reclassified dumps as hazardous waste sites and waste sinks as "drinking water" supplies. By redefining common environments, federal legislation both reacted to public concern and at the same time redirected it.

This chapter will trace the emergence of environmental awareness in New Orleans through two examples: the Agriculture Street Landfill and the city's drinking water supply, the Mississippi River. In both instances, what was once objectionable became toxic, and what was invisible became a measurable threat. These basic reclassifications had profound effects at the neighborhood, metropolitan, and national levels.

GARBAGE TO HAZARDOUS WASTE[3]

BACKGROUND

During the nineteenth century, New Orleans had relied on the Mississippi to transport its refuse to the Gulf of Mexico—out of sight, out of mind.[4]

A failed attempt to substitute a reduction/recovery system (discussed in Chapter 2) left the city with an inadequate garbage handling program at the outset of the twentieth century. Citizens offended by piles of refuse in the streets complained to both the Board of Health and the city Public Works Department. Each city agency hoped the other would solve the problem, but management by avoidance produced little improvement. Gradually the city took on an expanding authority over garbage service. In 1902 the commissioner of public works reported to the mayor that his garbage pickup routes covered a sizable portion of the city.[5] During the early twentieth century, city garbage haulers continued to shuttle refuse from the limited service area to the river, where barges dumped it into the muddy stream—about 92,763 tons in 1908.[6] In addition, many small neighborhood dumps near the rear of the city continued to receive refuse. Seeking to eliminate these nuisances, the city council passed an ordinance in 1906 that outlawed dumping or burning of garbage, refuse, or swill in empty lots.[7] Nonetheless, despite its ordinance, the city dumped and graded garbage to build up extensive low-lying sections of town.[8] By 1911, the city sent its refuse by the trainload to reclaim swampland and to areas such as the Agriculture Street dump.[9] Consequently, most low areas to the rear of the city remained nuisance zones, and the river continued to be a garbage sink.

When construction of the massive water, sewerage, and drainage projects began in the early 1900s (discussed in Chapter 3), the city rethought its garbage system as well. Technology offered relief to chronic water-related problems, and the Progressive Era administrators sought a similar solution for refuse disposal. In 1916, the city commenced a major effort to divert its garbage from the river and land dumps to incinerators. By 1929 it had spent about $1.2 million on five incinerators that were handling about 90 percent of the household garbage.[10]

All the while, one of the old dumps, located at the intersection of Agriculture Street and Almonaster Avenue, continued to receive the city's commercial refuse (Fig. 4.1). Opened in about 1909, the Agriculture Street dump occupied a site at the edge of poorly drained land and the rear of a low-income neighborhood. At its operational outset, the biggest concern was maintaining the access road through the mucky soils. Even in its early development, the dump attracted negative attention. Nuisance conditions forced public works officials to respond to complaints about flies and smoke. Following an outbreak of bubonic plague in 1914, U.S. Public Health

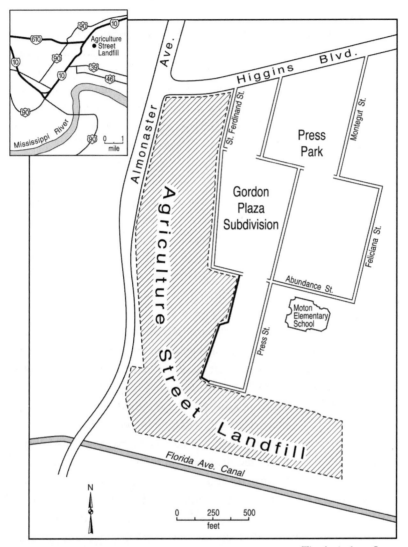

FIG. 4.1. AGRICULTURE STREET LANDFILL NEIGHBORHOOD. The Agriculture Street Dump/Landfill and publicly financed housing on its eastern flank. After U.S. EPA, *Record of Decision: Agriculture Street Landfill Superfund Site* (Dallas: U.S. EPA, Region 6, 1997).

officials provided assistance to local authorities to eradicate rats that thrived at the dump.[11] Local records reveal little about the operation of the dump during the 1930s, and although WPA funds underwrote the city's incinerators for most urban refuse, the Agriculture Street facility continued to receive wastes.[12]

During and after World War II, city funds for the more expensive garbage incineration dwindled. This led to greater and greater reliance on land disposal, particularly at the conveniently located Agriculture Street dump. Open burning there produced objectionable conditions. Smoke combined with offensive odors, mosquitos, and scavengers made the area a local nuisance. Increasing population density in the vicinity and rising expectations for better quality of life led residents to object to the operations. They branded the site as "Dante's Inferno"—a clear reflection of their dislike for open burning. In 1948, the state legislature intervened in city affairs and outlawed "open garbage or waste refuge dumps and burning of waste refuge" within the limits of cities having incinerators and populations greater than 300,000. In effect, the legislature enacted a statute that applied exclusively to New Orleans.[13] To avoid losing the Agriculture Street facility, the city sidestepped the state law by converting the dump to a landfill. By eliminating open burning and regularly compacting and covering the daily garbage deliveries, the city reengineered the dump as a sanitary landfill.[14]

In spite of the city's expressed intention to create a sanitary landfill, local residents observed little short-term improvement. Neighbors claimed that debris floated in open water-filled pits for up to four months before being buried and that the city even left uncovered remains from cemeteries on the dump's surface. Area residents also charged that open fires released thick smoke clouds into their homes. In sum, they asserted that the site was not being operated as a sanitary landfill—despite its nominal reclassification. Residents demanded that the parish grand jury compel the city to comply with the state law.[15] City officials responded by spraying DDT on the site to control insects and argued that the site was not a health hazard.[16] Objectionable conditions persisted, partly due to the lack of adequate fill at the site,[17] and thirty-seven residents appealed to the courts to close the dump in 1951.[18] Ultimately, the city convinced the jurists that the sanitary landfill method was a safe method for garbage disposal and that it had no other viable means to handle refuse.[19] By 1953 the dump operators apparently devised a method to use decomposed garbage as cover and claimed that this eliminated the old problem posed by inadequate fill.[20] Nonetheless, residents still found reasons to complain. In 1954, neighborhood residents campaigned for a bond issue to fund a new incinerator to replace the landfill. When that motion failed, residents objected to the lingering presence of flies and smoke.[21] Only in 1958, a decade after the legislature outlawed dumps in the city, did the city finally close the Agriculture Street Landfill.[22] But smoldering underground fires persisted at the site into the 1960s.[23]

Despite its change in designation from dump to landfill, the Agriculture Street disposal site remained a nuisance to neighbors until the 1960s. Yet after the final use of the site as an emergency dump for debris produced by Hurricane Betsy (1965), neighbors finally ceased their opposition.[24] Apparently, they no longer saw the dump as a long-term threat but had come to perceive the dump's operation and the associated byproducts—flies, smoke, rats—merely as undesirable nuisances.

A LANDSCAPE OF TRAGEDY

As discussed in Chapter 2, nuisances are conditions that are inherent in an activity that occurs at a site, whereas hazards are more deeply rooted. The transition of the Agriculture Street Landfill from a nuisance to a hazardous waste site represents a major shift in the public's perception and understanding of environmental activity at the site. Several related factors contributed to this transition. First, the neighborhood underwent a major demographic change from the early 1950s to the early 1990s—from white to primarily African American. As part of the demographic shift, public housing, built with federal support, encroached on the former landfill during the 1970s. Second, the federal government passed the Superfund Act (the Comprehensive Environmental Response, Compensation, and Liability Act, also know as CERCLA) in 1980. Procedures put in place by this act ultimately designated the landfill a priority hazardous waste site and set in motion a series of reactions by residents and environmental agencies. Events following the landfill's reclassification as a serious hazardous waste site and the public response to them have created a landscape of tragedy.[25]

From the 1950s to the 1980s, there was considerable demographic change in the neighborhood. Census tract 16 to the south of the dump went from 50 to 99 percent African American. The tract that encompassed the dump experienced a major population increase and went from 57 percent to 87 percent African American. New Orleans's population as a whole also underwent a transformation as the proportion of black residents increased from 32 percent in 1950 to 55 percent in 1980.[26] The landfill's most vocal opponents in the early 1950s had been largely white—at least those whose opposition was reported by the newspapers. By the time the federal Superfund Act came into play, the Agriculture Street neighborhood residents were overwhelmingly black.

By the 1980s the neighborhood's changing racial geography had situated the area in the midst of environmental justice debates. Several studies in the 1980s charged that African Americans bore an inordinate burden in the placement of landfills and other objectionable facilities.[27] Labeled as examples of "environmental racism," these high-profile situations prompted further examination of the geographic relationship of race and locally unwanted land uses. Investigators demonstrated that complex factors, including historical neighborhood development, real estate practices, income levels, and political influence, all entered into the equation and they employed more inclusive terminology such as environmental equity and environmental justice.[28] President Clinton made environmental justice a mandate for federal programs in 1994, and in 1995 the U.S. Environmental Protection Agency (EPA) espoused a formal environmental justice policy. It stipulated that "no segment of the population, regardless of race, color, national origin, or income, as a result of EPA's policies, programs, and activities, suffers disproportionately from adverse human health or environmental effects, and all people live in clean, healthy, and sustainable communities."[29]

While the dump's development in a largely white neighborhood at the turn of the century was obviously not a case of environmental racism, events following the landfill's 1965 closure must be considered through the lens of environmental justice. The low-income Ninth Ward was chronically denied public services.[30] As early as 1949, the city began to encroach on the dump with developments specifically for African American citizens. Plans for a black recreation center prompted the city to shift active filling from the eastern flank of the dump to the west. In fact, this shift prompted one of the early outcries from the then white neighborhood.[31] It also reflects a view that the city considered the filled land property it could develop—albeit for African Americans and not whites. This action imposed temporary nuisance costs on white residents to the west, but more importantly the city's white leadership brought its black citizens closer to the dump—exercising, to use Laura Pulido's term, white privilege.[32]

Beginning shortly after the dump's closure in 1965, additional encroachments on the landfill took place under municipal authority with federal funds. Seeking locations for public housing, local officials decided the municipally owned vacant land that had been the dump provided excellent unused ground. Construction on the first of two projects began in 1969 (Fig. 4.1). Press Park contained several townhouses with payment programs that allowed low-income public-housing residents to become homeowners. This development occupied a considerable area east of the closed landfill. A second mixed-development project, Gordon Plaza, received federal assistance in the late 1970s. It included single-family homes, apartments for senior citizens, and a strip shopping center. Like Press Park, it consumed land on the eastern flank of the dump, with the single-family homes backed up to the former landfill's core. There was little concern about hazards during the development of these projects, although engineers worried about subsidence on the former dump and its potential impact to building foundations.[33] Consequently, the main fill area remained vacant. As the neighborhood took shape, it became home to about a thousand residents, primarily African Americans, by the time of the 1990 census. Some of these residents contend that the EPA's management of the landfill exemplified environmental injustice, rather than the environmental justice mandated by the agency's policy.

Congress passed the Superfund Act in response to the discovery of several high-profile abandoned hazardous waste dumps in the late 1970s, including Love Canal in Niagara Falls, New York, and the Valley of the Drums in rural Kentucky. The act authorized the EPA to identify and prioritize sites that presented an immediate threat to public health and the environment. Using a variety of legal means that sought to make polluters pay for environmental damage they had caused, the federal agency would then oversee cleanup of the worst sites. To start this process, the EPA compiled a list of potential sites for evaluation. The inventory, known as the Comprehensive Environmental Response, Compensation, and Liability Information System, or CERCLIS, contained over forty thousand sites at one point in time. A prioritization process known as the hazards ranking system enabled the EPA to identify locations demanding prompt remediation. These were placed on the National Priorities List (NPL). Over the life of the Superfund program, the EPA has placed more than 2,000 sites on this list and had cleaned up 757 at the time of the act's twentieth anniversary in 2000.[34]

Over the course of more than twenty years, Superfund has evolved from a risk-based, litigation-driven, technically oriented site cleanup program to one that places greater emphasis on negotiated settlements, voluntary cleanups, and community involvement. These approaches differ from the initial orientation and often have placed U.S. EPA personnel and their state counterparts in awkward positions. Trained and experienced in evaluating technical criteria, in recent years they have found themselves dealing with less precise methods of social policy. President Clinton's 1994 executive order on environmental justice further clouded the agency's responsibilities by insisting that it determine whether there was unequal application of the law to minority or low-income populations.[35] The agency had no technical methods to gauge environmental justice. The Agriculture Street Landfill situation illustrates the complex and sometimes unsatisfactory results when science meets neighborhood concerns.

Using its original scoring method in 1986, the EPA gave the Agriculture Street Landfill a hazards ranking score of 3 (28.5 is necessary for inclusion on the NPL).[36] The initial methodology did not consider human ingestion of contaminated soil as a direct exposure. Consequently, relatively high lead levels in the soil around the landfill did not significantly influence the score. Furthermore, since residents did not consume local groundwater, there was no possibility of lead ingestion from this pathway, and again the presence of lead did not raise the score.

In 1993, local activists began pushing the EPA to conduct a second Superfund evaluation. President Clinton's 1994 executive order to consider environmental justice concerns in all federal projects added incentive to move forward with a new scoring.[37] Although the rescoring process is relatively rare, with only 4 out of more than 700 sites in the EPA's Region 6 undergoing a second evaluation, the environmental justice mandate brought the EPA back to Agriculture Street. Armed this time with a new methodology that considered soil as a direct "pathway" for contaminants, the agency discovered that the site's hazards ranking score had skyrocketed from a 3 to 50.[38] This high score placed the site on the NPL and completely changed public opinion of the site.

Geographer Kenneth Foote has coined the term "landscapes of tragedy" to refer to places associated with tragic events. Society, he argues, responds to such locales in different ways. At one extreme, "sanctification" is the process of setting aside a place of tragedy, dedicating it to the memory of fallen heroes, and providing long-term maintenance. Civil War battlefields such as Gettysburg or Vicksburg exemplify this landscape type. "Obliteration" is the opposite extreme. Society seldom chooses even to remember horrific events such as mass murders, and complete removal often becomes the favored treatment. Between these two extremes are "dedication" and "rectification." Dedication involves marking the site with a memorial to recall the event, but not the preservation and maintenance of the full territory associated with the tragedy. Memorials to the Johnstown flood or the Texas City explosion represent this response. Rectification occurs when the site is "put right and used again." Evidence of the tragedy is removed, although policies might be enacted to prevent repeat events. The Chicago fire, for example, prompted new building codes that transformed the urban landscape in other ways.[39]

Superfund sites like the Agriculture Street Landfill can be viewed as "landscapes of tragedy." Events at these sites resulted in threats to public health and the environmental threats and often in serious neighborhood disruption. Contamination can lead to personal illness, natural resource damage, community dislocation, and property devaluation. Evaluation of sites for inclusion on the NPL involves technical procedures for identifying and scoring potential threats. The scoring process leads to the formulation of technical remedial plans. While these methods may call for the consideration of economic issues, they contain no formula to evaluate neighbors' sentiments about the site's listing. Community relations programs, developed well after Superfund was set in motion, seek to incorporate public opinion in the EPA's planning but not to gauge and react to neighbors' responses to the identification of a seriously contaminated site in their midst.[40] Yet graffiti on homes and other buildings immediately reveals residents' true concern with unseen hazards.

Those living near a Superfund site may view the range of adverse consequences, such as illness, property devaluation, or environmental damage, as tragic. This is particularly evident at sites where environmental injustice charges arise, but cleanups at Superfund sites have few parallels with remedies at sites of tragedy. In the twenty-year history of Superfund site remediation, there is no example of a site that could be classified as a sanctified place, although Love Canal is set apart and has long-term maintenance. Sites in Butte, Montana, that have been included in local historical interpretation, come close.[41] For the most part, however, Superfund seeks to remove conditions that create hazards and effectively achieve either rectification or obliteration. Rectification can generally be achieved without uprooting a community, whereas obliteration can involve removing both the hazard and the neighborhood.

In New Orleans, residents of the Agriculture Street Superfund site neighborhood had greatly varying ideas about how to deal with their landscape of tragedy. Superfund designation attached a tragic specter to the place. Long before the Superfund designation, neighbors referred to the dump as "Dante's Inferno" and fought to close it. When it was closed, it ceased to be a nuisance. The formal NPL designation has evoked mixed reactions from neighbors. Some residents believe it best to repair the situation through rectification (or putting the place back to work); others desire obliteration (removal and relocation). Not only are there divisions within the community about how to address the site, but the responsible federal agency looks at it from yet another perspective. Where the residents see tragedy, the EPA sees a twofold problem: a site remediation and an environmental justice remedy. These disparate views contributed to a protracted battle over the Agriculture Street Landfill cleanup that has been couched in terms of risk and property value and not in terms of landscape, attachment to place, and neighborhood self-determination—which seems to be at the dispute's core. The landscape now bears an obvious record of the Superfund activity— a large bare field ringed by a tall fence with warning signs along with protest signs in the yards of homeowners. While the agency's NPL designation of the site created a tragic conflict, both the agency and the residents have erected signs declaring it a landscape of tragedy.

THE ROUTE TO TRAGEDY

By the early 1980s, the public housing around the landfill was sheltering a viable neighborhood, and the need for an elementary school became apparent. This initiated the recasting of the former dump from a nuisance into a hazard, and thereby into a landscape of tragedy. At the request of neighborhood residents, the Orleans Parish School Board began taking steps to build an elementary school on the edge of the former dump. In 1985, long after it acquired the site and well into the design process, the board learned that soil tests indicated elevated lead levels. Some of the school board members expressed concern that this might pose a health threat to students, and a mere two weeks before groundbreaking ceremonies, the board debated abandoning the site. State environmental authorities, however, insisted that a clay cap installed over the fill would protect students from exposure.[42] Some community members, on the other hand, suggested that the concern over hazardous materials "could be a sham to avoid building the school."[43] This response reflected frustration with the school board's slow pace in replacing a school that had already been demolished in an older portion of the primarily low-income, African American neighborhood. Ultimately, the board, under pressure to provide a neighborhood school and fearing huge losses if it abandoned the plan, initiated construction and opened the Moton Elementary School in 1986. It made one concession to residents' environmental concerns by implementing a lead monitoring program for neighborhood children.[44]

Thus in Superfund's early phases, local residents downplayed concerns about hazardous materials in the environment. They wanted a school and saw the discussion over hazards as a ploy to deny them a basic service. Their attitudes changed quickly as soil testing expanded to the neighborhood as a whole. Analysis revealed that lead in the residential section reached four times the safe level and rose even higher over a vacant portion of the dump.[45] Residents received warnings to keep their children out of the unused area and avoid tracking dirt into their homes, but they also heard reassurances that the neighborhood remained a safe place to live. Understandably, they became confused by the mixed messages from public health and environmental officials.

Confusion continued over the next decade and engendered distrust of public officials. At the core of public apprehension was a perceived reversal by the EPA in the site's Superfund evaluation. The fact that the score leaped from a lowly 3 to 50 and thereby required inclusion of the site on the NPL undercut public confidence in the process, while at the same time it firmly attached a hazards label to the site.[46] It also set into motion the various EPA programs to remediate the site and to deal with community concerns. One of the first steps was to enclose the dump's undeveloped portion with a tall chain link fence topped with razor wire and posted with numerous warning signs. This became an undeniable fixture in the landscape that spoke to the persistent hazards that underlay the neighborhood.

As part of Superfund's community relations program, the EPA took several steps to keep the community involved in and informed of its efforts. It offered an open house during the second scoring of the site, and in 1994 it opened a community outreach center—another obvious landscape element that bespoke environmental contamination. That same year, the EPA issued its community relations plan, outlining its intent to open communication with residents and involve community leaders in selecting the ultimate remediation plan.[47] In addition, it sought to follow the National Environmental Justice Advisory Council's public participation plan, which seeks to "encourage public participation in all aspects of environmental decision making."[48] Once the EPA had placed Agriculture Street on the NPL, there was brief hope that the site would be remediated in short order. But things did not work out that way. Community members doubted the earnestness of the EPA, and as quickly as the environmental agency acted to address one concern, new issues erupted. Serious differences of opinion emerged within the community, and city officials quickly found themselves at odds with both the EPA and the community. When the school board decided to close the Moton Elementary School in 1994 due to concern over contaminants on the property, the empty building and the warning signs hung on its fence became additional reminders of the Superfund designation. Thus the relatively new school became the most prominent symbol of hazards in the emerging landscape of tragedy.

The first in a series of contested positions centered on public health concerns. A 1995 study found contaminants over the former landfill, but none at serious levels[49]—contradicting studies from the 1980s. Only lead occurred at levels that warranted an immediate response and this was only in the undeveloped portion of the dump site. The EPA had already conducted a "removal" action and fenced this area off to prevent direct human contact in 1994.[50] Authors of the 1995 health study concluded that there was no immediate threat to neighborhood residents, and a local toxicologist told journalists that lead levels were worse in other sections of the city. Furthermore, analysis of neighborhood children's blood lead levels showed a steady drop from 70 percent above recommended concentrations in 1986 to only 11 percent above recommended levels in 1994.[51] A 1996 public health assessment also found that only the site's undeveloped portion was a "public health hazard." It concluded that the residential areas posed "no apparent public health hazard" and that the Moton School site posed "no public health hazard." A 1997 Louisiana Department of Health investigation concluded that most cancer rates for the Agriculture Street neighborhood were "not statistically different from what is expected as compared with the regional rates," although breast cancer did stand out above regional averages. The study, how-

FIG. 4.2. SIGN IN RESIDENT'S YARD DEMANDING BUYOUT. Photo by author.

ever, did not establish a causal link between environmental conditions in the neighborhood and breast cancer.[52] These findings did not appease area residents, however. They saw the report's findings as contradicting the Superfund designation, and their skepticism contributed to a critical reception to subsequent government-financed studies.

In spite of the health studies, neighborhood activists began insisting on a Superfund-financed buyout. They claimed that they were living on "toxic, God-forbidden land" and could not sell their houses anywhere near market value following the Superfund designation (Fig. 4.2).[53] The EPA responded that conditions did not warrant a buyout and relocation, which has been a rare response.[54] The government's remediation plan called for removal of contaminated soil, installation of a fiber barrier, and placement of clean soil on all affected properties. This option, with a price tag of about $10 million, projected far less expense than the estimated $33 million for remediation and relocation. Furthermore, not all residents favored the relocation option. Older residents, allied with those living in adjoining neighborhoods, wanted remediation without evacuation to avoid dismantling the community.[55] Unlike the relocation advocates who saw children threatened and property devalued, the older residents saw greater value in community ties than real estate. In the absence of a unified community, the EPA responded to the citizens who agreed with its plan, strictly followed its guidelines, and implemented a strategy in accord with its mandate to safeguard public health and natural resources (not property values) at the least cost.

The City of New Orleans, which was the sole Potentially Responsible Party (PRP) as long-term owner and operator of the site, initially distanced itself from community members seeking a buyout. Superfund made the city liable for buyout costs, and economic hard times during the 1980s left the city coffers in no condition to underwrite this option. By 1997, municipal leaders, comfortable that the EPA was not going after the city as a PRP, finally began making public statements about Agriculture Street. Both the mayor, Marc Morial, and the neighborhood's city council representative, Ellen Hazeur-Distance, adopted a middle position, trying to make all residents happy without incurring any costs to the city. They embraced a "hybrid" remedy that called for soil replacement along with a buyout option *only* for those demanding relocation.[56] This option would have added only about $6 million to the price tag, well under the complete remediation/relocation proposal.[57]

As city officials deliberated the hybrid plan, the EPA made adjustments of its own. In response to input from residents and lobbying by city officials, the EPA retained plans to remove contaminated soil from the landfill, transport it to another location, install a geotextile liner over the dump site, and excavate and replace soil from residences.[58] By removing the contaminated soil, the federal agency would physically eliminate the principal risk and raise the price tag. In September 1997, the EPA announced its "final" $20 million plan, which incorporated concessions to the neighborhood, but not relocation.[59]

The EPA's plan did not satisfy those demanding a federal buyout, and the mayor, using carefully chosen words, declared the federal plan "a grave injustice" to area residents.[60] Following the plan's announcement some semblance of local cooperation emerged. The city and the local congressional delegation expressed support for the hybrid plan, which would allow residents to receive federal relocation funds if they wanted them.[61] In order to force the EPA to consider this option, Louisiana congressman William Jefferson inserted a directive into the 1998 Superfund budget to freeze the agency's soil removal and replacement funds.[62] Thus local opponents of the EPA's plan began a series of tactical moves that would drag out rather than expedite the remediation process. Nonetheless, the EPA moved forward against the local current. In an attempt to block work, the local citizens group that favored a buyout sued for a temporary restraining order in January 1998. The suit claimed that the EPA's remediation would not protect residents from lead and arsenic tossed into the air by earthmoving equipment.[63] The federal judge threw out the case in March, noting that a restraining order would undercut the EPA's efforts to effect a prompt site cleanup.[64] The obstructionist tactics delayed cleanup efforts, but they did not secure funding for relocation.

The city took the lead in the second phase of delaying tactics in early 1998. Since it owned the vacant property, the city blocked remediation by denying EPA cleanup contractors access to the site for several months. When the EPA sought to move forward without city permission, the mayor charged the agency with "totalitarian" tactics and claimed that the EPA's actions made its "commitment to environmental justice ring hollow." EPA officials responded that if the city so desperately wanted a major relocation, then as lead PRP, it should pay the cost.[65] When the city remained silent on paying for the relocation, the federal environmental agency moved forward by issuing an administrative order granting itself access to the city-owned property in February 1999.[66] Although unwilling to underwrite relocation, the mayor assigned the city attorney's office the task of challenging the EPA order. Arguing before a federal district judge, the city claimed that it was being treated differently than other landowners, who had been given a choice whether or not to allow remedial actions, and that the cleanup would expose residents to airborne contaminants stirred up by the work crews.[67] In early March, the judge issued a temporary restraining order. After the EPA presented its case several weeks later, the judge ruled that access to city-owned land was essential for removing the threat of chemical hazards. This cleared the way for unimpeded remediation.[68] Cleanup pressed ahead during the spring and summer of 1999, but attempts to thwart the EPA continued.

Neighborhood activists, by now allied with national and international environmental organizations such as Greenpeace, took their case to a United Nations forum in Geneva and to EPA officials in Washington. Residents convinced an EPA official to search for relocation funding following a May 1999 meeting in the nation's capital. Nothing turned up, even under revised agency guidelines for executing a relocation.[69] In their next attempt to block work, residents charged that the contractors were removing only 1 foot of soil in the residential area, not two as the plan called for, and they requested a procedural review. Timothy Fields, EPA's Superfund chief, agreed to inspect conditions personally and determine if the remediation crew was adhering to the plan.[70] After a site visit in June, Fields concluded work was progressing satisfactorily and approved the 1-foot removal modification (digging deeper would have entailed moving water, sewer, and other buried utilities). Following his visit, he announced that the agency would stand by its original plan—which did not include relocation funds. This infuriated neighborhood activists, who charged the EPA with misleading them and repeatedly dashing their hopes. In an attempt to redirect community outrage, Fields issued a statement reminding residents that the city of New Orleans was the sole PRP and recommending that if they wanted relocation support, they should approach the city.[71] By midsummer, crews had made significant progress on capping the undeveloped portion of the landfill and replacing soil in the residential area. This did not mollify residents, especially those who protested the EPA efforts by refusing to let contractors carry out work on their property. Of sixty-seven property owners in Gordon Plaza, forty-two protested the plan by denying EPA crews access to their land.[72]

Some hope remains for local residents who filed a class-action suit in 1993 seeking damages for property devaluation, health problems, and relocation costs. A state judge ruled in September 1999 that neighborhood residents along with former students and teachers at Moton School could pursue this case against the city, the housing authority, and the school board. The plaintiffs claimed the public housing projects and the school were built with knowledge of contaminants, and therefore agencies involved knowingly placed residents at risk.[73] While this action did not change the remediation plan, it may eventually lead to compensation for residents wishing to relocate. But the suit delayed the cleanup process, put affected parties back into the courts, and obscured the community-based resolution sought by the environmental justice strategy.

As remediation was underway, the landscape was replete with evidence of the contamination tragedy. In addition to the fenced dump and closed school, an EPA trailer served as headquarters for the cleanup team. Heavy equipment lumbered in and out of the site, and smaller earthmovers invaded individual yards to remove soil and install new sod. Homeowners erected protest signs demanding relocation. Gradually, however, the landscape is becoming "rectified." In fall 2001, the parish school board reopened Moton

School, following the EPA's decision that it should be removed as an active unit of the Superfund site.[74] The federal environmental agency declared the remediation effort complete in May 2002 and began removing evidence of an active cleanup operation.[75] Some remain dissatisfied with the agency's failure to relocate families, but the remediation has put the neighborhood back to use.[76] As elsewhere, rectification of this landscape of tragedy will make way for something approximating normal activity in the future.

The EPA's approach and the neighborhood response to the Agriculture Street Landfill cleanup are similar in several respects to those for hazardous waste elsewhere. EPA officials saw the "tragedy" in terms of technical cleanup criteria and achieved their objectives. Residents saw the tragedy in terms of long-term health risks and property devaluation. While the remediation may have removed future health risks, it did not expunge prior exposures, nor did it restore property values. These issues have arisen at other Superfund sites without the same level of contention. Perhaps what sets the Agriculture Street Landfill site apart is the tendency in New Orleans to enlist the federal government to pay for solutions to the city's problems while at the same time attempting to control the process locally—a pattern also seen in nineteenth-century efforts to construct flood protection levees. A fundamental distrust of federal intervention has roots in the early Creole response to federal authorities after the Louisiana Purchase and during the Civil War.[77] This apprehensiveness about federal authority reappears in the struggle for clean drinking water.

FROM NAVIGABLE RIVER TO DRINKING WATER [78]

EARLY POLLUTION CONTROL

A second set of environmental concerns emerged in conjunction with the great river that passes by New Orleans. Both French and Spanish colonial authorities had identified the Mississippi River as a navigable waterway, and when the United States acquired the Louisiana Territory in 1803 it continued that legal designation. One of the key concerns behind the U.S. purchase was to preserve one fundamental right associated with navigable waterways—unimpeded passage. Thus early legal concern with the river focused on its utility as a route for watercraft. In addition, riparian landowners under the principles of Louisiana civil law had the right to expect undiminished quantity and quality of water flowing by their properties.[79] Louisiana courts had upheld damage complaints along smaller watercourses,[80] yet well into the twentieth century it was practically inconceivable that the quality of the Mississippi could be degraded sufficiently to cause harm. Increasing sewage releases from towns and cities, however, along with the arrival of numerous waste-discharging petrochemical manufacturing plants along the corridor between Baton Rouge and New Orleans demonstrated that there were limits to the mighty river's dilution capabilities. Louisiana's initial response to pollution had been to protect the state's waters for agriculture and as habitat for aquatic life—based on conservation principles. Policy commonly expressed explicit concern with the river as drinking water source, but such expressions did little to compel action through the 1960s. Ultimately, the fact that New Orleans relied on the river for its drinking water prompted an environmental stance and thereby altered protections offered waterways in general and the Mississippi in particular. As in its struggle to get external assistance with flood protection, Louisiana needed federal relief in securing upstream pollution control. By the 1970s, state and federal laws safeguarded the river not just as a navigable waterway or fish habitat but as the drinking water source for more than a million residents in the lower valley with a variety of rules and regulations that supplemented traditional legal protections.

Louisiana's first explicit water pollution law, passed in 1910, protected agricultural crops and aquatic life. Specifically, it forbade discharges of oil, salt water, and "other noxious or poisonous gases or substances that would render said water unfit for irrigation purposes or would destroy fish in said streams." Drafted specifically to defend rice growers in southwest Louisiana from oil-field brine releases, it also showed concern with wildlife. Yet it made no mention of drinking water supplies.[81] A second act (1924) expanded protection to "all the natural waterways and canals" from releases of salt water, oil, or other substances. Like its predecessor, it explicitly safeguarded fish but not drinking water supplies, and it placed the state's conservation agency in the enforcement role.[82] Early pollution law protected traditional economies, such as agriculture and commercial fisheries, over new economic activities like oil extraction. Because of its seemingly gargantuan diluting capacity, however, the Mississippi River remained largely outside the pollution discussion at this time. During the development of New Orleans's early-twentieth-century water supply, sediment filtration was the only issue discussed.[83]

With the expansion of Louisiana's oil and natural gas fields, petroleum companies realized the opportunities for refining crude along the lower Mississippi. Beginning in 1909, corporations such as Standard Oil began acquiring riverfront property and constructing refineries upstream from New Orleans. Petrochemical developments accelerated during the 1940s as the federal government underwrote refining capacity in the South in general and along the Mississippi in particular. Encouraged by a variety of locational factors such as ready access to crude oil, ample rural land, and ample fresh water for transportation, process, and waste disposal needs, modern refineries rose from the sugarcane fields.[84] By 1951, there were fifty-one plants along the lower river, and six produced petrochemical products.[85] The number of refineries in the state expanded from 175 in 1947 to 255 in 1967, and the value of their production jumped from $52 million in 1939 to $584 million in 1958.[86] Industrial development clustered along the Mississippi. By 1971, sixty major petrochemical plants occupied land on the river's flanks.[87] Riverside sites were desirable because manufacturers could use the water for industrial processes and waste transport. And it was not just petrochemical plants that discharged effluent into the river. Along with municipalities, numerous metallurgical plants and other assorted industries relied on the Mississippi as a waste sink.

During the early stages of its industrial buildup, Louisiana recognized the need for a pollution control agency. Following a model employed in other states, the legislature created the Stream Control Commission in 1940. The commission's legislative mandate was to regulate waste disposal into *any* waters of the state. Representatives from the state's conservation agency, the attorney general's office, and the public health department reflected its charge to prevent pollution that would "destroy fish life or be injurious to the public health."[88] Despite a dual responsibility to protect aquatic life and potable waters, much of the commission's early attention focused on aquatic life.

The Stream Control Commission (SCC), administratively placed in the state wildlife agency, crafted its first rules in 1941. Those rules prohibited the discharge of oil-field brines and oil in concentrations sufficient to harm aquatic life or livestock or to affect the receiving water's palatability. Given the host agency's orientation, the SCC's initial emphasis on fish was not surprising, and apparently there was sufficient enforcement to irk waste releasers. Charging that the rules singled out the oil producers while ignoring other polluters, the Texas Company claimed that the SCC had denied the industry due process in crafting the law and treated it unfairly by restricting its discharges in already brackish coastal waters. A federal court, however, ruled that the commission was acting within its legitimate authority and thereby affirmed the state's ability to protect its vital fisheries.[89]

Despite the Texas Company's grievances, the commission was very mindful of the oil industry's need to release wastes and demonstrated that it would not be antagonistic toward business interests. Reflecting this concern, the commission proclaimed that one of its first achievements was establishing a cooperative relationship among sportsmen, industrialists, and agriculturalists.[90] In addition, the petroleum refiners' pollution control organization, which funded its own waste disposal research, sponsored biologists working for the state. The industry-paid investigators evaluated the toxicity of refinery wastes and helped establish tolerable limits for the state's waterways.[91] Such efforts, which paralleled activity in Texas, represented a step by industry to control technical expertise.[92] By defining what constituted pollution, industry influenced the state's enforcement activity. Managing pollution research also enabled the industry to retain trade secrets, a powerful argument in deferring government investigations into particular industrial processes or waste streams. The commission also cooperated with industry in seeking to reshape public opinion about fish kills. Claiming that well-meaning citizens often attributed dead fish to industrial discharges, fish and wildlife scientists pointed out that sometimes naturally occurring events, such as salt water intrusion or temperature-related oxygen depletion, were the culprits.[93] In this collaborative atmosphere, most pollution control efforts focused on smaller streams and not the Mississippi River, where the large industries clustered during the 1940s.

Government concern, however, was not limited to aquatic life. As early as 1942, the state health agency received complaints that oil released into the Mississippi was causing taste and odor problems in Gretna (a New Orleans suburb on the river's west bank). An investigation identified Gulf Distilling as the problem's source. Refinery officials responded by extending the plant's discharge lines farther out into the river to ensure more complete mixing and dilution.[94] State officials also worked with Shell Oil to restrict its releases to the Mississippi just upstream from New Orleans's water intakes in the late 1940s. In perhaps the only instance of complete diversion of wastes from the river during this period, Shell initially impounded its oily effluent on site and then later diverted it to Lake Pontchartrain via a canal and a bayou.[95]

The plant's proximity to New Orleans (22 miles upstream from the water intake) was an obvious factor in the state's insistence that wastes stay out of the river. Although the state demonstrated concern about industrial wastes close to New Orleans, federal authorities noted threats coming from farther up river. In 1951 the U.S. Public Health Service (USPHS) asserted that "industrial wastes from Baton Rouge may affect the New Orleans water supply if the concentration becomes high enough."[96] The report discounted the immediacy of the problem, however, when it pointed out that dilution adequately handled existing discharges. Shell's waste diversion combined with the river's vast dilution capacity minimized state action against industrial polluters.

In 1951, the SCC issued new rules requiring industries to apply for waste discharge permits. In their applications, manufacturers had to submit a detailed engineering analysis of the content and volume of their proposed releases.[97] Despite this SCC-collected accounting, apparently the state public health agency, with primary responsibility for potable water supplies, did not receive the information. When the USPHS solicited information on industrial waste sources from its state counterpart in 1953, Louisiana reported only five companies along the Mississippi River, although there were many municipal sewage discharges. The number of plants reported by the state was far below the USPHS's own 1951 tally of fifty-eight. In its 1958 report on municipal and industrial sources, the USPHS indicated that the five plants along the lower Mississippi all discharged their wastes into canals or ditches and not directly to the river.[98] Thus the state-supplied information failed to reveal the actual level of industrial waste disposal. In addition to the federal health agency, in 1956 the U.S. Geological Survey pointed out that industrial pollution of the Mississippi was an "ever present danger" at New Orleans. More than anything, the federal reports exposed the state's apparent inattention to the Mississippi as a threatened municipal water source. While the federal agencies sounded alarms in the 1950s, the state regularly permitted industrial discharges to the river. Of thirty-seven applicants between 1958 and 1966, the state approved all but one.[99] Furthermore, out of 163 enforcement actions taken by the state from 1950 through 1959, only 1 was against a refinery.[100] The SCC's cooperative posture did little to discourage use of the Mississippi River as a waste sink.

The ambivalence of Louisiana state regulators was not wholly atypical in the early 1950s. Water pollution primarily remained a state legal responsibility, although the federal government was offering greater technical assistance with waste-related issues. States sought to attract and retain manufacturing operations and the jobs they brought. Although most states rewrote their water pollution laws after World War II, cooperation, not confrontation, was the enforcement approach.[101] On huge interstate waterways like the Mississippi River, states had little ability to alter upstream discharges. Additionally, most southern states left water pollution responsibilities in the hands of wildlife and fisheries departments. They typically responded to fish kills—the canaries of the waterways—but did not carry out systematic monitoring. Thus at a time when industry had exhausted most by-product recovery options to prevent stream pollution,[102] the states had not yet begun rigorously enforcing environmental protection policies.

By the late 1950s, however, this was beginning to change. In response to complaints about taste and odor problems caused by industrial discharges of organic chemicals, Louisiana's Wildlife and Fisheries Commission established sampling stations on the Mississippi River to monitor water quality.[103] In the early 1960s they required industries to report toxic and taste-causing discharges, and eighteen petrochemical plants along the lower Mississippi participated.[104] Federal agencies also began to develop river-basin monitoring systems in the 1950s. The U.S. Geological Survey reported on water quality in 1956 and again in 1959.[105] The USPHS tabulated municipal and industrial waste discharge sources in the early 1950s and reported similar information on water sources in 1958.[106] In addition, the USPHS had set up a massive pollution surveillance system on the nation's waterways by the early 1960s. By 1962 it was regularly monitoring a variety of pollutants, including organic chemicals, radioactivity, and most traditional measures of water quality such as biochemical oxygen demand, dissolved oxygen, and dissolved solids.[107] Surveillance enabled these agencies to track water quality over time and identify abnormal conditions. However, while monitoring established baseline conditions, it imposed no restrictions on use of the river for disposing wastes.

Industries and municipalities continued to use the river both as their primary disposal option and as a potable water source (see Fig. 4.3), but a massive spill in 1960 exceeded the waterway's diluting capabilities, forcing authorities to rethink their reliance on the river for both of those uses. A pipe rupture at a Baton Rouge refinery released a sizable quantity of phenols into the river. When combined with chlorine at water treatment facilities, phenols produce an obvious and very objectionable taste. The state Water Pollution Control Division reported that the obviously contaminated water drove New Orleans residents to the verge of panic. Bottled water sales soared, while distributors had to discard tons of foodstuffs and cases of soft drinks afflicted by the foul water. No longer was pollution just an inconvenience for consumers. The 1960 spill sent shock waves through the population and directly affected grocers, soft-drink bottlers, and other businesses. The state reacted by creating an emergency warning system to alert downstream municipal water treatment plants of spills that would impact their supply.[108] This response assumed that normal water quality did not pose a public health problem but spills could exceed tolerable conditions and have an adverse impact on water supplies. The plan required industries that spilled contaminants into the river to contact the state health agency, which would in turn warn water plant operators to shut off their intakes. Manufacturers could continue to release spills, while the real burden for protecting consumers lay with the public water suppliers. Industry only had to share information about abnormal releases with the state; it was up to public water supply operators to prevent pollutants from reaching consumers.

CONTROVERSY AND RESPONSE

Shortly after the 1962 publication of Rachel Carson's dramatic and influential work *Silent Spring*,[109] Louisiana and the communities and industries along the lower river found themselves in the midst of a national environmental struggle. Carson demonstrated that toxic chemicals used to control pests had long-lasting environmental impacts. As the nation grappled with its conflicting desires for a pest-free existence and a less toxic environment, an agricultural chemical (endrin) killed millions of Mississippi River fish. The massive fish kill of 1963–64 dramatized the consequences of industrial waste disposal in the river and altered public response to the threats it posed.

The 1963–64 event was one in a series Louisiana experienced in the early 1960s. In both 1961 and 1962 toxic conditions proved fatal to about 250,000 fish. These were large kills but were not entirely unusual in a state where sugarcane farmers relied on chemicals such as endrin to fight off sugar borers. Pollution problems had occurred occasionally during the cane harvest when grinding mills in south Louisiana released toxic concentrations of endrin to small rivers and bayous. The state had sought to eliminate such situations by banning the application of endrin during the forty-five days

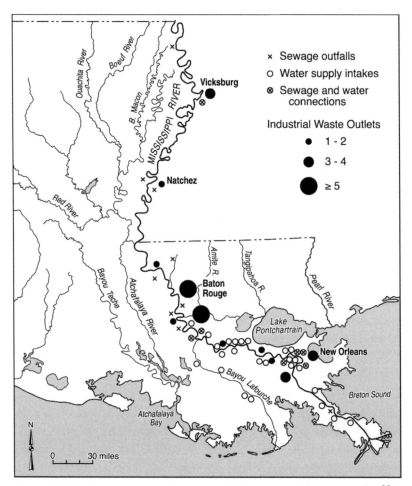

FIG. 4.3. INDUSTRY AND WATER USE ALONG THE MISSISSIPPI RIVER, 1969. New Orleans's water intakes were downstream from a massive industrial cluster in the 1960s. After U.S. Department of Health, Education, and Welfare, *Conference in the Matter of the Interstate Waters of the Lower Mississippi River: Proceedings* (Washington: U.S. Department of Health, Education, and Welfare, 1969).

before harvest.[110] The 1963–64 event fell outside the normal grinding period and killed fish well upstream from sugarcane cultivation and processing areas. But more significant was the number of fish affected: an estimated five million were killed. This placed the 1963–64 event in an entirely different category from the earlier episodes. With a public attuned to chemical hazards by Rachael Carson and regular reports on the incident in the *New York*

Times, it became a national story and prompted congressional hearings. Was this the beginning of the "silent spring"? Senator Abraham Ribicoff, an ardent foe of agricultural pesticide use, chaired hearings in Washington to find out, while Louisiana authorities sought answers from federal agencies.[111]

The USPHS reviewed the sampling logs of its water quality monitoring network. Its scientists quickly ruled out low river stage and inadequate dilution, deficient dissolved oxygen, extreme temperatures, and viruses. Continuing their search, USPHS investigators discovered one consistent factor —endrin was present in the flesh of most of the dead fish. Exactly where it came from they were unable to say initially.[112] With this evidence in mind, researchers reexamined water quality samples taken during the summers of 1960, 1961, and 1962. Elevated endrin concentrations appeared in New Orleans's water each year, but not at the next observation point upstream— Vicksburg. This evidence suggested that the previous kills, which occurred during the pesticide-use season, were tied to sugarcane cultivation. In the fall and winter of 1963–64, however, high endrin levels appeared to have traveled downstream from West Memphis, past Vicksburg and to New Orleans. This ruled out sugar-grinding operations and suggested a Memphis-area source for the toxic chemical.[113]

USPHS investigators quickly turned their attention from farmers to chemical manufacturers and soon pointed an accusatory finger at the sole endrin manufacturer in the lower Mississippi Valley—Velsicol Chemical Company's Memphis facility. Close scrutiny of the plant revealed high endrin concentrations in the waste sludges that lined company ditches and in local streams used to transport waste to the Mississippi River. In addition, the USPHS suspected that endrin seeped into the river from a landfill used by Velsicol. Rinse water from barrel-cleaning operations presented still another source of endrin wastes entering the river.[114] Through its discovery of these poor waste management practices, the USPHS concluded it had found the problem's source.

Pesticide opponents had hoped to exploit the event to restrict agricultural chemical uses, but the fact that industrial waste disposal was the source redirected the official response. USPHS and local governments pushed Velsicol to clean up its operations and shift its waste outflow from a water sink to a land sink.[115] Although Velsicol challenged the USPHS findings, the company had few industrial allies. In general, chemical manufacturers breathed a collective sigh of relief when the government scientists singled out Velsicol. As long as the cost to the industry was just one plant cleanup, and not widespread legal restrictions on pesticide use, corporate officials realized they had survived the controversy relatively unscathed. Indeed, after Velsicol's diversion of its wastes to a rural landfill far from the river and marked decrease in endrin use by farmers, there were no repeat fish kills on the scale of the 1963–64 event.[116]

After the fervor died down, several key changes in perceptions about the environmental issues surrounding the 1963–64 fish kill remained. Industrial wastes in general—not just large reported spills—became a primary point of concern. Small, ongoing releases had contributed to the fish kills and had proven that toxic elements were present in the river at all times. The USPHS and other agencies began to view the river as a huge ecological system. No longer were they concerned only with discharges immediately upstream from drinking water sources. The far-reaching impact of endrin convinced the USPHS that pollutants could travel hundreds of miles and that its monitoring system could help detect them. Finally, greater awareness of the potential impact on human health emerged from the disastrous fish kill. As part of the investigation, officials found endrin in the New Orleans water supply, although at what they deemed insignificant levels.[117] This discovery alerted public officials and the scientific community to the fact that toxic substances could be found in drinking water supplies far removed from the pollution's source.

New Orleans's reliance on the river for its drinking water drove local pollution policy over the next decade. Although the state health department had touted the success of its emergency warning system in 1960, by 1967 the system was largely ineffective because offensive tastes and odors had become constant problems. The Department of Health called for full-time surveillance on the river between Baton Rouge and New Orleans as the only way to address chronic "chemical" and "oily" tasting water and fish. The persistence of pollutants convinced state officials that regular discharges, not spills, caused intolerable water quality.[118] Conditions in the lower Mississippi also prompted federal investigators to analyze New Orleans's drinking water as a potential carcinogen. While the analysis was inconclusive, the foul tastes and suspected health threats prompted the SCC to appeal to the newly formed Federal Water Pollution Control Administration (FWPCA) to help resolve these problems.[119]

Responding to Louisiana's request, the FWPCA (later to become part of the U.S. EPA) deployed scientists to analyze both industrial effluent and public water supplies. Their research began in 1969 and lasted into 1971. Reviewing industrial discharge tabulations, investigators found seventeen manufacturers who were releasing sizable quantities of phenols to the river. While no single plant was responsible for the foul-tasting water, the impact of the plants' combined waste output of 8,400 pounds per day exceeded the taste threshold. The federal assessment exposed failings in the state's permit review system, which considered each proposed discharge individually and not as part of a combined total.[120] The EPA concluded that the industries released "significant quantities of hazardous and/or undesirable pollutants to the Mississippi River in Louisiana" and that these wastes were the "principal cause of persistent oily-petrochemical tastes in downstream water supplies and fish." Using new analytical techniques on raw river water, it was able to identify organic chemicals in trace amounts, which it declared were "a potential threat to the health of 1.5 million people who consume this water." In the absence of regulations explicitly prohibiting such discharges, the EPA called for the removal or at least reduction of "hazardous discharges to the river" by both industry and municipal treatment plants.[121]

While the federal investigation was underway, the SCC took action that paralleled the EPA's eventual conclusions. It reviewed all industrial permits and pressured industries to halt releasing the specific organic chemicals identified by the EPA as problems—namely chloroform, benzene, and bischloroethyl ether.[122] Calling for removal of these wastes clearly shifted enforcement from traditional pollution concerns, such as bacteria and BOD, to chemical wastes. The state's efforts were effective to a degree and prompted some of the larger manufacturers to divert wastes from the river either to land dumps or to deep geologic formations using injection wells.[123] But while Louisiana officials could press plants along the state's own chemical corridor to withhold releases to the river, they could not prevent toxic organic chemical discharges upstream. As the great sewer for the country's midsection, the Mississippi River transported wastes from Pittsburgh, Minneapolis, Kansas City, and points in between past the Crescent City. This complex brew became the focal point for ensuing efforts to enact a federal safe drinking water act.

As part of a national campaign to secure passage of the Safe Drinking Water Act (1974), Ralph Nader and others testified before Congress in 1973 that water supplies on the Ohio River contained potentially harmful organic

chemicals. Nader also suggested that high cancer rates in New Orleans resulted from contaminated drinking water. He charged that New Orleans
officials had been unwilling to cooperate with his investigation of the city's
water filtration system, which seemed to suggest, Nader implied, that they
had something to hide.[124] His associates Robert Harris and Edward Brecher
continued the exposé of tainted water supplies in 1974 as they pushed for
cities to adopt activated carbon filters, which could reduce organic chemical pollution. By this time affiliated with the Environmental Defense Fund,
Harris took the campaign for safe drinking water to the American public
through a three-part series in the popular magazine *Consumer Reports*. He
claimed that an exceptionally high cancer rate in New Orleans was due to an
environmental source—probably the drinking water. While Harris allowed
that New Orleans's water was not "necessarily worse than most other cities,"
he sparked resentment within the Louisiana public health community and
stimulated a lively national debate.[125] Harris also charged that cancer mortality among males who consumed Mississippi River water was 15 percent
higher than among those who did not.[126] Officials in New Orleans and their
counterparts in the EPA quickly proclaimed the city's water safe.[127] The
damage was done, however, and bottled water sales soared again in New
Orleans. Public confidence in the municipal water was undercut further by
a report that workers in city hall drank bottled water while at the same time
declaring the city's supply safe.[128]

Nader and Harris and Brecher's campaign ultimately proved successful
when Congress passed the Safe Drinking Water Act in 1974. But while the
act would help improve the quality of New Orleans's drinking water, the
reputation of the city's drinking water supply was smeared beyond repair,
despite local, state, and federal officials' criticism of Harris and Brecher's
reports.[129] At the national level, new federal policy initiatives took aim at organic chemicals in drinking water supplies and pushed to provide more complete treatment. The act broadened the EPA's mission to include monitoring and regulating tap water as well as raw river water and placed equivalent
emphasis on requirements for water treatment plants and sewage works.
This meant downstream water users had greater responsibilities for cleaning
up the damage done by upstream dischargers. The new federal act did not
reverse traditional riparian residents' rights to expect water quality undiminished by upstream communities. However, while the Clean Water Act (1972)
called on upstream dischargers to treat their effluent to maintain drinkable

water sources, it also raised municipal responsibilities to cleanse contaminants from the water they took from the river. Since the common sand filtration and chlorination systems did not remove organic chemicals, cities like New Orleans faced considerable challenges in order to upgrade their water treatment facilities.

New Orleans took no immediate steps to alter its treatment system, but it grappled with the new federal mandates. The massive industrial presence on the lower river continued to affect water quality, and taste-producing phenolic compounds commonly exceeded the recommended level for public water supplies into the late 1970s.[130] In response to the Safe Drinking Water Act, the New Orleans Sewerage and Water Board began an EPA-sponsored research program on the use of granulated activated carbon to remove organic chemicals. While continuing to use and rehabilitate its existing sand filters, the water utility examined the viability of the alternate purification technology. In 1980, the Sewerage and Water Board concluded that the more costly activated carbon system offered negligible benefits, and consequently the board abandoned its research on the treatment option.[131] Beginning in 1981, the Sewerage and Water Board complained that an increasing number of unauthorized industrial releases to the river plagued its treatment capabilities.[132] Industry-friendly enforcement practices of the Reagan era apparently gave industry license to resume discharges into the river, and pollutants from these releases were reaching the New Orleans water supply. In response the Sewerage and Water Board replaced chlorine with chloramine to reduce some organic chemicals produced by reactions with chlorine, and this new practice improved the water's taste.[133]

The grand irony was that, with the improved taste, New Orleans won a national award for best-tasting water in 1984. After battling organic chemical tastes for over thirty years and exactly a decade after the controversy over toxins in the water erupted, the Sewerage and Water Board entered a sample of its product in the First Annual Great Invitational International Water-Tasting Challenge. Judges concluded that New Orleans's water was the best of eight entrants. More a friendly competition than a serious evaluation, the outcome made the point that New Orleans had made progress with removing many of the taste-causing ingredients in its water. One of the judges allowed, however, "Safe doesn't have anything to do with taste."[134] Reflecting that opinion, public consumption of bottled water remained strong despite the taste prize.

Even as federal laws required upstream communities and industries to clean up their discharges to the Mississippi River and the treatment facility took measures to improve the water's taste, the city resisted federal guidance on treatment methods, and public apprehension about New Orleans's water quality persisted. Dixie Brewing Company, the city's only remaining brewery, which had relied on river water up until that time, initiated efforts to obtain spring water from the north shore community of Abita Springs. Dixie executives claimed they sought this replacement source out of their commitment to quality. Feeling pressure from national brewers whose advertisements touted pure water sources, the local beer maker sought to disassociate itself from the tainted drinking-water supply. A state law blocked its efforts to obtain Abita Springs water, but the brewery was able to gain access to a groundwater source in an adjoining parish.[135]

In the post–World War II era, invisible toxins became the central concern both at the Agriculture Street Landfill and in New Orleans's public water supply. Detection of minute quantities of harmful substances redefined these concerns, previously considered nuisances, as hazards. Considering the landfill as an ecological system, the EPA examined various "pathways" by which lead could move from the soil to neighborhood residents. Acting on its new environmental justice mission and adding direct soil ingestion to its hazards ranking formula, the EPA suddenly placed Agriculture Street Landfill on its National Priorities List. This decision left an indelible imprint on the neighborhood. As part of its effort to employ science and technology to remediate the environmental situation, the EPA helped create a landscape of tragedy by labeling the site as hazardous. Residents underscored the tragedy with graffiti and signs in their front lawns decrying the situation. As the cleanup effort ended and the neighborhood school reopened, the federal agency declared the environment had been restored to a safe condition, although many residents remained unsatisfied. The reclassification of the site from a nuisance to a hazard, along with public acceptance of environmental principles, fundamentally altered public reaction to the landfill. As a "hazard" it attained a persistent stigma, which created an inescapable situation for low-income, minority residents living in subsidized housing near the site. The city's traditional resistance to federal intervention complicated the attempted resolution.

The redefinition of river pollution as a public health hazard rather than merely a biological threat also marked the arrival of environmental concerns in Louisiana. Although the state identified oil industry wastes as a menace to its waterways in the early twentieth century, initial pollution control focused on protecting agriculture and aquatic life and reflected conservation attitudes. Gradually, public discontent with increasing taste and odor problems shifted to alarm over the toxic substances that caused those conditions. Protections at both ends of the pipeline—restrictions on industrial discharges, supplemented by increased expectations for water treatment—reflect the application of environmental principles to protect consumers who rely on large waterways for their drinking water. The post–World War II period brought many other environmental issues to the fore, both in New Orleans and across the nation, but the responses to the Agriculture Street Landfill and the public water supply crisis exemplify how the city dealt with old problems under new circumstances.

CHAPTER 5

COMBATING NEW FLOOD HAZARDS

PERHAPS THE GREATEST territorial expansion of American cities occurred in the period following World War II. Unlike the development of
suburbs that had previously been made possible through streetcars and other
public transportation, post–1945 suburbanization was tied to expanding networks of highways that enabled commuters to live farther from the city center and eventually led to the development of "galactic" cities containing numerous clusters of office and commercial land uses along freeways, with
residential areas filling the interstices. Numerous environmental impacts accompanied this unprecedented growth.[1] Farmland and open space loss, wildlife displacement, air pollution, and runoff-induced flooding were all unavoidable byproducts. New Orleans's suburbanization produced all these
effects, but the process also involved challenges not encountered in most
other cities, particularly with regard to flooding.

Lake Pontchartrain is a permanent barrier to New Orleans's growth to
the north, and vast wetlands inhibited expansion to the east and west before
1940. By the 1930s, drainage and landfilling efforts had successfully reclaimed

wetland between the city and the lake, and in the postwar years similar campaigns dewatered marshlands for tract housing eastward from the city and westward into Jefferson Parish. Boom years in the petroleum industry fueled population increases and demand for suburban homes in these former wetlands. Financial good times coupled with mosquito eradication programs and air conditioning made life bearable in the lower delta's steamy climes. Drainage engineering made it feasible to construct suburbs in what had at one time been largely uninhabitable land. Although we may associate automobile suburbs with West Coast urbanization, there was a Gulf Coast variant—albeit one that faced important environmental problems unknown in the arid West.

In the western states there is a common saying that water flows toward money. In water-scarce areas, those who can afford to secure water rights are able to direct the precious fluid toward their property. In the Crescent City the situation is reversed. Built entirely on an alluvial floodplain, subsequently surrounded by levees to keep out floods from the Mississippi River, and now sinking under its own weight, the city and its suburbs must collect and pump out an average 60 inches of rain that falls annually into what is often described as a giant bowl. All residential or commercial construction within the basin sheds rainfall, adding to surface runoff, and is subject to periodic flooding from storms that exceed the drainage system's short-term capacity. The city and its occupants have situated themselves in harm's way. Within the general pattern of flood risk, water flows away from money— that is, away from the property of those who can afford to live in less flood-prone areas and those with the influence to secure adequate publicly financed water-removal services.

The geographer Gilbert White has argued that urban dwellers tend to occupy floodplains after structural flood protection devices such as levees have been erected.[2] Yet building on the floodplain was unavoidable in New Orleans—even the highest ground on the natural levee was a product of regular river inundations. Certainly the city hid behind its levee system, constructed initially at its own expense and later taken over by the federal government (see Chapter 1). To expel periodic high water within the encircling levees, the city has relied on a massive canal and pumping system. Even after the initiation of a federal program in the late 1960s to discourage both floodplain occupancy and structural flood protection, New Orleans had little choice but to continue collecting and pumping excess rain dropped by storms passing over the city. It is more than just a false sense of security that propels structural flood protection. As historian Martin Melosi argues, the adoption of one key infrastructure system creates a dependence on that system, despite the adoption of building codes and other land-use approaches to flood protection.[3]

EARLY FLOOD CONTROL EFFORTS

By the 1890s an effective levee system prevented regular river inundations, but New Orleans's internal drainage efforts were piecemeal, disjointed, and largely ineffective. A fractured city government from early statehood to the mid-nineteenth century fostered the construction of three independent open canals fed by street drains to transport water from the high ground of the natural levee to the backswamps behind (away from the river) the city (see Chapter 2). The principal aim of these and later-nineteenth-century projects was to remove floodwaters washing over the city from the Mississippi River or Lake Pontchartrain and to reduce the amount of standing water and groundwater that contributed to public health problems and inhibited the city's growth. Relieving storm-induced urban flooding was a secondary issue.[4] Only as the city achieved the primary objectives did the secondary concerns become obvious. Simply put, once the bowl was securely in place, rain began to fill it. Protection against one flood hazard guaranteed the city's long-standing struggle with the second.[5]

A vastly improved barrier, maintained by the Mississippi River Commission, lined the river by the early twentieth century and withstood several critical tests. Water rose to 23 feet or higher at New Orleans in 1907, 1910, and 1914, but the levees held. In 1922 crevasses spilled water onto rural farmland upstream, but a relief outlet below the city eased pressure on the municipal levee.[6] During the spring of 1927, one of the most devastating floods in the valley's history broke through levees upstream. Thousands fled their homes, hundreds died, and crops drowned in the fields. New Orleans's leaders pressed for an artificial outlet to save the city's levees, and with the governor's approval, the U.S. Army Corps of Engineers dynamited a hole in the levee just below the city at Caenarvon on April 29. The human-created crevasse allowed water to flow across the largely uninhabited St. Bernard Parish wetlands. While this response displaced trappers and fishermen and destroyed the valuable muskrat harvest for years, it achieved the city's objective by lowering the water level at New Orleans.[7] The levees, with some desperate modifications, protected the city from even the worst river floods by the 1920s.

In the midst of the battle against the great 1927 flood, the problem of internal flooding became all too obvious. In February over 5 inches of torrential rain fell on the city. It completely overwhelmed the city's pumps and caused flooding, particularly in the bottom of the bowl and in low areas along Bayou St. John. As city officials worked feverishly to shore up the levee system against the threatening river, the heavens unleashed a far worse flood within the protective barriers. In April a second storm dumped 14 inches into the city's raised perimeter. Serious flooding occurred in the bottom of the bowl, the former backswamp neighborhoods, and even in better-drained neighborhoods. High water disrupted transportation lines and commerce for several days. Drainage system inadequacies coupled with this exceptional rainfall triggered appeals for improvements.[8] While the levees fended off the river, the "bowl" did not have a lid to shed spring rains that rose within its confines.

The drainage system that failed in 1927 was part of the late-nineteenth-century citywide drainage effort designed to provide coordinated sewerage, drainage, and water systems to meet existing needs and future growth. One of its main purposes was to open previously undeveloped lands and accommodate increasing demand for more usable real estate. Any space within the sprawling city limits that had not been built up was waterlogged swamp or marsh. In 1900 the Sewerage and Water Board began work on open drainage canals and pumps that would equip New Orleans to follow other cities into the new century with an adequate infrastructure.[9] The original design sought to move about 5 inches of rain in a 5-hour period, or about 22,091 cubic feet per second. Due to its high cost, the project was completed in three phases; the first phase provided only 5,400 cubic feet per second capacity by 1920. Although incomplete, the system successfully transformed sizable territory by lowering the water table. With the economic prosperity of the 1920s, the system enabled rapid urbanization in the bottom of the bowl and toward the lakefront (see Chapter 3). However, despite promising results during dry spells and even following modest storms, a series of intense downpours surpassed the system's capacity in the 1920s and caused serious flooding particularly in neighborhoods in and around the city's lowest ground. This spate of inundations and resulting citizen complaints prodded the drainage authority to resume efforts to achieve the original specifications. In the meantime, however, there had been considerable construction and street paving within the drained territory. Coupled with land subsidence, which offset pumping capacity, the increased runoff from impervious cover rendered the latest improvements inadequate by the time they were completed in 1928.[10]

Following the 1920s improvements, New Orleans entered a period of relatively infrequent extreme downpours and few major tests of its drainage system.[11] This is not to say there were no internal floods. There were several hurricane-induced inundations, although the most serious damage from those events resulted from structural failures. As the metropolitan area expanded toward the lakefront, first in the city itself and in Jefferson Parish after World War II, suburbs sprang up on what had been a wide marsh and swamp buffer between the city and the lake. Before urban sprawl reached this zone, hurricane winds driving waves from the lake across the wetlands caused little damage other than to the lakefront entertainment districts and private houses built on stilts. But when these wetlands were leveed and drained, the residential districts that were developed in these buffer areas were at risk.

In 1922 the state authorized the Orleans Levee Board to begin a major overhaul of 5.5 miles of lakefront between the mouth of the New Basin Canal and the Industrial Canal. This project was part of Governor Huey Long's public works program, which won the favor of voters and enabled his associates to profit.[12] Despite devious political motives, it had a profound impact on the lakefront and property values. Its principal features were a sinuous, stepped seawall that rose 9.6 feet above sea level some distance from the existing shoreline and new land built on the lake bed. After the seawall was in place, the levee board pumped sediment from Lake Pontchartrain's bed into the area landward of the new barrier, creating extensive new acreage. Completed in 1934, the "made land" was devoted to a mixture of mostly high-value residential development and recreational land uses.[13] Adjacent Jefferson Parish constructed a 6-foot-high lakefront protection levee in 1926 as part of its overall drainage improvements.[14] Thus a long line of human-made barriers stood between the lake and newly drained territory and encouraged residential expansion into the former wetlands.

No serious hurricane had buffeted the city since 1915, but a storm in September 1947 demonstrated the new lakefront suburbs' vulnerability. A hurricane packing 112-mile-per-hour winds tracked westward across Lake Pont-chartrain, pushing gulf water into the lake and then shoving it up against what proved to be a hapless shoreline protection system. Waves topped the seawall in Orleans Parish and inundated nearly 9 square miles, with water 2 feet deep covering a quarter of that area. Resting on highly compressible subsoils, the Jefferson Parish levees had subsided in the two decades since their construction and provided even less protection than the Orleans Parish seawall. The storm-propelled waves inundated over 30 square miles of Jefferson Parish.[15] Obviously the lakefront barrier was not up to the task.

Both Orleans and Jefferson parishes promptly set to work correcting the structural deficiencies. With assistance from the Corps of Engineers, they gradually raised the levees to about 14 feet by the 1970s.[16] While this barrier has prevented a repeat of the flooding produced by the 1947 storm, subsequent hurricane-driven water still found breaches in the levee system. Hurricane Flossy in 1956 tossed water over the lakefront levees and inundated a large portion of the Gentilly neighborhood, and the storm surge burst through low gaps in the levee to flood industries along the Industrial Canal.[17] Hurricane Hilda again revealed weaknesses in the levees, causing damages to businesses along the Industrial Canal in 1964.[18] Both of these storms also disrupted transportation and battered lakefront camps, but their impacts were eclipsed by two more impressive hurricanes.

Hurricane Betsy bore down on the city in September 1965 after pummeling the Louisiana coast with winds up to 160 miles per hour. Winds raced through the city at 100 miles per hour overnight on September 10. The worst flooding occurred when the tidal surge breached the west levee of the Inner Harbor Navigation Canal (formerly the Industrial Canal). Water in low-lying areas reached 8 feet. More than seven thousand homes suffered damages along with more than three hundred industries. The Corps of Engineers reported that waves overtopped the lakefront seawall, but a secondary levee built after 1947 prevented inland damages. Likewise, the levee prevented any noteworthy damages in lakefront areas of Jefferson Parish.[19] Hurricane Camille was a legendary Gulf Coast storm whose most intense winds passed well east of New Orleans in August 1969. While the hurricane devastated Mississippi's coastline, New Orleans's levee system successfully protected most of the city from flooding. Nonetheless a levee section along the Inner Harbor Navigation Canal failed due to wave-powered scouring at its base, and water poured into residential areas. Most houses in the inundated area stood on piles, so there was only moderate damage, but residents' lives were seriously disrupted. More serious damage occurred in the Venetian Isles subdivision of far eastern New Orleans when water rose above the floor level of many newer homes.[20] Betsy and Camille affected areas not protected by the lakefront bulwarks and caused damage largely due to levee failures along the Inner Harbor Navigation Canal. Such were the consequences of development that relied on structural protection. In New Orleans, the inadequacy of structural protection was greatly exacerbated by the fact that the bowl can accumulate water more quickly than it can be pumped out.

Before effective implementation of the National Flood Insurance Program (NFIP), established in 1968, New Orleans's reliance primarily on structural protection had been the normal pattern across the country since the early twentieth century.[21] Residents unwittingly bought their way into areas of risk as soon as drainage projects reclaimed urban wetlands. This pattern, seen nationally, of urbanization in high-risk areas following completion of engineering works that allowed such expansion ultimately led to federal policies like the NFIP that were aimed at shifting from structural to land-use flood-protection practices.[22]

RECENT FLOOD CONTROL EFFORTS

Since the completion of the late-1920s drainage projects, there have been several fundamental changes to New Orleans's land-use patterns. The territory needing drainage has expanded dramatically. The original 1895 plan called for draining 13,349 acres, but by 1950 over 49,000 acres lay within the system's domain, and by 1983 the area had expanded to over 90,000 acres.[23] Much of the urban sprawl had pushed into former wetlands along the lakefront and to the east of the city. Construction of houses, shopping malls, parking lots, and other commercial structures associated with the expansion increased runoff. Although New Orleans's population peaked in 1960 and has since declined, the acreage requiring drainage has continued to expand, and water-shedding surfaces no longer in use have not generally been removed. Meanwhile, adjacent and suburban Jefferson Parish has experienced rapid population growth and related urbanization from 1950 through 1990. It followed the New Orleans model by building an extensive grid of drainage canals equipped with pumps to remove water within the levee system that rings the parish's built-up territory. As in the central city, groundwater removal from the underlying peaty soils caused subsidence—indeed sinking ground has been a bigger problem in the suburbs than in New Orleans's older neighborhoods. Also, serious flooding has occurred since the passage of the National Flood Insurance Act, which seeks to discourage structural flood protection projects and to encourage a land-use approach.[24]

Two prominent urban flood issues have emerged during the last three decades in New Orleans—one urban and the other suburban. The remainder of this chapter will focus on two representative areas that have been the foci of major drainage system renovations. The first is the Broadmoor neighborhood, situated near the "bottom of the bowl" and developed during the 1920s in conjunction with drainage improvements (Fig. 5.1). A brief comparison with the Ninth Ward will also be offered to highlight differences from another city neighborhood. The second area includes neighborhoods in suburban west bank Jefferson Parish, which grew rapidly after 1950. The Broadmoor district is a mixed-income area with influential neighbors. When the pumps that serve Broadmoor become overwhelmed, water quickly backs up into higher-income neighborhoods. Residents in these adjoining tracts, allied with a new majority African American citizenry, have successfully promoted significant flood improvement projects using their political clout. The suburban west bank neighborhoods are lower- to middle-income and do not have such influential neighbors. Most high-income neighborhoods in Jefferson Parish are located on the opposite side of the river. While these neighborhoods have endured some flooding, they have suffered less than their west bank counterparts and consequently have not supported efforts to fund parishwide drainage improvements. As a result, west bank residents have resorted to citizen law suits, augmented by a federal suit against the drainage authority, to impel flood protection projects.

Much of the postwar flooding in these areas has occurred since 1978, when a spate of intense rainfalls prompted a reexamination of flood management systems. Flood control efforts in New Orleans by this time took place within the framework of the NFIP. Created by federal legislation, the program first mapped 100-year floodplains and charged communities with developing land-use-based flood protection policies; once such local policies had been implemented, residents could purchase federally underwritten flood insurance policies. The basic intent was to force a shift from structural

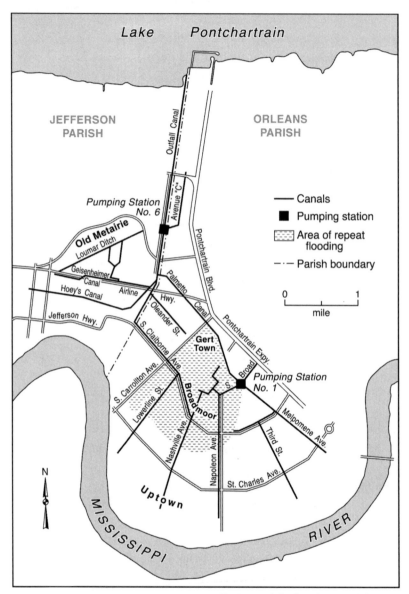

FIG. 5.1. BROADMOOR DRAINAGE SYSTEM. Drainage of the Broadmoor and Uptown neighborhoods depends on buried canals and pumps that lift the runoff to lake level. The shaded area is the zone of concentrated repeat claims for flood insurance. After Linfield, Hunter, and Gibbons, Inc., *Seventeenth Street Canal Drainage Basin Study* (New Orleans: New Orleans Sewerage and Water Board, 1983), and New Orleans Sewerage and Water Board, *Drainage Improvements to the Broadmoor Neighborhood: Pre-Application to the Statewide Flood Control Program* (New Orleans: New Orleans Sewerage and Water Board, 1998).

protection to a system wherein planning and construction codes inhibit inappropriate development in flood-prone areas and those who choose to live in high-risk zones pay the cost for protection through insurance premiums.[25] Although flood insurance subscription in Louisiana was well above the national average by the early 1970s, neither New Orleans nor suburban Jefferson Parish fully employed the land-use controls necessary to make the program effective. Much of the metropolitan area is within the 100-year floodplain defined by the NFIP.[26] Given the topographic situation and the early-twentieth-century approach, structural flood abatement remained essential.[27] Despite both the structures and the high insurance subscription rate, frequent flooding left Federal Emergency Management Agency (FEMA) administrators exasperated with the frequency of repetitive payments.

BROADMOOR

On May 3, 1978, a storm dumped more than 9 inches of rain in New Orleans, with more than 5.5 inches falling at one gauge in two hours.[28] This storm vastly exceeded the drainage system's capabilities for expelling rainfall and became the standard by which future events were measured. While streets turned into rivers throughout the city, the Broadmoor section was particularly hard hit. Much of it is below sea level, and the drainage system funnels runoff from a huge crescent-shaped area along the river into this low area, where it is then pumped out of the "bowl." When input exceeds pumping capacity, this low-lying area serves as a reservoir, and as the pumps labor to catch up, standing water rises higher than in other sections of the city. This is what happened in May 1978, when water rose as high as 3.5 feet, damaging more than 1,700 structures.[29] The Uptown and Old Metairie[30] districts in turn suffer overflow when the pumps' capacity is exceeded and water can no longer flow down the gentle gradient into the bowl. Typically flooding in New Orleans gradually fills streets, spills over into yards, and eventually rises into houses. Most homes in the older sections were built with flooding in mind (Fig. 5.2). They were constructed either on piles a couple of feet above the ground or with utility spaces at ground level and the living areas 5 to 6 feet above the ground. Nonetheless, some 71,500 homes throughout the city were estimated to have suffered a total of $71 million in damages from the 1978 event, to say nothing of commercial and public facilities.[31]

FIG. 5.2. RAISED HOUSE IN BROADMOOR NEIGHBORHOOD. Raised housing dating from the 1920s is common in low-lying neighborhoods. By enclosing the ground level, home-owners increased the risk of flood damage. Photo by author.

Less than a year later, on February 6, 1979, there was a 5-inch rain event that caused somewhat less damage.[32] In fairly rapid succession, further in-undations occurred on April 2, 1980 (over 7 inches); April 13, 1980 (over 8 inches); and June 10, 1981 (almost 7 inches). The second 1980 storm be-came the new benchmark for flood planners, replacing the barely two-year-old standard. It produced extensive damage throughout the city, but the low-lying districts such as Broadmoor and nearby, low-income Gert Town felt the brunt.[33] Water again rose over 3 feet and damaged 1,690 homes in Broadmoor.[34] Both the intensity and the duration of this storm completely overwhelmed the drainage and pumping system, allowing waters to back up into the city's highest areas, such as Uptown and even the French Quarter. A highly localized 2.33-inch rainfall on April 30, 1981, caused serious flood-ing in the Uptown and Broadmoor sections again.[35] This sequence of in-tense precipitation events and consequent flooding stirred a public reaction, as business owners and residents who had known no flooding in fifty years suddenly became victims several times in four years.[36] One entrepreneur charged that his business was flooded three times between 1978 and 1981, but had endured no similar damages in the preceding 26 years at the same location.[37]

Initially, voters of all income levels throughout the city, with fresh memories of repeated floods and enjoying relative prosperity fueled by the state's oil industry, approved a capital improvement project to modify the ineffective drainage system.[38] Uptown business owners lobbied for the drainage improvements, and low-income residents, including much of the city's African American population (a 55 percent majority in 1980), supported the measure because they too stood to benefit. The Sewerage and Water Board began designing modifications to the canal and pumping stations serving the hard-hit neighborhoods. With a goal of upgrading the system's capacity from a half an inch per hour to the old standard of 5 inches in 5 hours, the board began a ten-year improvement project. Specifically, engineers designed it to increase the pumping capacity for the Uptown and Broadmoor neighborhoods by 30 percent and to enlarge the canals and sewers leading to the pumps.[39]

Heavy rains did not await the completion of these improvements, however, and repeated flooding prompted property owners to complain to the drainage authority again. Drainage officials blamed increased impervious cover as the culprit—due in part to the absence of restrictions on construction in flood-prone areas—but took no action on this particular problem. As the public debate continued, the rains kept coming, bringing more flooding. On April 24 and 25, 1982, storm clouds dumped about 4.5 inches of rain, damaging nearly 1,400 structures, and more than 10 inches fell on April 7, 1983, affecting even more buildings (1,775) than the great 1978 flood.[40] Following these events, Uptown and Broadmoor residents pressed their concerns through the Uptown Flood Association, a neighborhood organization whose membership included influential citizens. Its leaders expressed some hope that they were making headway with the drainage authority.[41] The Sewerage and Water Board also received pressure from neighboring Jefferson Parish, which relied on the New Orleans pumps to drain a portion of the suburban parish, including Old Metairie, a high-income neighborhood.[42] Responding to the public clamor, the drainage authority revealed its ten-year systemwide upgrade in a 1983 master plan that once again relied on structural means by enlarging pumping capacity and making the canal and sewer system more efficient.[43] Despite steady progress on the improvements, precipitation continued to pound the city and flood neighborhoods during the implementation period.[44] Generally, damage totals declined in the Broadmoor neighborhood, and a 9-inch rainfall in 1988 affected only eight hundred buildings.[45] An enormous deluge in 1995 unleashed some 12 inches of precipitation, causing particularly severe damage throughout the urban area, but only 455 houses in Broadmoor suffered losses.[46]

Despite what might be viewed as a trend toward reduced impacts, federal agencies began seeking ways to trim government costs for flood recovery. Broadmoor and adjoining neighborhoods continued to be flood prone. Seeking to deflect liability, the Sewerage and Water Board claimed that impervious cover caused the continued flooding after its extensive improvements.[47] The municipal planning agency argued that conversion of ground utility spaces to apartments had increased the incidence of claims. Continued subsidence along with street construction that obstructed drainage added to the ponding effect in the low area.[48] Whatever the causes, the Sewerage and Water Board, under federal pressure, applied for state funding to help enlarge the pumping capacity for the Broadmoor neighborhood once again.[49] In the mid-1990s, at the request of local authorities with considerable support from the state's congressional delegation, the U.S. Army Corps of Engineers stepped in to assist the New Orleans area communities develop a more comprehensive flood-control program and thereby offset some of the heavy repetitive claims under the NFIP. The cornerstone of the Corps' proposed work in Orleans Parish was to enlarge the capacity of the pump serving Broadmoor and adjacent neighborhoods.[50]

Other approaches to flood protection had been gaining some acceptance. Although the city began participating in the NFIP in 1975, effective compliance was not prompt. New Orleans revised its 1950s construction standard that called for slabs to be a foot above the natural ground to one that required them to be 18 inches above the highest point of the curb adjacent to the property. The lowest support beams for houses raised above ground level on piers had to be 24 inches above the curb rather than 24 inches above natural ground.[51] Despite the new codes, it was not until the 1980s that inspectors received training in floodplain management policies and began to enforce them. City building inspectors only began making systematic inspections for compliance with flood protection standards in the 1990s. Some inspectors rejected numerous permit applications in the late 1990s, due either to insufficient floor elevations or inadequate site improvements to minimize flooding.[52] These steps, of course, had little impact in older districts, which were densely built up and still had to rely on structural measures such as pumps and canals. Furthermore, with the economic downturn caused by the oil bust and population losses between 1980 and 2000, far less construction occurred to which the new standards might be applied. The city granted about 1,000 single-family-unit construction permits in 1964, compared to about 500 in 1985 and around 360 per year in the late 1990s.[53] The city applied for and in 2001 received federal grant money to raise homes in areas with repetitive flood insurance claims. Touted by FEMA officials as "the best kind of disaster program," two grants totaling about $1.8 million raised only seventeen houses scattered throughout the city.[54] Despite such efforts, however, the city remains reliant on structural measures to manage flood hazards, especially in older districts.

With federal financial assistance, the Sewerage and Water Board worked on a series of related drainage projects in the Broadmoor neighborhood in early 2001. Crews opened large cavities in the "neutral grounds" (the local term for medians) of Claiborne and Napoleon avenues. Piledrivers and other heavy equipment rattled buildings, and some residents charged that the construction was causing damage to their homes. After waiting decades for relief from flooding, residents found the construction efforts a threat to their property.[55] The drainage system's effectiveness remained to be tested.

Tropical Storm Allison delivered a test. Allison, a slow-moving tropical depression, stalled over south Louisiana in June 2001, releasing more than 20 inches of rain in some locations. Although precipitation totals were substantial, the fact that moderate rains fell over a four-day period allowed the drainage system to keep pace with the deluge. There was some street flooding, but there was virtually no reported residential damage in New Orleans.[56] This test of the drainage system convinced some that improvements were finally meeting the citizens' needs.

In September 2002, Isidore, a hurricane downgraded to tropical storm status, revealed some lingering weaknesses in the system. Part of New Orleans received as much as 23 inches in 8 hours as the storm moved inland from the Gulf of Mexico. As much as 4 inches fell in one hour and overwhelmed the expanded and improved drainage system. Major streets, including South Claiborne Avenue, which passes through Broadmoor, became impassable, and even the central business district suffered temporary street flooding. The most disturbing revelation was that high waters closed Interstate 10 for more than twenty-four hours. Because the interstate is one of the few evacuation routes from the city, this failure of the drainage system received critical attention. A project to improve the pumping capacity at the low point in the interstate was under way at the time of the storm and should alleviate that potential drainage bottleneck.[57] Nonetheless, that project and other ongoing improvements reveal the never-ending need for flood control improvements within the bowl.

The growth of mixed-income residential areas in the city's lowest section stemmed directly from drainage improvements completed in the early twentieth century. Thus the structural approach lured encroachment into areas of highest risk—although there was nowhere else to go. Given New Orleans's topography, structural means have remained the principal approach to alleviate socially constructed hazards created by previous municipal works. Although the opportunity to raise or remove houses in harm's way exists for those with the financial resources, this option has never supplanted traditional canal and pumping solutions within the city. The adoption of NFIP guidelines was too late to affect building practices in the lowest sections of the city. Ironically, many older raised homes stand higher than new homes built to NFIP guidelines. Officials charged with floodplain management complain, however, that enclosing ground-level garages that did not meet pre- or post-NFIP guidelines has been the greatest cause of repeat flood claims.

THE NINTH WARD

A second flood-prone area in the city warrants mention. The Ninth Ward has long been a low-income section of the city and has endured chronic neglect in terms of city services.[58] The ward's lower sections have been victimized repeatedly by flooding. Hurricane Betsy in 1965 produced serious flooding in the area. A winter storm in 1983 drove water from the gulf into the Industrial Canal, and when the levee board failed to close floodgates, water rose up to 3 feet high in the neighborhood. Inaction on the part of the levee board prompted residents to file a suit seeking compensation for damages.[59]

Since the creation of the NFIP, the area has suffered from the same storms that saturated Broadmoor. In May 1978 more than 1,000 structures suffered damage, in April 1983 high water affected 1,570 buildings, and the May 1995 event flooded over 1,200 structures. Like the Broadmoor area, this neighborhood has had frequent repeat claims for federal flood insurance. The fact that high-income residents have the same concerns about flooding as low-income residents and African American populations has broadened public support for flood control measures within the municipal limits. As a result, the city applied for state funding to improve the structural flood control facilities—mainly enlarging the canal's capacity to match that of the pumps they feed. Although it is a low-income neighborhood, the Ninth Ward seemed to be getting treatment comparable to that of the more affluent areas around Broadmoor. In both instances, structural controls remained the only feasible option.

Jefferson Parish occupies territory on both banks of the Mississippi River immediately upstream from New Orleans. Urbanization in this parish was limited primarily to the narrow natural levee and the narrower-still Metairie Ridge before 1940. On the east bank, canals, levees, and pumps built in the 1920s enabled some residential expansion into wetland areas, but these structural controls were not wholly effective. The levee along the lakefront subsided and permitted inundations in 1937 when the Corps of Engineers first opened the Bonnet Carré spillway to divert Mississippi River floodwaters into Lake Pontchartrain. Following the severe 1947 hurricane, which drove even more water from Lake Pontchartrain over the deteriorated levees, the parish began a major effort to improve its east bank drainage system. With enlarged pumping capacity and strengthened lakefront barriers in place by 1952, the parish was able to drain residential neighborhoods, which enabled rapid suburbanization in the second half of the twentieth century (Fig. 5.3). Population soared from 53,441 in 1950 to 290,000 in 1980—driven largely by white flight to the east bank bedroom suburbs. Unlike the older residences in the central city, most suburban Jefferson Parish housing was post–World War II slab construction. Significant land subsidence (as much as 2 feet) followed drainage, lowering large portions of the parish below sea level. Consequently, all drainage requires pumps to lift water into either the Mississippi River or Lake Pontchartrain. With increased land cover, the system designed in the early 1950s became inadequate by the late 1970s, and regular structural upgrades have been required.[60]

Jefferson Parish straddles the Mississippi River, and drainage systems on the east and west banks operate separately. Land use and demographics are also distinct on the opposite sides of the river. On the west bank, working-class residential and industrial land use also initially clung to the river (Fig. 5.4). Newly created drainage districts gradually expanded the ter-

FIG. 5.3. EAST BANK DRAINAGE SYSTEM, 1951. Suburban growth in postwar Jefferson Parish depended on wetland drainage. Sub-District No. 1, largely undeveloped in this 1951 photograph, witnessed nearly complete development by the 1970s. Frank Photograph Collection. Courtesy The Historic New Orleans Collection, Museum/Research Center, Accession No. 1974.25.18.122.

ritory available for development during the twentieth century. Each new district pushed the usable land back from the river by utilizing canals and pumps to transport runoff and groundwater through ring levees into the backswamp. As on the east bank, structural means had opened considerable territory—some 35,000 acres—to development by 1980. Industry had occupied most of the best drained land on the west bank, leaving the more recently drained and topographically lower area for residential use.[61] Drainage improvements have concentrated residential areas in former wetlands, which face the greatest flood risks due to their low-lying situation.

Although the parish relies heavily on its structural flood control system, many homeowners have purchased federal flood insurance. At the program's outset, area developers expressed fears that flood insurance costs would halt residential expansion in Jefferson Parish, but there was exceptionally high participation in the insurance program, with more than ten thousand policyholders in 1974. That number grew to more than 61,000 in 1993.[62] By the early 1980s, all construction was required to comply with NFIP guidelines,

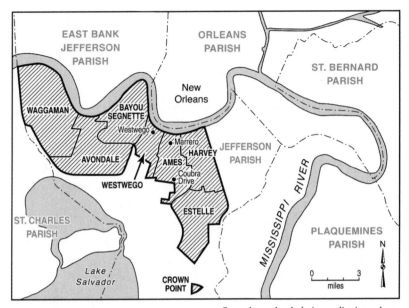

FIG. 5.4. WEST BANK DRAINAGE DISTRICTS. Several west bank drainage districts rely on canals and pumps to transport water out of the levee-enclosed residential developments into the backswamp. Coubra Drive is in one of the lower developed sections of suburban New Orleans. After URS Company, *West Bank Master Drainage Study*, vol. 1, *Report* (Gretna, LA: Jefferson Parish Public Works, 1981), plate 1.

but housing construction and regular inundations continued without interruption, and during the 1980s Jefferson Parish led the country in flood insurance claims.[63] Despite steps toward land-use flood protection, ultimately the structural system controlled water movement out of the drainage districts, and when the system was overwhelmed, NFIP guidelines proved worthless. Reliance on structural flood control offered residents a false sense of security without modifying land-use patterns. Furthermore, high insurance premiums produced a resistance to additional support for publicly financed drainage improvements. People did not want to pay for flood protection twice.

The great storm of May 3, 1978, brought severe flooding to suburban Jefferson Parish as it did to New Orleans. Initial reports suggested some thirty thousand homes sustained approximately $65 million in damages. Particularly hard hit were neighborhoods in the west bank community of Marrero. In the storm's wake, parish officials claimed that uncontrolled growth was

157

the problem, not the drainage system's inadequacies. Yet private development was not the sole cause. The Coubra Drive neighborhood in Marrero suffered exceptionally severe flooding. Built in a borrow pit where contractors had removed fill for neighboring streets, the neighborhood became a reservoir during heavy rains. The U.S. Department of Housing and Urban Development financed the construction of homes in the Coubra Drive area as part of a special federal program to assist moderate-income renters become homeowners. Thus the neighborhood was constructed as a publicly funded project and was not an example of uncontrolled private development.[64] In effect, two uncoordinated public programs were working in direct conflict with one another and exacerbating the system's inadequacies.

Unlike voters in New Orleans, the Jefferson Parish electorate rejected a tax hike to pay off bonds to finance drainage system improvements after the 1978 flood. A large white majority on the east bank (77 percent), who bore less of the flood's impact than African Americans on the west bank, rejected the proposed tax. Shortly thereafter heavy winter rains again flooded approximately one hundred homes in Marrero and the Coubra Drive neighborhood.[65] The April 1, 1980, flood also hit the west bank hard, with some of the worst flooding in the greater New Orleans area occurring around Coubra Drive and nearby Westwego.[66] Two weeks later, an even more copious rainfall dropped 14 inches on the West Bank and seriously flooded parts of Westwego, contributing to more than $150 million in damages in Jefferson Parish.[67]

Weary of the excessive and repetitive flood insurance claims, FEMA filed suit against Jefferson Parish in 1981. Hit with over $53 million in claims following the May 13, 1980, flood and claims of more than $93 million between 1978 and 1982, the federal agency charged that the parish and several other defendants were negligent in providing adequate flood protection and that they were not compliant with NFIP standards. Following a preliminary federal victory, the federal appeals court sided with the parish, asserting that the floods were "acts of God."[68] Even though the parish was not in complete compliance with the NFIP guidelines, the court ruled it was not wholly liable for damages. An eventual settlement called for the parish to pay the federal government $1 million and to come into compliance with the NFIP. In addition, the parish had to develop a flood-reduction plan that would require that new construction follow flood-reduction procedures and would prohibit construction within the 100-year floodplain. Additionally, the parish had to improve its drainage and pumping system substantially.[69]

Following this judicial ruling, the parish undertook flood reduction studies to minimize the effects of future inundations. The solutions were largely structural, underscoring the parish's path dependence on its historical practices.[70] It also made improvements in floodplain management practices. Building codes now call for slabs to be 18 inches above the crown of the road in front of new homes and for floors of elevated homes to be at least 18 inches above the road's crown.[71] Any new home built in repetitive loss areas must be raised above the 100-year flood level.[72] Despite the dubious distinction of having the most repetitive loss claims in the United States—5,106 homes —the parish claims that most of those are for structures built before the implementation of NFIP guidelines. Furthermore, the parish cites the drop in all claims from 2,580 after the 1995 flood to only 61 total claims after Tropical Storm Allison in 2001 as measurable progress in flood prevention prompted by the federal lawsuit.[73]

In addition to the federal legal action, the parish faced private lawsuits alleging inadequate flood protection. Marrero homeowners filed a class-action suit against the parish in 1985 charging that their neighborhood's drainage canal provided inadequate flow to the nearest pump, and water typically backed up in their streets.[74] Before the courts could deliver a decision, storms in 1988 again inundated the same neighborhoods, damaging more than three hundred homes.[75] Shortly thereafter, the state supreme court approved an expansion in the number of plaintiffs in the suit against the parish. Following the huge 1995 flood that damaged more than twelve thousand east bank homes in largely upper-income sections of Jefferson Parish, lawyers filed a second round of citizen suits against the parish. Charging that an ongoing construction project caused a canal to back up, the homeowners sought relief as a group. In this case, the Louisiana Supreme Court ruled that the plaintiffs needed to establish a basis for their suits individually, yet the class remained intact.[76] By February 2000, the construction firm had offered $4 million in settlement money, and the parish proffered $19 million in prompt drainage improvements but no compensation for damages.[77] The courts approved this arrangement, and once again the parish embarked on more structural remedies.

Including the twelve thousand homes on the east bank, the 1995 storm caused an estimated $545 million in damages in Jefferson Parish. The scale of the FEMA claims and the overall costs drew the parish into the regional drainage program administered by the Corps of Engineers. As part of the effort to provide improved flood protection to New Orleans proper, the Corps quickly evaluated drainage needs and authorized over $170 million for Jefferson Parish structural improvements. None of the Corps' massive Southeast Louisiana Flood Control project involved land-use provisions.[78] So even though FEMA was encouraging steps to deter development in flood-prone areas,[79] the Corps continued to plan and finance reduction of flood risks via structural means and thereby encouraged flood-zone development. Only the fact that the parish, particularly the east bank, had begun losing population offset any encroachment into flood zones.[80] The copious precipitation brought by Tropical Storm Allison in 2001 caused only minor street flooding in Jefferson Parish, suggesting the Corps' improvements were producing some benefits.[81] Tropical Storm Isidore's 20 inches of rain in 2002 caused street flooding in Jefferson Parish, but property damage did not compare to that caused by earlier events.[82]

Construction continues in low-lying areas of Jefferson Parish—there is nowhere else to build. Indeed, development is underway adjacent to neighborhoods that have endured serious flooding in the past. Enlarged drainage canals and pumping capacity remain the primary means of flood protection.

Despite a trend toward land-use approaches to flood protection in other cities, New Orleans and its suburbs continue to rely chiefly on structural methods—even with various floodplain management policies in place. These structural mechanisms did indeed lure additional population into flood zones before 1960, but there has been a net out-migration from both Orleans and Jefferson parishes in recent years—although new construction continues in the suburban parish. Expectations for protection have increased, but planning based on past events rather than potential future occurrences continues to leave areas exposed to high water during the most extreme events.[83] In this respect, the New Orleans metropolitan area is similar to other urban places, despite its unique topography.

While huge storms can produce devastating impacts across metropolitan New Orleans, the most severe damages are not spread uniformly across the urban territory. Broadmoor, the Ninth Ward, and Marrero have endured inordinate suffering. The levees that protect the city from the river have become a trap for rain that collects in these low areas. Recent federal land-use approaches offer little benefit for long-urbanized tracts.

The response time for structural improvements is slow at best, and the structural system is under continual modification. Securing funding and then planning and building massive engineering works is not a rapid process. As the city, its suburbs, and now the Corps of Engineers enlarge pumping systems and canals, repeat flooding continues to occur, often highlighting the need for improvements that are already under construction. With the greatest incidence of flooding occurring in areas built before the NFIP, the cycle of flooding and structural improvements is the only viable option for drainage authorities. Citizens who opt not to wait for improvements can move to higher ground across the lake in the Florida Parishes, and many with resources to do so have joined the migrants relocating to the north shore. Suburbanization has also leaped westward across the Bonnet Carré spillway into St. Charles Parish.

While New Orleans and Jefferson Parish face similar challenges, the responses of the city and the suburban parish have differed. Broad-based citizen demand for improvement exists in the city, while minority populations who have endured the worst flooding in the suburbs have been unable to mobilize an effective political response. In recent years, the city has accepted land-use control of future development as a means of flood protection to a greater extent than the suburban parish has. In 1992 the city adopted a plan calling for restrictions on wetland development and for wetlands to be used as flood-retention basins.[84] Measures such as building codes are still largely irrelevant to the older and lowest sections of the city, however. The parish, on the other hand, while forced by the FEMA lawsuit to manage land use more effectively for flood protection, has petitioned the Corps of Engineers to fill more than 2,000 acres of wetlands above the level of projected floods —further reducing floodwater retention capacity.[85] Such outlooks reflect fundamentally different perspectives on nature's power and how to respond to it. All in all, New Orleans and its suburbs will never be able to rely on land-use approaches the way other cities do. Rains will continue to fall, and the city and the suburbs must manage development of flood-prone areas with that in mind. Protecting the city from flood risks remains a chronic concern.

CHAPTER 6

REINTRODUCING WETLAND ENVIRONMENTS

FOR MORE THAN two centuries, New Orleans's builders struggled to expel the soggy wetlands from within their city. Early settlers saw little value in the swamps after they had harvested the virgin cypress forests, and marshes held no value as urban real estate. During the early 1700s the city had grown along the natural levee, a narrow band of relatively high ground deposited by recurring river floods, and by the time of Louisiana statehood (1812) several faubourgs extended into the miasmatic backswamps. Levee construction along the river coupled with canal excavation toward the lakefront were the key colonial public works projects to drain water from the city and thereby reclaim the swamps and marshes. Only after a viable flood protection barrier was in place by the mid-nineteenth century and the effective completion of major drainage systems by the 1920s were developers able to extend streets and subdivisions across the marsh to the Lake Pontchartrain shore. In addition to expanding usable real estate, the massive drainage projects greatly reduced disease threats that had plagued the city for two centuries. To accommodate post–World War II suburbanization, wetland drainage pressed westward into adjacent Jefferson Parish, into the marshes east of New Orleans, and southward beyond the natural levee on the Mississippi's west bank.[1] By the late 1960s, there was sufficient technical capability and real estate demand to complete the conquest of wetlands within the city limits.

Yet after more than two centuries, the drive to enlarge the drained territory was reversed. Since about 1970, fundamental changes in public attitudes toward the environment in general and wetlands in particular impeded the Crescent City's ever-expanding drainage program. While the city will never abandon its existing drainage system or abate ongoing improvement efforts, it has shelved some expansion plans. There has arisen an overwhelming urge to protect marsh and swamp in and near the city, along with programs designating wetlands as relics of Louisiana's natural history. This chapter traces the public's abandonment of the belief that the city is no place for a swamp and the replacement of that belief with policies and practices that preserve wetland tracts. Beyond sentiments about wetland protection, a second underlying attitude shift was also necessary. This involved adopting the concept that nature could provide a public utility. In order to justify the preservation of wetlands, society first had to embrace the notion that these preserves would serve as educational settings and provide necessary ecological services. Although these preserves are thought of as "nature," they are in fact highly modified environments that are maintained at considerable effort. By examining the forces and ideas behind the creation and maintenance of the Audubon Zoo swamp exhibit, the Audubon Louisiana Nature Center, the National Park Service's Barataria Preserve, and the Bayou Sauvage National Wildlife Refuge (Fig. 6.1), this chapter considers these sites as landscapes shaped to resemble preurbanized environments that function in an urban setting as part of an evolving concept of parks and open spaces and stand as concrete evidence of public attitudes and environmental policies. The transformation and preservation of wetlands reflect urban land-use practices that are vastly different than those of a century ago and as a result are creating a very different urban landscape.

NATURE IN THE CITY

At their core, the four examples discussed in this chapter represent efforts to replicate or set aside parcels of a precolonial lower Mississippi River delta

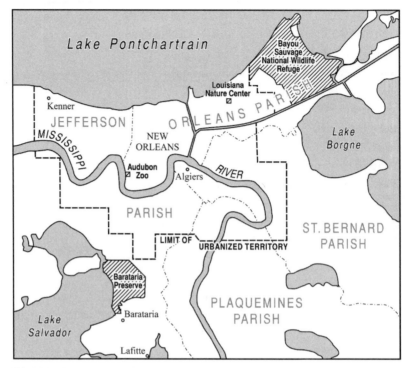

FIG. 6.1. WETLAND EXHIBITS AND PRESERVES.

environment. Envisioned as places where the public could come in contact with and learn about native flora and fauna or where actual vestiges of nature could survive, they were all post–1970 creations or delineations. In this respect they reflect a conspicuous trend in public policy toward preservation of wetland and urban open space.[2] The impulse to create and preserve wetlands in urban settings was also part of another process—the management of the nonhuman world within America's most highly urbanized places. Rural wetlands have received considerable attention,[3] but New Orleans's wetlands are within the *direct* reach of urban influences. The growth of cities in the early twentieth century prompted both rural and urban drainage efforts. The city, as a market for agricultural produce, propelled rural floodplain drainage to create farmland to feed growing urban immigrant populations in the Midwest and along the eastern seaboard.[4] This was an indirect outreach of urban economic influences into rural hinterlands. Wetlands in the path of expanding cities also underwent drainage to eliminate disease threats and accommodate the direct expansion of urban land uses

—the Lake Calumet area in southeast Chicago, for example, became a major industrial district.[5] Thus economic factors also drove the conversion of marshes and swamplands that fell under the footprint of the urban juggernaut.

In Louisiana, urban wetlands were distinct from their rural counterparts. Though long considered harbors of pestilence, wetlands were platted as residential and commercial real estate, and thus cartographers applied an urban imprint upon them well before the construction of drainage canals, levees, or streets. Rural wetlands, by contrast, served as locales for hunting and fishing, logging, and oil drilling. When Louisiana set aside more than 200,000 acres of marsh habitat in the early twentieth century, it offered no comparable protection for urban parcels.[6] Hunters, fishermen, and a few tourists ventured out to enjoy the rural swamps and marshes, while urban tracts drew the developers' attention. Only in the last third of the twentieth century, with the emergence of public concern for wetlands accompanied by chemical control of mosquitoes, did city residents demand wetland creation and preservation within New Orleans.[7]

The Crescent City's residents, like their counterparts in other cities, have not severed their connections with nature. As historian Ari Kelman observed, although New Orleanians have manipulated nature in numerous ways to make a more secure settlement on the banks of the Mississippi, the levees and floodways that protect the city have not diminished the river's significance in the city's existence.[8] Likewise, the wetlands, long targets of attempted modification by engineers and developers, have remained a critical nonhuman element in this urban setting. The massive drainage works constructed to rid the city of public health problems and provide more space placed a huge financial burden on the partly-below-sea-level city because they merely diverted water and did not eliminate the conditions that created wetlands. Moreover, the dewatered peaty soils within the flood barriers subsided, causing problems for suburban construction. However, though nature has persisted as an element of the urban fabric throughout the city's history, efforts to showcase and preserve segments of the precolonial environment reflect a relatively recent campaign with an urban point of view.[9]

Rutherford Platt traces open-space development in urban America through the romantic, sanitary reform, City Beautiful, and garden city periods.[10] Parks developed during these periods endowed cities with lovely open spaces and provided access to an idealized nature in the city.[11] These parks emulated nature with the use of carefully landscaped terrain, and their creators believed they provided urban residents with spaces for emotional rejuvenation. New Orleans's Audubon Park traces its inception to the romantic period and its full-blown development to the City Beautiful period.[12] Since the 1970s, Platt states, an entirely different entity has emerged to serve the urban longing for open-space: valued for their climatic, hydrologic, and ecological contributions, expansive reserves are the current objective of open-space planners.[13] Such reserves reflect land managers' efforts to accommodate post−1970 federal environmental laws and a public demand that environmental considerations enter the urban development equation. The Endangered Species Act along with Section 404 of the Clean Water Act dramatically affected both rural and urban land management, and they compelled public bodies to protect certain areas. Public support for defending the environment enabled these laws' passage, although opposition has emerged. Recognition of wetlands' vital ecological functions has also inspired public support for their preservation. To permit the public to observe these functions at work, management policies have mandated public access to the protected areas—for education and recreation—thereby expanding their service role. Efforts to protect the Lake Calumet wetlands and the New Jersey meadowlands, for example, have paralleled the situation in New Orleans.[14] Through the act of designation, society has domesticated for public use places viewed as natural areas.[15] Even though the late-twentieth-century reserves have received less formal landscaping than traditional parks, the latter open spaces are not just wildlife preserves but must also satisfy the urban population's demands.

The founders of the four sites considered here did not see them as pristine. In fact, they were anything but. Indeed, as areas set apart both for wildlife and for humans, they blur the distinction between nature and artifice.[16] They are neither completely of nature nor of the city—more a hybrid landscape. Audubon Zoo's swamp exhibit is a zoological exhibit, crafted by designers and maintained by the staff. Landscape designers also created the Nature Center's swamp exhibit, although it is situated in a wooded tract that appears to some as untouched nature. Both are well within New Orleans's urbanized territory. The two larger reserves, Barataria Preserve and the Bayou Sauvage refuge, were wetlands long before European arrival to the lower delta. Nonetheless, prehistoric societies had acted upon these latter locales for millennia. Extensive human manipulation continued into the twentieth century as the city grew outward toward these tracts. Designating these properties as preserves did not initiate their preservation. As private property these tracts endured as viable habitat even without government management efforts. Nature was at work and human alterations had not eliminated all potential for wildlife support. Under the auspices of federal natural resource agencies these parcels have come under more thorough management plans than previously, and under such supervision they will continue to provide habitat for wild animals and plants, all the while being made accessible to the public. Wetland preservation in the New Orleans urban area, as much as protecting habitat and wildlife, provides people with physical and intellectual entry to marsh and swamp.

PUBLIC ATTENTION TO WETLANDS

Each of the organizations that created swamp exhibits or set aside wetlands shared a common objective: to introduce the urban public to this endangered habitat and to reveal the connections between the humanized and the nonhumanized world. Current wetland presentations build on an erratic history of swamp and marsh interest. Victorian-era artists discovered and painted the Louisiana swamp, while rugged hunters and fishers sought game in the wetlands. The latter group was instrumental in prompting conservation-oriented efforts to set aside massive rural wildlife refuges. Unlike the more recent urban efforts, the early-twentieth-century refuges were both spatially and conceptually distant from the city.

It has taken more than a century of popular tourism in the New Orleans area for guides and promoters to make wetlands a destination for urban tourists. Travel literature and sightseeing tours traditionally emphasized the city's cultural landscapes—the French Quarter, the aboveground cemeteries, and lavish mansions—along with nightclubs. Hunters, by contrast, could hire guides to take them into the rural swamp. A nineteenth-century guidebook touted alligator hunting as "a favorite sport," but lamented the decline in game: "There are not as many alligators in the suburbs of New Orleans as there were before the skins of the mighty saurians became commercial commodity. . . . You will have no difficulty in finding as many alligators as you want in the innumerable bayous and lakes just back of Algiers."[17] Located outside the city, the hunter's wetland was a place where men could camp in palmetto lodges, like the ones built by native peoples centuries before, and hunt wildlife. This experience was not urban.

Victorian America witnessed a surge of interest in the wetlands as a place to observe sublime and picturesque nature. Longfellow's tale of Evangeline described the cypress swamp as an ancient cathedral,[18] and James Hamilton's painting *Bayou in Moonlight* portrayed a swamp that was the domain not just of the rustic hunter but of rural beauty. During the 1870s and 1880s, artists gathered in New Orleans and from there ventured into the swamp searching for suitable scenes to capture to canvas.[19] Apparently inspired by their romantic images, George Coulon embarked upon a 350-mile voyage through the Atchafalaya Basin—a vast wetland west of New Orleans—in search of "virgin nature."[20] Both visual and narrative presentations of Louisiana's wetlands directed attention to the rural swamps and marshes, but tourism in the early twentieth century relegated such adventures to sportsmen and artists.

The Federal Writers' Project guide to New Orleans noted that fishing and hunting remained popular attractions in the bayous and lagoons surrounding the city. It also suggested several automobile tour routes through the bayou country to places such as Barataria and Lafitte (both near the modern Barataria Preserve) where one could see oaks and cypress and the "trembling" prairie—a type of marsh often described as "land on water."[21] During the 1950s, guidebooks continued to point visitors toward routes *through* the rural wetlands where they might view Spanish moss or where men might go fishing and hunting in nearby parishes.[22] While families could observe wetland flora from the highway, only males typically penetrated the swamps in quest of game. Thus the Louisiana wetlands presented to tourists were either a picturesque backdrop of live oaks and cypress trees festooned with moss or an untrammeled wilderness where males could prey on waterfowl, alligators, and fish. In either instance, it was hardly an urban experience. Rather, to appreciate the wetlands, one had to leave the city—at least until the 1960s.

Tentative opportunities for urban tourists to penetrate Louisiana's wetlands began in the early 1960s when the large excursion boats added "bayou trips" to their customary river cruise offerings. Telephone book listings for sightseeing opportunities first included bayou trips offered by the *President* and the *Voyageur* in 1961.[23] Both multideck boats operated from the foot of Canal Street, the heart of the city, and took visitors on junkets along waterways that passed through swampland south of New Orleans. Large vessels with restrooms and food service transported these excursions and allowed tourists to glimpse wetlands similar to the ones that could be seen on automobile tours but with all the comforts and convenience of an urban river cruise.

From this modest beginning, several related influences sparked additional interest in the wetlands during the 1970s. Louisiana environmental activists made the Atchafalaya Basin their cause célèbre as they battled with the Corps of Engineers over its management of the massive wetland. At issue was a series of Corps of Engineers proposals to stabilize the engineering works that provided flood protection for the lower Mississippi River valley. Environmentalists feared that these plans would upset the basin's ecology and disrupt both commercial and sport fishing and hunting. Traditional fishermen and hunters shared some fundamental objectives with environmental organizations, and they worked to block the plan's more destructive elements.[24] Tapping a growing awareness, C. C. Lockwood, a Louisiana nature photographer, further aroused public concern over the Atchafalaya in the 1970s with his colorful images of the basin.[25] National environmental organizations encouraged exposure to the bayous and wetlands surrounding New Orleans by promoting tours for those willing to propel themselves in canoes.[26] Concerns raised by such efforts coalesced into a movement to create urban wetlands.

Tour operators also responded to growing public interest in rural swamps. Beginning in 1980, New Orleans telephone directories included advertisements for "swamp tours," and the number of swamp tour operators has since escalated. By 1990 eight services placed their advertisements in the New Orleans telephone book, and by the late 1990s a score of operators advertised in various media.[27] No longer were the tours conducted on large river boats, but the new swamp adventures traveled in single-deck (twenty-to-eighty-passenger) boats that could negotiate smaller bayous and canals (Fig. 6.2), offering a much more intimate experience. These operators set up bases outside the city, pulling passengers away from the tourist bubble and into the wetlands at the urban fringe. Indeed, swamp tour operations have docks near the Barataria Preserve or the Bayou Segnette State Park, and one cruises

FIG. 6.2. SWAMP TOUR BOAT. Commercial swamp tour craft on Bayou Segnette at Marrero. Photo by author.

through the Bayou Sauvage refuge. Improved access to the rural wetlands both fueled public interest in wetlands and served a growing demand.

EXHIBITING WETLANDS

The compulsion to construct natural enclaves and put them on display in New Orleans emerged over a fifteen-to-twenty-year span beginning in the 1970s. At the root was a growing social concern about nature in general and wetlands in particular.[28] At the national level, public articulation of the environmental significance of wetlands emerged in the 1956 U.S. Fish and Wildlife Service report *Wetlands of the United States*. Although largely rural in its orientation, the report noted federal apprehension over the vulnerability of wetlands as waterfowl habitat in the northeast due to urban land-use pressures.[29] Several years later, participants at a national conference deliberated the need to preserve space for outdoor recreation and claimed that "the first task is to provide recreation for the metropolitan areas," where land was the most precious.[30] At another conference organized to address "nature in the city," one commentator noted that "nature is rapidly disappearing from our urban environment as an annual 1 million acres of land give way to urbanization."[31] Obviously, the open-space and wetlands preservation advocates saw urban land as a key part of the discussion. Even in the South, long considered lagging in environmental activism, the Atchafalaya Basin controversy was only one of several regional controversies in the early 1970s.[32] The fact that most open space in south Louisiana is also wetland made swamps and marshes an easy choice for preservation efforts. Though southern environmentalism remained largely rural, urban environmental concern in line with national trends developed in New Orleans, and the initial environmental campaigns in Louisiana led to the creation of two wetland educational exhibits in the city.

AUDUBON PARK ZOO SWAMP EXHIBIT

In New Orleans, it took shame to stir local action with an urban focus. A 1966 account of the whooping crane's perilous situation nationally pointed out that New Orleans's Audubon Zoo housed seven of the birds, which were to be the centerpiece of the Fish and Wildlife Service's captive breeding experiment. Faith McNulty, the gifted nature writer, described the zoo as having a "shabby air of ease."[33] Shortly thereafter, a local journalist used harsher language, referring to the zoo as a "zoological ghetto" and an "animal concentration camp."[34] In addition to the abysmal conditions at the zoo, McNulty argued that "its lack of trained staff or special facilities make[s] it an unlikely site for a crucial experiment in aviculture."[35] Indeed, her remarks were an oblique reference to the sudden death the previous year of the female of the zoo's successful mating pair. With the whooping cranes' fate in the allegedly incompetent hands of the New Orleans zoo, many in the wildlife conservation movement were troubled.

Publicly humiliated, zoo supporters organized to improve conditions at the municipally supported facility.[36] As a first step, in 1971 a local research organization evaluated whether the zoo should be rejuvenated in situ or rebuilt from scratch at a new location. Ultimately, the study advocated keeping the zoo at its existing site—part of a large City Beautiful–era park designed by the Olmsted firm—but with major improvements, namely larger and more naturalistic settings for the animals.[37] In a dramatic departure from the traditional zoological park practice of exhibiting rare and exotic animals, the researchers called for exhibits "emphasizing the natural resources of Louisiana."[38] At a time when the official state bird, the brown pelican, had virtually disappeared[39] and the emblematic megafauna of the Louisiana wetlands, the alligator, was under serious threat,[40] the report suggested that

FIG. 6.3. ALLIGATOR EXHIBIT AT THE AUDUBON ZOO. The barren, concrete-lined alligator pond at the old Audubon Park Zoo was replaced by a swamp exhibit that provides more natural habitats for the alligators and other exhibited species. Photo by author.

local fauna serve as the key attractions (Fig. 6.3). This strategy sought to include the rare but to replace the exotic with local fauna, and it represented a critical turning point in attitudes toward the local swamps and marshes. Specifically, the new view was that the public had a responsibility to *protect* wetland fauna and flora purely for their environmental role and not just *conserve* them for the benefit of hunters and trappers. Furthermore, this responsibility was an urban imperative; it suggested that hope for wetlands lay with the nation's majority—urban residents—who were woefully unfamiliar with the natural environments surrounding them.

A schematic plan for the zoo's rehabilitation showed a Louisiana exhibit larger than the entire grounds at the time. Within this area, a swamp exhibit would "include spectacular aquatic birds peculiar to Louisiana together with extensive exhibits of alligators and other appropriate swamp life."[41] A conceptual drawing showed a "tracked" African Queen–like launch motoring past the alligators on the banks of an artificial bayou to "increase the excitement" of the exhibit. In order for this exhibit to become a reality, a portion of the natural levee had to be reworked, secure exhibit facilities built, and animals acquired. The plan underwent some alterations from its initial conception, progressing from a Disneyesque ride to a walk-through exhibit that attempted to replicate both the biophysical and cultural landscapes of the Louisiana wetlands.[42] Native plantings and structures modeled after vernacular buildings found in the nearby swamp created the ambiance of the Atchafalaya Basin. Touted as an effort to preserve "a vital part of the state's heritage" when it opened in 1984,[43] planners intended the exhibit to convince urban residents that they actually had visited a Louisiana swamp. Today, raised walkways allow visitors to see alligators, pelicans, herons, egrets, and a variety of ducks in naturalistic settings consisting of ponds surrounded by cypress and other native vegetation. Since its opening, the swamp exhibit has consistently been the zoo's leading attraction.[44] One key impetus for creating this type of nature exhibit in the city was to replicate a bit of a rapidly disappearing and increasingly inaccessible swamp. Zoo officials accomplished this purpose without the advantage of preexisting swamp at the site; consequently the exhibit's creation was not a direct part of the subsequent effort to set aside and preserve wetlands.[45] Nonetheless, it was fundamentally part of the same social impulse and contributed to local concern about wetlands, as did its suburban counterpart, the Louisiana Nature Center.

LOUISIANA NATURE CENTER

At about the same time as the zoo overhaul, a group of private citizens organized in 1972 to create a nature education center. A board consisting of local civic and university leaders secured a two-acre site, buffered by an eighty-acre city-owned woodland in rapidly urbanizing eastern New Orleans, which became the Louisiana Nature Center.[46] The nature center's staff justified its existence with the argument that most city residents had not seen the marshlands that encircled the metropolis and that they had no appreciation for the ecological and economic significance of these wetlands to the city and the state. The staff asserted that the center's purpose was to stimulate "an awareness and understanding of our total environment, natural and altered, . . . and to develop a sense of responsibility for the care and wise use of the environment."[47] Like the zoo supporters, the nature center advocates did not think that their small tract would actually preserve nature, but they planned to use their tiny wooded setting to illustrate nonhuman processes and promote understanding of the environment within the city. Among the center's first major projects was to create a swamp. On the once marshy site that had been drained for residential and commercial development, creating a swamp entailed excavating two ponds (one for catfish and one for crawfish), planting cypress trees and other swamp vegetation, and erecting a raised walkway through the exhibit.[48] The center's management plan called for planting native species that were not found at the site while at the same time battling exotic plants and animals within its limited grounds.[49] Although not as thoroughly crafted as the zoo exhibit, the nature center's swamp had to be created, literally, in a location where there had never been a swamp and then maintained through human agency.

Both the zoo improvements and the new nature center reflected a desire to employ nature in an educational capacity. Exhibits at both venues were intended to inform the urban public about the significance of Louisiana's best-known but receding habitat. They both presented wetlands that planners thought urban youth needed to encounter—either through a zoo exhibit or a small woodland in the midst of suburban sprawl. Neither of these projects included plans to acquire large tracts of land or set aside existing wetlands. Although the nature center eventually leased a total of eighty-six acres from the city and participated vigorously in the creation of the Bayou Sauvage refuge, the center itself did not significantly deflect conversion of wetland to suburb. The zoo's site was on the natural levee, some of the highest ground in the city, and the nature center occupied former marshland that had already been drained by the time of its inception. Neither effort actually preserved wetland, and swamp exhibits at both locales had to be artificially constructed.

New Orleans advocates for nature preservation were part of a larger national movement, and Louisiana was in synch with the times.[50] A spate of late-1960s and early-1970s federal environmental laws began to impede wholesale wetland development in the New Orleans area. Most notably, Section 404 of the Clean Water Act (1972) prompted court decisions that expanded wetland protection from those adjacent to navigable waters to those beyond major waterways.[51] Filling or draining wetlands under this law required permits from the Corps of Engineers, whose permitting process provided the public a means to question and comment on proposed wetland alterations. Armed with legal tools, local wetland protection advocates stalled seemingly relentless development pressures in eastern New Orleans.[52] Protection efforts rested on arguments that wetlands served vital ecological purposes with benefits to humans—flood retention, wildlife habitat, and groundwater recharge. In New Orleans, wetlands also served as a vital buffer to coastal erosion.[53]

By the mid-1970s public attitudes toward wetlands in New Orleans were undergoing a fundamental shift. Civic embarrassment over the zoo controversy and the near extinction of two emblematic state creatures, increased public attentiveness to environmental issues, and new federal legislation and supporting case law led to major programs to reconfigure the geography of wetland management, to set aside islands of nature. Once viewed as impassable mires that bred disease and provided a livelihood for reclusive "swamp rats," wetlands acquired an entirely different image in public opinion as vital habitats and ecosystems.[54] Socially reconstituted and legally protected, swamps and marshes became desirable locales, worthy of protection, investigation, and recreation—even in urban areas.

PRESERVING URBAN WETLANDS

Along the Gulf Coast, private land ownership has dominated since colonial times, so any effort to create public reserves required the transfer of titles to a public entity. This was the case when private foundations set aside vast tracts of rural Louisiana marsh as refuges in the early twentieth century.[55] These efforts operated on conservation principles and principally sought to sustain waterfowl populations for sport hunters. These impulses differed from the late-twentieth-century efforts to preserve wetlands for their inherently desirable environmental conditions. In and around New Orleans after 1970, the driving motivation was to preserve a disappearing habitat, to maintain ecological and hydrological conditions, and to protect the city from relentless coastal erosion. The rise of public concern for wetlands, along with federal laws that inhibited unrestricted drainage, undercut development schemes that had long targeted the expansive wetlands.

In the early 1970s much of eastern Orleans Parish remained largely undeveloped marsh. With the exception of a few transportation routes crossing the area and some recreational facilities along the lake and bays, large privately owned marshlands lay ready for the same type of drainage and subdivision that had transformed much of the territory along the Pontchartrain lakefront. The restrictions presented by wetland regulations complicated a once straightforward technical process and increased development costs. Other complications also arose with marsh development. For example, in the early 1970s subsidence of drained marshlands in Jefferson Parish caused gas pipeline fractures, resulting in several dramatic explosions. Entire subdivisions built on recently drained peaty soils suffered fractured streets, driveways, and foundations. In some neighborhoods where builders used pilings to stabilize homes, the residences seemed to rise above the ground when the earth around them sank. Owners trucked in fill to raise lawns and close the gaps between foundations and the sunken ground. In some areas of Kenner (west of New Orleans), subsidence exceeded two feet.[56] Such complications prompted local ordinances that added costs to wetland development. Coupled with general economic malaise in the mid-1980s and the regulatory situation, the prospect of similar challenges in subsidence-prone east Orleans Parish effectively blocked further drainage projects in the area. As development ground to a halt, other options for wetlands entered the public discussion. At the forefront were plans to preserve sprawling urban examples.

BARATARIA PRESERVE

Talk of setting aside a larger wetland tract as a National Park property began in the early 1970s. When the National Park Service (NPS) first deliberated establishing a park that would include several sites representative of Louisiana's environmentally based traditions, its personnel expressed concern over a wetlands unit. Most of the potential locations around New Orleans were second-growth cypress swamp, canalized marsh, or landscapes extensively altered by human activity. NPS personnel feared that no potential property would meet the "integrity" standard required of a "nationally significant" natural area. Nonetheless the idea remained afloat under the rubric of a "cultural park," as opposed to a natural area, which would enable the removal of a passable, although not pristine, wetland from development pressures and permit urban residents access to this rapidly disappearing ecosystem.[57] An additional impetus may have come from the NPS's identification of wetlands as an underrepresented ecosystem in the nation's parks and one prioritized for acquisition. By the late 1970s discussions about a wetland unit recast as a preserve (the NPS designation for an area set aside primarily for its ecological characteristics) gained momentum. Despite significant human impacts to the area, NPS personnel determined that the Barataria Unit offered a representative sample of a rapidly disappearing ecosystem and thus qualified as a preserve.

At 1977 congressional hearings on the establishment of an 8,000-acre wetland unit, Louisiana's delegation predicted that it would "preserve" an important environmental setting while providing access for schoolchildren. Some local interests, however, saw another side of the picture. The 8,000-acre parcel, to be supplemented with an additional 20,000-acre "protection zone," would constitute a significant shift in property ownership and in their view threaten access and use by local fishermen, hunters, trappers, and oil prospectors. Local governments feared tax revenue losses and federal intrusion into local politics.[58] Louisiana's congressional delegation inserted language in the bill creating the new unit that resolved most local concerns and secured the bill's approval in 1978.[59]

As finally passed, the enabling legislation called for acquisition of approximately 20,000 acres for the Barataria Preserve of the Jean Lafitte National Historical Park and Preserve and a buffer or protection zone.[60] The new facility had a mandate to "preserve for the education, inspiration, and benefit of present and future generations *significant examples of natural and historical resources* [emphasis added] and to provide for their interpretation in such a manner as to portray the development of cultural diversity in the region."[61] In terms of the "natural" conditions, the Park Service was to preserve and protect the freshwater drainage patterns, the vegetative cover, the ecological and biological systems' integrity, and air and water quality. At the same time, and as a concession to local interests, the Park Service had to allow "traditional uses"—namely commercial fishing, trapping, and oil prospecting—within the service's overall management guidelines. The NPS also had to recognize private rights to some two hundred existing "camps," or fishing and hunting cabins. This created a difficult prospect for the park service within its mission to provide safe public access and protect the preserve's biological integrity. Yet the highly modified parcel of land, subject to sewage from neighboring towns, external drainage, tidal manipulations, and the presence of nonnative species, was not ecologically intact from the outset.

The site acquired by the Park Service contained several settings that represented the diverse ecological zones found in the lower delta. A transect across the park, which is roughly centered on a former Mississippi River distributary, would pass over the natural levee covered with live oak, down the back slope and its maple forest, and into the cypress–Tupelo gum swamp and out into a freshwater marsh. Human activity in the area has been extensive. Native peoples began building shell mounds about two thousand years ago. Timber removal, of both oaks from the higher natural levees and cypress from the backswamps, began in the early colonial period and lasted until the 1950s. Commercial cypress removal was most intense between about 1880 and 1925, when skidders used to pull the giant logs to collection points scoured sizable ditches through the wetlands. Land clearing and agriculture brought significant change to the natural levees, and relict field ditches still exist in reforested areas. Additionally, landowners built artificial levees along the natural levee crests to protect their crops, further altering the area's hydrology. More recently oil extraction companies cut larger canals throughout the Louisiana coastal plain, including the Barataria Preserve, and they constructed drilling pads, mounds of fill that now rise above the surrounding wetland. Over two millennia, human alteration to both the physical topography and the moisture-sensitive plant and animal life has been extensive.[62] This is the wetland that the Park Service acquired to manage as a natural and historical preserve.

Situated within an urbanizing region, the Barataria Preserve faced greater external threats than many other parks and consequently had to implement more extensive environmental management plans than its rural counterparts.[63] Of particular importance in the initial land protection plan, park authorities had to contend with flooding resulting from increased runoff in upstream urban areas and with the release of untreated sewage that entered park waterways. Levees constructed within the protection zone to protect neighboring suburbs had accelerated subsidence and thereby altered natural hydrological and ecological conditions. Canals allowed greater saltwater intrusion from the Gulf of Mexico.[64] In response to the dual issues of external threats and preexisting environmental modifications, the Park Service had to work with numerous agencies to develop management plans that maintained its resources within a larger complex regional ecosystem. With a mandate to preserve, protect, and interpret the natural values of the unit, the Park Service sought to reestablish preurban conditions of water quality, levels, and surface flow. Obtaining the desired outcome required extensive management. In order to maintain the preserve, some entity had to provide adequate sewage treatment for neighboring communities, divert storm runoff, and control water levels on flood-protection levees.[65] Each of these procedures required cooperative actions by other government bodies—which may not have shared the objectives of the Park Service.

Recognizing inherent conflicts between "traditional use" and "preservation," the park service carefully reviewed its impact on practices predating the creation of the preserve. Despite legislation mandating the toleration of numerous traditional activities, some came under regulatory pressure. The park curtailed annual burns of marsh grasses and digging of small canals, or *trainasses*, by trappers.[66] By outlawing motorized vehicles and filling traînasses, the park service has effectively blocked some traditional trapping activity, without explicitly banning locally important practices. At the same time, it permitted trappers to remove unwanted nonnative rodents known as nutria from the park territory. During the 1990–91 season, trappers captured more than two thousand nutria,[67] helping to protect marsh grasses and ensure better habitat for native species.[68] Wildlife management practices disrupted other traditional practices as well. Policies to protect alligators discouraged sport fishing within the park, while prohibitions against cutting wax myrtle branches, used to catch softshell crab, reduced this type of commercial fishing.[69]

Within the property acquired, as stipulated in the management plan, human oversight and husbandry of the environment has been a pervasive influence. Human action has become essential for the "natural" conditions that the Park Service desires to exist. Certainly nature abounds within this manipulated setting, and the NPS has sought to minimize influences from the highly altered surrounding territory. Nonetheless, the preserve's managers exerted considerable efforts to protect the property's ecology. Similar circumstances prevail at the wildlife refuge east of New Orleans.

BAYOU SAUVAGE NATIONAL WILDLIFE REFUGE

After the creation of Barataria Preserve, nearly a decade passed before Louisiana wetlands advocates could position themselves to bring about a more significant transfer of marsh from private to public management—in this case through the establishment of the Bayou Sauvage National Wildlife

Refuge. New Orleans East, a major land-development company with more than 20,000 acres of marshland within New Orleans's city limits, had struggled but failed to obtain approval to develop its sprawling wetland and lapsed into receivership during economic hard times in 1985. Faced with opposition to wetland drainage, Section 404 obstacles, and increasing costs for safely developing the peaty ground, New Orleans East transferred the property to South Point, Inc., a subsidiary of its financer, to manage. In a desperate attempt to get a return on its bad loan and unload the property, South Point began meetings with city, environmental, and federal officials. A proposal that appealed to the investors called for selling the marsh to the federal government as an urban wildlife refuge. This would ensure a fair market price for the entire tract, thereby securing the developer's investment and eliminating the need to "bank" a portion of the wetland under Section 404 and lose revenue on idled acreage.[70]

Environmental groups and city officials championed the proposed urban wildlife refuge in testimony before Congress in 1986. They claimed the refuge would help offset the rapid loss of Louisiana's trademark habitat, maintain marshland for educational purposes, and preserve wetlands for their essential ecological functions. Louisiana's congressional delegation pressed hard to establish the refuge, which was hailed as a means of protecting the habitat of some forty thousand migratory birds and a nursery for shrimp, crabs, and fish. One advocate argued that the area could only survive with human management, suggesting nature could not sustain this wetland tract without human intervention.[71] The only critical question came from the Fish and Wildlife Service. James Pulliam, the regional director, testified that the Bayou Sauvage area in eastern New Orleans had not been identified as a critical habitat using the service's normal prioritization system. While not opposing the designation, the service simply had not evaluated the site's importance in its larger wildlife protection plans.[72] The Louisiana delegation remained determined to deliver a refuge to the state and whittled away at the Fish and Wildlife Service representative's concerns. Ultimately, refuge advocates prevailed. Legislation passed in 1986 authorized the federal agency to acquire and manage more than 22,000 acres.[73]

Like the Barataria Preserve, the newly created Bayou Sauvage National Wildlife Refuge was a thoroughly reworked territory due to its urban fringe location. About 60 percent of the acreage was within the hurricane protection levee system and was subject to complete water-level management by

FIG. 6.4. DEVELOPMENT APPROACHES BAYOU SAUVAGE WETLAND, 1964. Looking eastward, the new interstate highway crosses what would become the Bayou Sauvage National Wildlife Refuge. Sutton Photograph Collection. Courtesy The Historic New Orleans Collection Museum and Research Center, Accession No. 1984.166.2.298.

the Corps of Engineers. Large lakes occupied excavations where crews had removed fill to raise interstate highway exchanges, and several canals and their spoil mounds traversed the area (Fig. 6.4). Additionally, the Fish and Wildlife Service's territory encompassed the largest sanitary landfill in the greater New Orleans area. Within the refuge territory, subsidence was causing marshland to disappear at a rate of more than 100 acres per year. Between 1956 and 1988 about half the marsh had sunk below the water level, although controlling water levels within the levee system could reduce the rate of marshland erosion.[74] Nonetheless, extensive marshes used by migratory waterfowl made up most of the property. The presence of levees and canals simply meant that the infrastructure to manage the environment was already in place.

The goals of the Fish and Wildlife Service's management plan were to (1) preserve, maintain, and restore natural habitat; (2) enhance and maintain wildlife diversity; (3) provide for public access, education, and research; and (4) foster a stewardship ethic. To accomplish these goals in an area already subject to substantial alteration, the service claimed that extensive management was essential. The master plan set in motion several procedures. The first and perhaps most critical was controlling water levels. Lowering the water levels in spring stimulated emergent vegetation, and raising levels in late summer maintained waterfowl feeding areas. Control of nuisance species was a second objective. This included mosquito eradication, the elimination of nonnative species such as water hyacinth by flooding with saltwater, and trapping nutria and feral hogs. Further, shoreline stabilization was necessary to prevent excessive coastal erosion. Key elements of this effort included creating wave-dampening barriers and stimulating oyster reefs along the shore outside the levee system.[75] Without human intervention, the wetlands would become a saltwater bay, and waterfowl would have to winter elsewhere. Human involvement at Bayou Sauvage was essential to maintaining the wetland and preventing its destruction by nonhuman processes.

The preserve and the refuge, along with additional restoration projects not mentioned here,[76] represent the latest phase in New Orleans's interaction with its largely wetland environment. Faced with restrictive laws, local interests recalibrated the value of wetlands by touting them as important educational and ecological resources. At the risk of assigning too much importance to the federal laws involved, it must be understood that development costs and other economic issues clouded the potential for full-scale wetland drainage and development. Nonetheless, convincing the federal government to purchase and manage more than 40,000 acres of wetlands within easy reach of downtown New Orleans has provided local and out-of-town visitors with ready access to a once remote environmental setting.

In addition to programs offered by the Park Service and the Fish and

Wildlife Service, swamp tourism facilities have sprung up in the vicinity of both properties. Thus both public and private enterprises permit entry to urbanized nature, but the interpretations of the wetlands offered to the public by commercial vendors and government agencies are in stark contrast.

Education material prepared by the NPS and the Fish and Wildlife Service introduce teachers and students to the wetlands. At the Barataria Preserve the theme "everybody needs a home" acquaints younger students (grades 4–5) with the notion of habitat—that all creatures need a place to survive. Older children learn about wetlands specifically and the various functions they perform. Facts about wetland loss are used to stimulate interest in preservation efforts and indicate human responsibility to manage wetlands.[77] Both education programs seek to satisfy science components of the state's curriculum objectives. Likewise, at the Bayou Sauvage National Wildlife Refuge, educators have compiled material for teachers that emphasizes the habitat and critical water resource functions of wetlands.[78] The literature prepared and circulated to teachers stresses the value of the habitat found within the preserves and the function it serves for both wildlife and human society. It also indicates that human action can have deleterious effects, but proper management can preserve these important settings. Students who visit the sites observe the wetlands as they walk along raised boardwalks through dense cypress-palmetto swamp or at viewing stands at the marsh's edge. Through the lense of ecological science they witness nature as a *home* to animals and as a fragile ecosystem—the environmental setting is the center of the interpretation. Armed with this scientific understanding, they learn that humans can intervene positively on behalf of the wetlands' residents. These educational programs present science as nature's benefactor, along with the concept that humans can use science to sustain nature.

Commercial tours offer an interpretation that is less attuned to the state curriculum guidelines and places the alligator at the center of attention. From the brochures placed in hotel lobbies to the paintings on their shuttle buses and their billboards, the tour operators have used the alligator as the central motif and the tour's main attraction. Typically a tour boat will depart its dock, cruise slowly along a waterway while the pilot points out swamp features such as cypress trees, the invasive water hyacinth, and blue herons. A brief lesson in terminology sometimes provides misconceptions about terms like *bayou* and *marsh*. Ultimately, the pilot navigates the boat to a location where alligators are known to lurk. Coaxed into view with marshmallows, chicken wings, or sausage, the alligators take food from the guide as the guests clamor to photograph the reptiles. There might follow a discussion of alligator trapping, along with uses of other swamp and marsh animals, but close contact with alligators is the excursion's highlight. On the return leg, pilots typically play some "Cajun" music and show off live snapping turtles and pet alligators.[79] There is little effort to present the wetlands as a fragile habitat or as a place deserving scientific attention. Rather, operators seek out megafauna to perform for the tourists—the wildlife becomes a commodity for the tour purveyors. The commodification does not end on the banks of the bayous, however. Sale of alligator jaws, teeth, and other body parts has reached unprecedented heights in recent years.[80] Tourists are able to take home trophies of their swamp adventure in the form of photographs or even animal artifacts. Thus the wetland presented to tourists is a wild, unhumanized nature—even though the alligators have been trained to approach the boats in search of treats.[81]

After more than two centuries of trying to exclude wetlands from their city, New Orleans's citizens embarked on a grand crusade to reintroduce swamp and protect marshes within the city. Levee and drainage system construction has enlarged the city's habitable territory, and mosquito extermination programs have dramatically reduced the threat of insect-borne disease. Consequently, the fear of the wetlands as harbors for disease had disappeared by the 1970s, and few could recall the long struggle to eliminate what had been considered a deadly habitat.

With much of the negative attitude toward wetlands forgotten, preservation proponents first had to create a demand to preserve this ecosystem. National environmental movements provided one impetus by sparking public concern about Louisiana's remaining rural wetlands and the threatened alligators. By literally creating swamp exhibits in the city zoo and nature center, citizens fostered understanding about local environments and wildlife, thereby contributing to public support for subsequent efforts.

The wetlands set aside as nature in New Orleans fit within a broader pattern of open-space preservation for biological and hydrological purposes prompted in part by federal laws. Nature, in such situations, must earn its keep by serving socially valued purposes such as maintaining wildlife diversity, educating the population, or providing a flood-control reservoir. In

New Orleans the additional chore of protecting the city from coastal erosion provides a particularly urgent rationale.

In setting aside actual swamp and marshland, local advocates found that while wetlands abounded, they were highly altered by human action. Both the Barataria Preserve and the Bayou Sauvage refuge required considerable management to offset intrusive urban influences and modifications carried out inside their borders. Thus the nature presented to the public is a hybrid, a domesticated breed, made accessible and maintained by human intervention. The NPS and the Fish and Wildlife Service work with the properties they inherited, and they actively manage the environments within their boundaries.

In New Orleans, as in other cities, human artifice has never erased the myriad forms and processes of nature. Efforts to wring the Crescent City's wetlands dry were among the paramount struggles of human interactions with the environment there. Despite two hundred years of human-induced drainage, extensive swamps and marshes remain in and around New Orleans. Thus the nature reintroduced has always been there; what society changed was its social value and ease of access. As urban residents began to explore swamp and marsh habitats, they discovered "nature" shaped by human agency and largely dependent on human management to survive.

EPILOGUE

ENVIRONMENT HAS ALWAYS MATTERED

Since its founding, New Orleans has faced a legion of challenges presented by its environment. Reconstructing the responses to these challenges is fundamental to understanding the urbanization of the territory the city now occupies. In New Orleans as in other cities, the environment matters. Although described in some cases as the antithesis of nature, cities are not, nor can they be, insulated from interaction with the environment. Every structural engineer who considers soil properties when designing a building's foundation understands this.[1] Sanitary engineers at the turn of the twentieth century knew that they had to deal with environmental factors when installing sewers and water supply systems.[2] For some reason, many urban geographers, perhaps seduced by the power of economic theories and models, did not share the engineers' appreciation for the environment in the city. Even those not captivated by the economic models have not given the environment its due place. In his brilliant overview of urban morphological development, James Vance scarcely touches on physical site characteristics.[3]

David Harvey's highly influential writings focus on power relationships constructed on capital rather than cities erected on terra firma.[4] Postmodern perspectives acknowledge nature but maneuver their discussions away from natural systems and toward social construction of nature.[5] Yet from its founding to the present, New Orleans offers insight into the significance of human interaction with the hydrology, geomorphology, climatology, and biogeography of an urban territory.[6]

Faced with dual water hazards—riverine floods and standing water—New Orleans's leaders embarked along two very different courses to deal with these dangers in the nineteenth century. Levees became the principal device to protect the city from inundation. Given its challenging topography, the city was initially unable to erect a sufficient barrier through combined corporate and municipal efforts. By externalizing the costs of levee construction, first to upstream agriculturalists, then to shippers tying up at the city's waterfront, and ultimately the Mississippi River Commission and the Corps of Engineers, the city was able to secure a well-tested protection system that has kept the river out for more than a century. Drainage proved a much more troublesome problem. To eliminate the water-logged conditions, which, according to contemporary beliefs, produced disease-causing miasmas, the city attempted to drain low-lying sites. Insufficient gradient made gravity-driven flow nearly impossible. Technological capabilities limited the volume of water that could be pumped out, and a politically fractured city administration frustrated the construction of a comprehensive citywide system. Its inability to contend with a high water table left New Orleans mired, literally, in a disease-prone setting that restricted urbanization to the better-drained natural levee. At the close of the antebellum period, New Orleans was poised for failure as the South's leading city. Hemmed in by its levees and surrounding wetlands, its precipitous drop from the country's sixth largest city in 1860 to fifteenth in 1900 was reasonably assured even without the Civil War. The environment did not determine the city's course, but it certainly mattered.

New Orleans continued to struggle with environmental problems during and after Reconstruction. The city sought to eliminate several troublesome nuisances, to use a contemporary term. These objectionable conditions were rooted in particular activities situated in specific places in the city. They diminished citizens' enjoyment of air and water. In response to the nuisance conditions, the city council passed ordinances and implemented public works programs to restrict the activities that made certain sectors unlivable.

It increasingly regulated sewage removal, garbage disposal, public water delivery, burial practices, and offensive industries. In general, the city sought a geographic solution and restricted nuisance-causing activity within the city limits—and thereby distorted economic land-use models. To offset undesirable conditions, the city created several small parks, planted trees along boulevards, and ultimately established a pair of large parks where citizens could enjoy the benefits of "nature." Creating amenity zones influenced surrounding land uses and values as well. Dealing with the environment consumed municipal government in the second half of the nineteenth century and had tremendous impacts on the city's growth.

As New Orleans followed other American cities into the Progressive Era, the distribution of its environmental improvement efforts exposed racial inequities. Instituting a major drainage, sewerage, and water delivery system, the city attempted to follow rational engineering principles that would ensure even delivery of municipal services throughout the city. However, pockets of inadequate service revealed Jim Crow tendencies and temporary failures in the municipal undertaking. Ultimately engineering efficiency prevailed and the city extended services to all quarters, but institutionalized racism in deed covenants limited housing choices among African Americans. Environmental transformation opened new residential areas to whites and blacks, but legal restrictions worked to create ever-larger and more completely segregated African American neighborhoods, typically in the city's poorest environmental settings.

In the post–World War II years, New Orleans entered the modern environmental era. New environmental definitions imposed by external regulatory agencies altered residents' expectations. Renaming a garbage dump a sanitary landfill and later a Superfund site fundamentally changed a neighborhood's perception of the former disposal site and made a previously desirable location a landscape of tragedy. Federal programs that revealed invisible toxins in the city's drinking water redirected municipal efforts to supply potable water and, more importantly, undermined public confidence in local tap water. Both of these issues reflected changing perceptions of human relationships with the environment and brought greater federal intervention into municipal environmental management, thus reducing local authority and the city's ability to shape its own solutions.

Residential infilling within the city created new environmental relations in old neighborhoods, while suburbanization carried New Orleans to the outer edges of reclaimable land by the 1980s. Successful drainage inside the municipal boundaries had emboldened home builders to develop housing tracts in some of the city's lowest sections during the 1920s, and a period with few major storms after 1930 led to inappropriate ground-level home improvements. When a period of record-setting storms began in the late 1970s, residents soon relearned the inadequacies of the local drainage systems. Despite a federal program to encourage land-use means to reduce flooding, New Orleans's topography renders it utterly dependent on structural means to control internal flooding. Likewise, in the sprawling Jefferson Parish suburbs, a levee and pump system remains the key flood-protection method. Federal lawsuits for failure to abide by flood-reduction planning aside, historical decisions to employ structural techniques still pervade New Orleans's response to localized flooding. As with the massive levees, the city and its suburbs are now dependent on the federal government to underwrite drainage.

After two centuries trying to exclude wetlands from the city, New Orleans has rediscovered the habitat that once so completely dominated the local environs. Due in part to federal restrictions on wetland development and the near elimination of valued fauna like the alligator, local organizations began creating swamp exhibits in the 1970s. With help from the local congressional delegation, activists worked to create a national park unit in the Barataria wetlands south of the city and a wildlife refuge to the east. By preserving and touting local wetlands, the city reversed a compulsion to transform nature into city. In recent years, an urge to bring nature back into the city has propelled these efforts. While the preserved wetlands are far from pristine, they reflect a fundamental shift in attitudes about nature and underscore a recognition that nature still exists in urban places.

ENVIRONMENT CONTINUES TO MATTER

If one looks at a map showing recent population growth in the New Orleans area it is obvious that during the last twenty years suburban development has leap-frogged well beyond the area that witnessed growth in the years immediately following World War II. Parishes on the north shore of Lake Pontchartrain—particularly St. Tammany—and St. Charles Parish upriver have experienced the most dramatic population increases. This development pattern bypassed the nearer Bayou Sauvage wetlands in favor of the better-drained north shore and followed the interstate highway beyond the LaBranche wetland and the Bonnet Carré Spillway. Thus New Orleans is still hemmed by wetlands that have deflected recent growth. Nature remains a constant issue in the city and its metropolitan area.

Massive and shallow Lake Pontchartrain makes the city vulnerable to natural disasters. Should a Class 5 hurricane blow water over the lakefront levees, the city could find itself under water for months. Evacuation would face serious bottlenecks due to the limited number of escape routes across the water-logged terrain—and some of those raised highways could be over-topped by storm-driven waves. Recent popular accounts paint a dire picture and suggest that federal authorities might not be willing to make the investment necessary to save a city that cannot afford to protect itself.[7] Global warming and sea level rise make this grim forecast all too likely.

On a very different scale, nature nibbles at key elements of the city's tourist industry. Visitors may notice small silver disks every 20 feet or so on the sidewalk as they amble through the French Quarter. These devices are part of the city-developed detection system that alerts property owners to the presence of Formosa termites—a particularly ravenous wood-eating insect that is literally devouring historic buildings, the city's prized live oaks, and anything else made of wood. There is real concern that they could destroy the historic fabric of the city and the shaded boulevards that make the city so attractive to tourists. An exotic import, the Formosa is one of the most recent natural threats to a city with a host of environmental problems. In addition, the arrival of West Nile Virus in the summer of 2002 ushered in a new mosquito-borne public health menace. While fatality rates from this disease have not come close to the devastation caused by nineteenth-century yellow fever epidemics in New Orleans, the disease and attendant mosquito control programs underscore the fact that the twenty-first-century city still exists within an environmental context.

The continuing significance of the environment in New Orleans is all too obvious. Levees and drainage canals are seldom out of view. Land reclaimed by the drainage they permit is sinking, while coastal erosion threatens the city externally. The levees constructed to protect the city from river and hurricane flooding leave it more vulnerable to flooding from intense rainfalls. The racial geography reflects historical efforts to transform undesirable acreage into prime neighborhoods for a segregated white elite, while neglecting areas occupied by poor blacks. In recent years, environmental laws and designations have prompted residents of New Orleans to rethink old garbage dumps, their drinking water supply, and the very wetlands that surround the city. The environment has mattered in every aspect of New

Orleans's development. Although New Orleans might offer exceptional examples of human-environment interactions in its geographic evolution, physical features have been equally important in shaping other cities.

Urban geography is as much a reflection of environmental dimensions as economic influences. This notion needs to find its way into urban geographic analysis and theory in a much more consistent way. One complication has been that economic theories sought sweeping generalizations. When the environment is considered, however, cities became unique places, not economically organized nodes in a great urban hierarchy. As an academic discipline, geography has tools to analyze both unique and general qualities. Site selection and initial settlement are directly influenced by local resources and hazards as well as larger economic networks and linkages. Physical conditions affect land uses within cities, and environmental impacts of land uses in one area affect land uses in surrounding areas. Transportation networks, internal and external, follow favorable topography and contribute to the evolving urban morphology. The least desirable environments became zones of poverty and neglect, while affluent citizens select the most favorable settings. Amenity landscapes, both natural and artificial, have an impact on surrounding urban spaces. Perhaps the key to a complete urban geography lies in accepting local environmental uniqueness and blending the facts of a particular city's setting with general concepts of urban development.

Mayor Marc Morial's complaint that New Orleans's founders selected a poor site speaks to the environment's singular importance in the city's urbanization.[8] Most other cities are able to rely on gravity to transport sewage and runoff out of and away from the urbanized territory. New Orleans, by contrast, had to make a massive investment in levees and canals, which also consume huge amounts of urban property, and it has to pay ever-increasing prices for fuel to lift runoff and sewage out of the city. These are hardly sustainable practices, and they eat up valuable financial resources. The presence of canals influences neighboring property values and makes the city deviate from the standard models of urban growth. Evidence of the efforts to wrest New Orleans from nature are pervasive in the city's landscape and its economic geography. Most importantly, the engineering, social, and economic systems put in place to lure the city from the mire must be modified regularly and maintained perpetually. Human effort, no matter how sophisticated, has never excluded an environment that continues to pervade urban life along the mighty crescent that sweeps by this unnatural metropolis.

NOTES

NOTES TO INTRODUCTION

1. "Mayor: N.O. Location 'Lousy Place to Put a City,'" *Baton Rouge Advocate*, 17 May 2001, 14A.

2. Peirce F. Lewis, *New Orleans: The Making of an Urban Landscape*, 2nd ed. (Santa Fe: Center for American Places, 2003).

3. Baron Marc de Villiers, "A History of the Foundation of New Orleans (1717–1722)," trans. Warrington Dawson, *Louisiana Historical Quarterly* 3:2 (1920): 157–251.

4. A fine discussion of New Orleans's relationship to the river is Ari Kelman, *A River and Its City: The Nature of Landscape in New Orleans* (Berkeley: University of California Press, 2003). Essays on New Orleans's environmental history appear in Craig E. Colten, ed., *Transforming New Orleans and Its Environs: Centuries of Change* (Pittsburgh: University of Pittsburgh Press, 2000). A lavishly illustrated work that examines New Orleans and its site is Richard Campanella, *Time and Place in New Orleans: Past Geographies in Present Day* (Gretna, LA: Pelican, 2002).

5. M. Le Page du Pratz, *The History of Louisiana*, ed. J. G. Tregle, Jr. (1774; reprint, Baton Rouge: Louisiana State University Press, 1975), 128–29. Du Pratz cites the discovery of a buried tree trunk in a well as evidence the river was building the land where New Orleans stood.

6. An excellent account of the formation of the land surface at New Orleans is Roger T. Saucier, *Recent Geomorphic History of the Pontchartrain Basin* (Baton Rouge: Louisiana State University Press, 1963), 18–21.

7. *Ibid.*, 18–21.

8. *Ibid.*, 18–21.

9. See Albert E. Cowdrey, *Land's End: A History of the New Orleans District, U.S. Army Corps of Engineers* (Washington: U.S. Army Corps of Engineers, 1977).

10. William Cronon, *Nature's Metropolis: Chicago and the Great West* (New York: W. W. Norton, 1991). Cronon has inspired a growing body of literature on urban environmental history—both internal and external in its scope. James Lemon has argued that North American cities benefitted from nature's largesse within a larger urban system. See *Liberal Dreams and Nature's Limits: Great Cities of North America since 1600* (New York: Oxford University Press, 1996). The present volume, by contrast, will maintain an internal focus.

11. The concept of "reworking nature" in a major urban area is developed by Matthew Gandy, *Concrete and Clay: Reworking Nature in New York City* (Cambridge: MIT Press, 2002).

12. See John G. Clark, *New Orleans, 1718–1812: An Economic History* (Baton Rouge: Louisiana State University Press, 1970), and N. M. Miller Surrey, *The Commerce of Louisiana during the French Régime, 1699–1763*, Columbia Studies in the Social Sciences, no. 167 (New York: Columbia University Press, 1916).

13. Lewis Mumford, "The Natural History of Urbanization," in *Man's Role in Changing the Face of the Earth*, vol. 1, ed. William L. Thomas (Chicago: University of Chicago Press, 1956), 382–98; Henry Lawrence, "The Greening of the Squares of London: Transformation of Urban Landscapes and Ideals," *Annals of the Association of American Geographers* 83 (1993): 90–118.

14. The classic example of this genre is Edward T. Price, "The Central Courthouse Square in the American County Seat," *Geographical Review* 58 (1968): 29–60. For an overview of urban landscape studies, see Michael P. Conzen, "Analytical Approaches to the Urban Landscape," in *Dimensions of Human Geography: Essays on Some Familiar and Neglected Themes*, ed. Karl Butzer, Research Paper 186 (Chicago: University of Chicago, Department of Geography, 1978), 128–65. A recent interpretation is Richard Schein, "Place of Landscape: Conceptual Framework for an American Scene," *Annals of the Association of American Geographers* 87:4 (1997): 660–80.

15. David Ward, *Cities and Immigrants: A Geography of Change in Nineteenth-Century America* (New York: Oxford University Press, 1971); Alan R. Pred, *The Spatial Dynamics of U.S. Urban-Industrial Growth, 1800–1914* (Cambridge: MIT Press, 1966); John Adams, "Residential Structure of Midwestern Cities," *Annals of the Association of American Geographers* 60 (1970): 37–62. Good overviews of urban landscape evolution are Larry R. Ford, *Cities and Buildings: Skyscrapers, Skid Rows, and Suburbs* (Baltimore: Johns Hopkins University Press, 1994), and Richard Harris and Robert Lewis, "Constructing a Faulty Zone: American Suburbs 1900–1950," *Annals of the Association of American Geographers* 88:4 (1998): 622–39.

16. John R. Borchert, "American Metropolitan Evolution," *Geographical Review* 57 (1967): 302–32.

NOTES TO PAGES 8-9

17. General overviews of these theories and models appear in Paul Knox, *The Restless Urban Landscape* (Englewood Cliffs, NJ: Prentice Hall, 1993), and Harold Carter, *The Study of Urban Geography*, 4th ed. (New York: Arnold, 1995). The clear exception to neglect of the physical environment in general urban texts is Risa Palm, *The Geography of American Cities* (New York: Oxford University Press, 1981).

18. At the height of the early-1970s environmental movement, several volumes appeared that emphasized the role of the environment in the city. See Brian J. L. Berry and Frank E. Horton, *Urban Environmental Management: Planning for Pollution Control* (Englewood Cliffs, NJ: Prentice-Hall, 1974), and Brian J. L. Berry et al., *Land Use, Urban Form, and Environmental Quality*, Research Paper 155 (Chicago: University of Chicago, Department of Geography, 1974).

19. James E. Vance, *The Continuing City: Urban Morphology in Western Civilization* (Baltimore: Johns Hopkins University Press, 1990).

20. An early study of urban ecological systems is Ian Douglas, *The Urban Environment* (Baltimore: Arnold, 1983). See also Rutherford H. Platt et al., *The Ecological City: Preserving and Restoring Urban Biodiversity* (Amherst: University of Massachusetts Press, 1994), and Rodney R. White, *Urban Environmental Management: Environmental Change and Urban Design* (New York: Wiley, 1994).

21. Kenneth Hewitt and Ian Burton, *The Hazardousness of a Place: A Regional Ecology of Damaging Events* (Toronto: University of Toronto Press, 1971); Robert Kates, "The Road Not Taken," *Annals of the Association of American Geographers* 77 (1987): 525-34.

22. Susan Cutter, *Living with Risk: The Geography of Technological Hazards* (New York: Arnold, 1993); Robert W. Kates, ed., *Managing Technological Hazards: Research Needs and Opportunities* (Boulder: University of Colorado Program on Technology, Environment, and Man, 1977); Joel A. Tarr, *The Search for the Ultimate Sink: Urban Pollution in Historical Perspective* (Akron, OH: University of Akron Press, 1996).

23. Joel A. Tarr and Gabriel Dupuy, eds., *Technology and the Rise of the Networked City in Europe and America* (Philadelphia: Temple University Press, 1988), and Martin V. Melosi, *The Sanitary City: Urban Infrastructure in America from Colonial Times to the Present* (Baltimore: Johns Hopkins University Press, 2000) are prominent examples.

24. Andrew Hurley, *Environmental Inequalities: Class, Race, and Industrial Pollution, 1945-1980* (Chapel Hill: University of North Carolina Press, 1995).

25. A spate of urban environmental histories has followed the pioneering work in Andrew Hurley, ed., *Common Fields: An Environmental History of St. Louis* (St. Louis: Missouri Historical Society Press, 1997). See Colten, *Transforming New Orleans and Its Environs*, Char Miller, ed., *On the Border: An Environmental History of San Antonio* (Pittsburgh: University of Pittsburgh Press, 2001), Martin V. Melosi, *Effluent America: Cities, Industry, Energy, and the Environment* (Pittsburgh: University of Pittsburgh Press, 2001), and Joel A. Tarr, ed., *Devastation and Renewal: The Environmental History of Pittsburgh and Its Region* (Pittsburgh: University of Pittsburgh Press, 2003).

26. For a discussion of the importance of environment in historical geography see Stanley Trimble, preface to *The American Environment: Interpretations of Past Geographies*, ed. Lary M.

Dilsaver and Craig E. Colten (Lanham, MD: Rowman and Littlefield, 1992), xv–xxii, and the essays on urban environments in a special issue of *Historical Geography* 25 (1997) guest edited by Christopher Boone.

27. In particular he states that water was essential in the city's economic viability. Gandy, *Concrete and Clay*, 74.

28. William Meyer, "Bringing Hyspography Back In: Altitude and Residence in American Cities," *Urban Geography* 15 (1994): 505–13; Craig E. Colten, "Chicago's Waste Lands: Refuse Disposal and Urban Growth, 1840–1990," *Journal of Historical Geography* 20:2 (1994): 124–42.

29. W. B. Meyer, "Urban Heat Island and Urban Health: Early American Perspectives," *Professional Geographer* 43 (1991): 38–48; Felix Driver, "Moral Geographies: Social Science and the Urban Environment in Mid-Nineteenth Century England," *Transactions of the Institute of British Geographers*, n.s., 13 (1988): 275–87; Pyrs Gruffudd, "'A Crusade against Consumption': Environment, Health, and Social Reform in Wales, 1900–1939," *Journal of Historical Geography* 21:1 (1995): 39–54; Graham Mooney, "Did London Pass the 'Sanitary Test'? Seasonal Infant Mortality in London, 1870–1914," *Journal of Historical Geography* 20:2 (1994): 158–74.

30. John Sheail, "Sewering the English Suburbs: An Inter-War Perspective," *Journal of Historical Geography* 19:2 (1993): 433–47; Catherine Brace, "Corruption, Pollution, and the Problems of Public Provision: The Garrison Creek Sewer Scandal in Late-Nineteenth-Century Toronto," *Historical Geography* 25 (1997): 113–23.

31. William B. Meyer, *Human Impact on the Earth* (Cambridge: Cambridge University Press, 1996).

32. Essays on this subject appear in William Cronon, ed., *Uncommon Ground: Toward Reinventing Nature* (New York: W. W. Norton, 1995).

33. Tristram R. Kidder, "Making the City Inevitable: Native Americans and the Geography of New Orleans," in Colten, *Transforming New Orleans and Its Environs*, 9–21.

34. New Orleans residents have developed directional lexicon based on places' position relative to the river. Making reference to a huge meander, these relative terms have little relation to the cardinal positions on a compass. Uptown is upriver, downtown is downriver. "Rear" refers to places away from the river, toward Lake Pontchartrain.

35. Robert Bullard, *Dumping in Dixie: Race, Class, and Environmental Quality* (Boulder, CO: Westview, 1990); Laura Pulido, "Rethinking Environmental Racism: White Privilege and Urban Development," *Annals of the Association of American Geographers* 90:1 (2000): 12–40.

36. Jacques Emel and Elizabeth Brooks, "Changes in Form and Function of Property Rights Institutions under Threatened Resource Scarcity," *Annals of the Association of American Geographers* 78 (1988): 241–52.

37. Melosi, *Sanitary City*.

38. Kenneth Foote, *Shadowed Ground: America's Landscapes of Violence and Tragedy* (Austin: University of Texas Press, 1997).

NOTES TO CHAPTER I

1. Baron Marc De Villiers, "A History of the Foundation of New Orleans (1717–1722)," trans. Warrington Dawson, *Louisiana Historical Quarterly* 3 : 2 (1920): 161–251, discusses the issues surrounding the city's founding.

2. William Darby, *A Geographical Description of the State of Louisiana* (New York: James Olmstead, 1817), 63.

3. For discussions of hazards and the social response see Kenneth Hewitt and Ian Burton, *The Hazardousness of Place: A Regional Ecology of Damaging Events* (Toronto: University of Toronto Press, 1971), and Ian Burton, Robert W. Kates, and Gilbert F. White, *The Environment as Hazard*, 2nd ed. (New York: Guilford, 1993).

4. D. O. Elliott, *The Improvement of the Lower Mississippi River for Flood Control and Navigation* (Vicksburg: U.S. Army Corps of Engineers, U.S. Waterways Experiment Station, 1932), 105; Jeffrey A. Owens, "Holding Back the Waters: Land Development and the Origins of the Levees on the Mississippi," (Ph.D. diss., Louisiana State University, 1999), 37–40, 77. The levee surrounding most of the city served the dual purpose of military defense. See Samuel Wilson, Jr., *The Vieux Carré, New Orleans: Its Plan, Its Growth, and Its Architecture* (New Orleans: Bureau of Government Research, 1968), 26–29, and Robert W. Harrison, *Alluvial Empire*, vol. 1, *A Study of State and Local Efforts Toward Land Development in the Alluvial Valley of the Lower Mississippi River, Including Flood Control, Land Drainage, Land Clearing, Land Forming* (Little Rock: U.S. Department of Agriculture, Economic Research Service, 1961), 54–56.

5. Philip Pittman, *The Present State of the European Settlements on the Mississippi* (1770; reprint, Cleveland: Arthur H. Clark, 1906), 41.

6. Owens, "Holding Back the Waters," 67, 81; Marcel Giraud, *A History of French Louisiana*, vol. 5, trans. Brian Pearce (Baton Rouge: Louisiana State University Press, 1991), 192–98.

7. Owens, "Holding Back the Waters," 158.

8. Robert W. Harrison, *Swamp Land Reclamation in Louisiana, 1849–1879: A Study of Flood Control and Land Drainage in Louisiana under the Swamp Land Grant of 1849* (Baton Rouge: U.S. Bureau of Agricultural Economics, 1951), 3.

9. "An Act Relative to Roads, Levees, and the Police of Cattle," *Acts Passed before the Second Session of the First Legislature of the Territory of Orleans* (New Orleans: Bradford and Anderson, 1807), 312–34.

10. Zadok Cramer, *The Navigator*, 8th ed. (1814; Ann Arbor: University Microfilms, 1966), 221; Fred B. Kniffen, "The Lower Mississippi Valley: European Settlement, Utilization, and Modification," in *Cultural Diffusion and Landscapes*, ed. H. Jesse Walker and Randall A. Detro, Geoscience and Man, vol. 27 (Baton Rouge: Geosciences Publications, Department of Geography and Anthropology, Louisiana State University, 1990), 3–34; Harrison, *Alluvial Empire*, 160.

11. New Orleans Conseil de Ville, "Resolution of the Common Council, 22 May 1805," Ordinances and Resolutions, 1805–1835, New Orleans Municipal Archives, microform AB 311, New Orleans Public Library, New Orleans.

12. "Regulations of Port of New Orleans" (no date); poster and monthly notes from the mayor indicating levee tax receipts, 1819, contained in New Orleans Municipal Records Collection, T-58, box 7, folder 7, Hill Memorial Library, Louisiana State University, Baton Rouge.

13. New Orleans Conseil de Ville, "Resolution Relative to a Protest in the Congress Concerning the Levee Tax," Ordinances and Resolutions, 1805–1835, New Orleans Municipal Archives, microform AB 311, New Orleans Public Library, New Orleans. Creole-American conflicts are discussed in Ari Kelman, *A River and Its City: The Nature of Landscape in New Orleans* (Berkeley: University of California Press, 2003), esp. 19–49.

14. Darby, *Geographical Description*, 56–57.

15. See John Monette, "The Mississippi Floods," *Publications of the Mississippi Historical Society* 7 (1903): 442. The 1785 flood broke through a crevasse and inundated New Orleans. See Elliott, *Improvement of the Lower Mississippi*, 105.

16. Edward Fenner, "On the Inundation of 1816," *Southern Medical Reports* 1 (1849): 56–62.

17. New Orleans Municipal Records Collection, T-58, 1812–1828, miscellaneous boxes, Hill Memorial Library, Louisiana State University, Baton Rouge.

18. "An Ordinance Concerning the Roads, Bridges, and Levees within the Liberties of the City of New Orleans" (approved July 28, 1815), *A General Digest of the Ordinances and Resolutions of the Corporation of New Orleans* (New Orleans: Jerome Bayon, 1831), 39–49.

19. Henry M. Brackenridge, *Views of Louisiana* (1814; Chicago: Quadrangle Books, 1962), 176–77.

20. Henry Righton, *Standard History of New Orleans, Louisiana* (Chicago: Lewis, 1900), 173.

21. Fenner, "On the Inundation," 56.

22. *Ibid.*, 58.

23. *Ibid.*, 61–62.

24. Monette, "Mississippi Floods," 444.

25. Elliott, *Improvement of the Lower Mississippi*, 107.

26. See First Municipality Council Index 1844–1852, New Orleans Municipal Archives, microform AB 300, New Orleans Public Library, New Orleans. The index lists municipal authorizations to purchase lumber and gravel to be used in levee maintenance and also indicates where levee repairs took place. The fracture of the city into three municipalities stemmed from conflict over control of the waterfront and between the American and Creole/immigrant political factions. See also Leon Soulé, "The Creole-American Struggle in New Orleans Politics, 1850–1862," *Louisiana Historical Quarterly* 40 (1957): 54–83. The city was reconsolidated in 1852.

27. P. O. Hebert, *Annual Report of the State Engineer to the Legislature of the State of Louisiana* (New Orleans: The Jeffersonian, 1846), 10–11.

28. P. O. Hebert, *Annual Report of the State Engineer to the Legislature of the State of Louisiana* (New Orleans: Magne and Weisse, 1847), 10–12.

29. Caleb Forshay, "Crevasse of 1849: A Chapter of the Hydrography of the Mississippi River," *Southern Medical Reports* 1 (1849): 63–70.

30. *Ibid.*, 70.

31. *Ibid.*, 70. See also Harry Kmen, "New Orleans's Forty Days in 1949," *Louisiana Historical Quarterly* 40 (1957): 25–45.

32. Edward Fenner, "New Orleans," *Southern Medical Reports* 1 (1849): 17–19.

33. "The Crevasse," *New Orleans Daily Delta*, 19 January 1850, 2.

34. A. D. Wooldridge, "Report of the Internal Improvements of Louisiana for 1849," *Documents of the First Session of the Third Legislature of the State of Louisiana* (Baton Rouge: 1850), 12.

35. *Ibid.*, 12–14.

36. For an extensive discussion of floodwater diversion through the Atchafalaya Basin, see Martin Reuss, *Designing the Bayous: The Control of Water in the Atchafalaya Basin 1800–1995* (Alexandria, VA: U.S. Army Corps of Engineers, Office of History, 1998).

37. Wooldridge, "Report of Internal Improvements," 14. This site became the location of the first outlet built in the 1930s.

38. U.S. Senate, *Report: The Swamp and Overflowed Lands in Louisiana*, Ex. Doc. 68, 31st Cong., 1st sess., 1950, 3.

39. In 1852 the New Orleans Common Council revised its levee law and assigned maintenance responsibilities to individuals who leased waterfront property for wharves and landings from the city. The ordinance required them to maintain a hard surface on the river side, fill any collapsed sections, and maintain the outer bulkheads. Henry T. Leovy, *The Laws and General Ordinances of the City of New Orleans* (New Orleans: Wharton, 1957), 335–36.

40. "The Levee," *New Orleans Daily True Delta*, 13 May 1862, 3; "Falling Fast," *New Orleans Daily True Delta*, 30 May 1862, 1.

41. "Bonnet Carre Crevasse," *New Orleans Daily Picayune*, 22 April 1871, 1; "City Flood—Hagan Avenue," *New Orleans Daily Picayune*, 4 June 1871, 2.

42. Henry Abbott, "Analysis of Floods Subsequent to that of 1858," *Annual Report, Chief of Engineers*, part 1 (Washington: U.S. Army, 1875), 581.

43. Elliott, *Improvement of the Lower Mississippi*, 162–63; Harrison, *Alluvial Empire*, 146–49.

44. Elliott, *Improvement of the Lower Mississippi*, 166.

45. "Backwater: Rear of City Inundated," *New Orleans Daily Picayune*, 22 April 1890, 1; "The Inundation," *New Orleans Daily Picayune*, 23 April 1890, 1; "Submerged Suburbs," *New Orleans Daily Picayune*, 24 April 1890, 1.

46. Excellent accounts of the 1927 flood appear in John M. Barry, *Rising Tide: The Great Mississippi Flood of 1927 and How It Changed America* (New York: Touchstone, 1997), and Kelman, *River and Its City*, 157–96.

47. Ann Vileisis, *Discovering the Unknown Landscape: A History of America's Wetlands* (Washington: Island, 1997), 44–47; Conevery Bolton Valenčius, *The Health of the Country: How American Settlers Understood Themselves and Their Land* (New York: Basic Books, 2002), 133–52. Discussions of traditional French use of wetlands appear in Matthew Hatvany, "The Origins of the Acadian Aboiteau," *Historical Geography* 30 (2002): 121–38, and Karl Butzer, "French Wetland Agriculture in Atlantic Canada and Its European Roots: Different Avenues to Historical Diffusion," *Annals of the Association of American Geographers* 92 (2002): 451–70.

48. Claude C. Sturgill and Charles L. Price, eds., "On the Present State of the Province of Louisiana in the Year 1720, by Jean Baptiste Bernard de la Harpe," *Louisiana Historical Quarterly* 54:3 (1971): 45.

49. Donald W. Davis and Randall A. Detro, "New Orleans Drainage and Reclamation: A 200 Year Problem," *Zeitschrift fur Geomorphologie*, n.s., 34 (May 1980): 87–96; Giraud, *History of French Louisiana*, 206–8. See also Wilson, *Vieux Carré*, 19, 26–29.

50. Laura L. Porteous, trans., "Sanitary Conditions in New Orleans under the Spanish Regime, 1799–1800," *Louisiana Historical Quarterly* 15:4 (1932): 611.

51. James Pitot, *Observations on the Colony of Louisiana from 1796 to 1802*, trans. Henry C. Pitot (Baton Rouge: Louisiana State University Press, 1979), 110.

52. Pitot, *Observations on the Colony*, 111. One aspect of nineteenth-century etiology that puzzled physicians was the frequent outbreak of disease along the New Orleans waterfront— the high ground. Medical practitioners addressed this source area with quarantines, following the contagion theory of disease. See Jo Ann Carrigan, *The Saffron Scourge: A History of Yellow Fever in Louisiana, 1796–1905* (Lafayette: Center for Louisiana Studies, 1994), esp. 77–80.

53. Noah Webster, *A Brief History of Epidemic and Pestilential Diseases* (1799; New York: B. Franklin, 1970).

54. M. Le Page du Pratz, *The History of Louisiana*, ed. Joseph G. Tregle, Jr. (1774; Baton Rouge: Louisiana State University Press, 1975), 128–29.

55. Pitot, *Observations on the Colony*, 110.

56. William Darby, *The Emigrant's Guide to the Western and Southwestern States and Territories* (New York: Kirk and Mercein, 1818), 235.

57. Jabez W. Heustis, *Physical Observations and Medical Tracts on the Topography and Diseases of Louisiana* (New York: T. and J. Swords, 1817), 39.

58. Timothy Flint, *A Condensed Geography and History of the Western States, or the Mississippi Valley*, vol. 1 (1828; Gainesville, FL: Scholar's Facsimiles and Reprints, 1970), 557.

59. Fenner, "New Orleans," 23.

60. New Orleans Board of Health, *Annual Report of the Board of Health of the City of New Orleans for 1849* (New Orleans: 1850), 9.

61. E. H. Barton, *Report to the Louisiana State Medical Society on the Meteorology, Vital Statistics, and Hygiene of the State of Louisiana* (New Orleans: Davies and Son, 1851), 39–40. See also Dell Upton, "The Master Street of the World: The Levee," in *Streets: Critical Perspectives on Public Space*, ed. Zeynep Celik, Diane Favro, and Richard Ingersoll (Berkeley: University of California Press, 1994), 277–88.

62. Du Pratz, *History of Louisiana*, 239. For a discussion of colonial and antebellum forest removal see John H. Moore, "The Cypress Lumber Industry of the Lower Mississippi during the Colonial Period," *Louisiana History* 24 (1983): 25–47, and John A. Eisterhold, "Lumber and Trade in the Lower Mississippi Valley and New Orleans, 1800–1860," *Louisiana History* 13 (1971): 71–91.

63. Porteous, "Sanitary Conditions in New Orleans," 614–15.

64. C. C. Robin, *Voyage to Louisiana*, trans. Stuart O. Landry (1807; New Orleans: Pelican, 1966), 32–33.

65. Darby, *Geographical Description*, 73; Timothy Flint, *Recollections of the Last Ten Years* (1826; New York: Knopf, 1932), 303–4; Harriet Martineau, *Retrospect of Western Travel* (New York: Harper and Brothers, 1838), 263; Fenner, "New Orleans," 17.

66. New Orleans Canal and Banking Company, *Report of a Committee of the Directors on the Canal and Other Works* (New Orleans: 1831).

67. "An Act to Provide for the Draining and Clearing of Marshy Grounds and Cypress Swamps Situated between the City of New Orleans, Its Incorporated Suburbs, and Lake Pontchartrain" (New Orleans: Brusle and Lesseps, 1839), 3–4.

68. New Orleans Board of Health, *Annual Report*, 10.

69. Barton, *Report to the Louisiana Medical Society*, 40.

70. E. H. Barton, *The Cause and Prevention of Yellow Fever Contained in the Report of the Sanitary Commission of New Orleans* (Philadelphia: Lindsay and Blakiston, 1855).

71. In 1847 the city council authorized the city surveyor to buy trees for a promenade. First Municipality Council, Index 1844–1852, New Orleans Municipal Archives, microform AB 300, New Orleans Public Library, New Orleans.

72. In all likelihood, the forests in the 1860s were mostly second-growth cypress stands. See N. P. Banks, Approaches to New Orleans (map), U.S. Army, Department of the Gulf, 1863. In rural areas upstream, Henry Shreve led an aggressive campaign to remove riparian forests to prevent snag formation. See Ari Kelman, "Forests and Other River Perils," in *Transforming New Orleans and Its Environs: Centuries of Change*, ed. Craig E. Colten (Pittsburgh: University of Pittsburgh Press), 45–63, and Craig E. Colten, "Cypress in New Orleans: Revisiting the Observations of Le Page du Pratz," *Louisiana History* 64 (2003): 463–77.

73. John Duffy, "Nineteenth-Century Public Health in New York and New Orleans: A Comparison," *Louisiana History* 15:4 (1974): 325–37; Carrigan, *Saffron Scourge*, 55.

74. Heustis, *Physical Observations*, 41–42.

75. Fenner, "New Orleans," 26.

76. Barton, *Report to the Louisiana Medical Society*, 35–36.

77. Edward Fenner, "Claiborne and Girod Canals," *Southern Medical Reports* 2 (1850): 53.

78. John S. Kendall, *History of New Orleans*, vol. 2 (Chicago: Lewis, 1922), 565; James S. Winston, "Notes on the Economic History of New Orleans, 1803–1836," *Mississippi Valley Historical Review* 11:2 (1924): 218; T. P. Thompson, "Early Financing in New Orleans," *Publications of the Louisiana Historical Society* 7 (1913–14): 16–17.

79. "The Canal of Carondelet," *Louisiana Gazette*, 9 July 1810, 2.

80. Flooding produced by northerly winds remained a problem into the 1840s. Fenner, "New Orleans," 19.

81. Thomas Jefferson, letter to M. du Plantier, 24 September 1808, Tulane University Special Collections, M 998, New Orleans.

82. Flint, *Condensed Geography and History*, 557.

83. Earth Search, Inc., *National Register Evaluation of New Orleans Drainage System, Orleans Parish, Louisiana*, report no. COEMVN/PD-98-09 (New Orleans: U.S. Army Corps of Engineers, 1999), 10.

84. George E. Waring, Jr., and George W. Cable, *History and Present Condition of New Orleans, Louisiana* (Washington: U.S. Department of the Interior, 1881), 53.

85. Wilton P. Ledet, "The History of the City of Carrollton," *Louisiana Historical Quarterly* 21 (1938): 228–29; Thompson, "Early Financing in New Orleans," 24–27.

86. "Act to Provide for the Draining and Clearing," 5–8.

87. Kendall, *History of New Orleans,* 565.

88. Soulé, "Creole-American Struggle."

89. George T. Dunbar, *Report on the Draining of the Back Lands beyond Claiborne Street* (New Orleans: Brusle and Lesseps, 1840).

90. Fenner, "New Orleans," 17–18.

91. "Special Report on the Fevers of New Orleans, 1850," *Southern Medical Reports* 2 (1850): 83.

92. A detailed analysis of the 1853 epidemic is found in John Duffy, *Sword of Pestilence: The New Orleans Yellow Fever Epidemic of 1853* (Baton Rouge: Louisiana State University Press, 1966).

93. Reported in Earl F. Niehaus, *The Irish in New Orleans* (Baton Rouge: Louisiana State University Press, 1965), 32.

94. Barton, *Cause and Prevention of Yellow Fever,* 219.

95. "Report of the Board of Health," *Documents of the Second Session of the Third Legislature of the State of Louisiana, 1857* (New Orleans: John Claiborne, 1857).

96. New Orleans was not alone among southern cities that were unable to develop comprehensive municipal public works in the antebellum period. See Carl V. Harris, *Political Power in Birmingham, 1871–1921* (Knoxville: University of Tennessee Press, 1977), and Stuart Galishoff, "Germs Know No Color Line: Black Health and Public Policy in Atlanta," *Journal of the History of Medicine and Allied Sciences* 40 (1985): 22–41.

97. Lewis G. de Russy, *Special Report Relative to the Cost of Draining the Swamp Lands Bordering on Lake Pontchartrain* (Baton Rouge: J. M. Taylor, 1858).

98. Louis H. Pile, *Report on Drainage Communicated to the Common Council* (New Orleans: Bulletin, 1857).

99. Flint, *Recollections of the Last Ten Years,* 290–317; Flint, *Condensed Geography and History,* 542.

100. Benjamin H. Latrobe, *The Journal of Latrobe, 1798–1819* (New York: D. Appleton, 1905), 242–43.

101. "Special Report on the Fevers of New Orleans," 122.

NOTES TO CHAPTER 2

1. Edward Barton, "Report upon the Sanitary Condition of New Orleans," in City Council of New Orleans, *Report of the Sanitary Commission of New Orleans on the Yellow Fever Epidemic of 1853* (New Orleans: Picayune, 1854), 388–98.

2. For a critical discussion of beliefs in environmental influences on public health see, Felix Driver, "Moral Geographies: Social Science and the Urban Environment in Mid-Nineteenth-Century England," *Transactions of the Institute of British Geographers,* n.s., 13 (1988): 275–87.

3. Jacque L. Emel and Elizabeth Brooks, "Changes in Form and Function of Property Rights Institutions under Threatened Resource Scarcity," *Annals of the Association of American Geographers* 78:2 (1988): 241–52. The shift from common-law solutions to regulatory approaches is

often associated with common property resources such as fish and water but is evident in the more clearly defined rules and regulations supervised by administrative bodies.

4. Galen Cranz, *The Politics of Park Design: A History of Urban Parks in America* (Cambridge: MIT Press, 1982), esp. chaps. 1 and 2. See also Terence Young, "Modern Urban Parks," *Geographical Review* 85 (October 1995): 535–51, and Rutherford H. Platt, "From Commons to Commons: Evolving Concepts of Open Spaces in North American Cities," in *The Ecological City: Preserving and Restoring Urban Biodiversity,* ed. Rutherford H. Platt, Rowan A. Rowntree, and Pamela Muick (Amherst: University of Massachusetts Press, 1994), 21–39.

5. Barton, "Report upon the Sanitary Condition," 390–91.

6. The basic concept of nuisance law is described in Rutherford H. Platt, *Land Use and Society: Geography, Law, and Public Policy* (Washington: Island, 1996), 98–100.

7. Charles Richardson, *A New Dictionary of the English Language* (London: Bell and Daldy, 1863), s.v. "nuisance."

8. Robert Hunter and Charles Morris, eds., *Universal Dictionary of the English Language* (New York: Peter Collier, 1897), s.v. "nuisance."

9. Despite Louisiana's use of French civil law rather than English common law, there were similarities between the two with regard to nuisances. Territorial courts ruled that the city of New Orleans could regulate activities that affected cleanliness or public health. P. J. Benjamin and T. Slidell, comp., *Digest of the Reported Decisions of the Superior Court of the Late Territory of Orleans,* rev. and enl. ed. (New Orleans: E. Johns and Co., 1840), 465. State courts heard suits charging both private and public nuisance conditions and similar offenses in other states. Edward White and William Dart, *The Louisiana Digest Annotated,* vol. 5 (Indianapolis: Bobbs-Merrill, 1918), 567–74.

10. See William B. Meyer and Michael Brown, "Locational Conflict in a Nineteenth-Century City," *Political Geography Quarterly* 8:2 (1989): 107–22; Craig E. Colten, "Historical Hazards: The Geography of Relict Industrial Wastes," *Professional Geographer* 42 (1991): 143–56; Graham Taylor, *Satellite Cities: A Study of Industrial Suburbs* (New York: Appleton and Co., 1915). Discussions about increasingly stringent water pollution laws regulating nuisance conditions appear in Ted Steinberg, *Nature Incorporated: Industrialization and Waters of New England* (Amherst: University of Massachusetts Press, 1991), and John T. Cumbler, *Reasonable Use: The People, the Environment, and the State, New England, 1790–1930* (Oxford: Oxford University Press, 2001).

11. The city contracted to clean out various sections of the Claiborne Canal in 1860. New Orleans Surveyor's Records, Specification Book, vol. 3, *1860–1865,* 141–44, New Orleans Municipal Archives, microform KG 630, New Orleans Public Library, New Orleans.

12. Benjamin F. Butler, *Butler's Book of Everyday Reference* (Boston: A. M. Thayer, 1892), 393–413; Howard P. Johnson, "New Orleans under General Butler," *Louisiana Historical Quarterly* 24:2 (1941): 46–49.

13. "Board of Engineers to Mature and Recommend Some General and Harmonious Plan for the Present and Future Draining of the City of New Orleans," pamphlet (New Orleans: Simmons and Co., 1869), 4, Hill Memorial Library, Louisiana State University, Baton Rouge.

14. Most other cities were able to install water-carriage systems to transport sewerage. With limited gradient and a portion of the city below sea level this option was infeasible in New Orleans. See Joel A. Tarr, Francis C. McMichael, and Terry Yosie, "Water and Wastes: A Retrospective Assessment of Wastewater Technology in the United States, 1800–1932," *Technology and Culture* 25:2 (1984): 226–63.

15. Many cities in the second half of the nineteenth century relied on corporations to furnish basic municipal services. See Martin V. Melosi, *The Sanitary City: Urban Infrastructure in America from Colonial Times to the Present* (Baltimore: Johns Hopkins University Press, 2000), esp. 73–90. New Orleans made attempts to manage its public utilities but generally relied on private or voluntary organizations due to "municipal poverty," particularly during Reconstruction. See James Breeden, "Joseph Jones and Public Health in the New South," *Louisiana History* 32 (1995): 341–70, and Joy J. Jackson, *New Orleans in the Gilded Age: Politics and Urban Progress, 1880–1896* (Baton Rouge: Louisiana State University Press, 1969), 172–75, 203.

16. Henry J. Leovy, *General Ordinances of the City of New Orleans* (New Orleans: Wharton, 1857), articles 543 and 544, 178–79.

17. Gordon Gillson, *Louisiana State Board of Health: The Formative Years* (New Orleans: Louisiana Board of Health, 1967), 112; New Orleans Street Commissioner, Ledger of Accounts, 1858–1860, 1, New Orleans Municipal Archives, microform LC 510, New Orleans Public Library, New Orleans; Stanford Chille, "The Yellow Fever, Sanitary Condition, and Vital Statistics of New Orleans during its Military Occupation, the Four Years 1862–1865," *New Orleans Journal of Medicine* 23 (July 1870): 586. See also Breeden, "Joseph Jones and Public Health."

18. Margaret Humphreys, *Yellow Fever and the South* (New Brunswick: Rutgers University Press, 1999), 4; Jo Ann Carrigan, *Saffron Scourge: A History of Yellow Fever in Louisiana, 1796–1905* (Lafayette: Center for Louisiana Studies, 1994), 113–118, 165.

19. Joseph Holt, "Report of Sanitary Inspector, First District," in *Annual Report of the Board of Health of the State of Louisiana, 1879* (New Orleans: Graham, 1880), 46. The First Sanitary District comprised the American Sector from Canal Street uptown to Felicity Street, Wards 1, 2, and 3. Privies did pose potential public health threats in terms of typhoid and cholera.

20. William Schupert, "Report of Sanitary Inspector, Third District," in *Annual Report, 1879*, 109. The Third Sanitary District extended downstream from Esplanade Avenue to the military barracks, Wards 7, 8, and 9.

21. Tabulations of privy conditions in each of the sanitary districts appear in *Annual Report, 1879*, 46–193.

22. Joseph Holt, "The Evil and the Remedy for the Privy System of New Orleans," in New Orleans Auxiliary Sanitary Association, *Domestic Sanitation* (New Orleans: Hansell, 1879), 6–7. Another contemporary estimate proposed that New Orleans residents dumped over 500,000 tons of excreta into their privies annually, while only 25,000 tons were removed to the river. Plan and Specifications with Approximate Estimate of the Cost to Perfect the Drainage of the City (New Orleans: Graham and Son, 1889), 15.

23. The Second Sanitary District included the French Quarter and extended between Canal Street and Esplanade Avenue (Wards 4, 5, and 6), and the Fourth Sanitary District included the Garden District, stretching from Felicity Street uptown to Toledano Street (Wards 10 and 11).

Algiers on the west bank made up the Fifth Sanitary District, and the uptown neighborhoods constituted the Sixth. Joseph Holt, "History of the Yellow Fever Epidemic in the Fourth District," Excerpt from the Annual Report of the Board of Health for 1878, 8–9, Hill Memorial Library, Louisiana State University, Baton Rouge. The call for water closets followed the practices employed in other cities. See Tarr, McMichael, and Yosie, "Water and Wastes," 226–63.

24. Edwin L. Jewell, *Jewell's Digest of the City Ordinances* (New Orleans: 1887), Ordinance 4077 (enacted 1877), 76–77.

25. Breeden, "Joseph Jones and Public Health"; Jackson, *New Orleans in the Gilded Age,* 172–77.

26. New Orleans Auxiliary Sanitary Association, *Report of the Flushing Committee* (New Orleans: Dunn and Brothers, 1881), 7–8.

27. New Orleans Auxiliary Sanitary Association, *Report of the Flushing Committee,* 3–4, and Edward Fenner, Annual Address of the New Orleans Sanitary Association, 13 November 1880 (New Orleans: Dunn and Brothers, 1880), 11–12.

28. "Report of the Committee on Sewerage and Drainage to the City Council," 3 August 1880, Drainage and Paving vertical file, Jones Library, Tulane University, New Orleans; John Roy, Report on the Drainage and Sewerage (New Orleans: Rivers, 1880). The Memphis system, designed by George Waring, was an extremely influential municipal sewerage system. See Joel A. Tarr, "The Separate vs. Combined Sewer Problem: A Case Study in Urban Technology Design Choice," *Journal of Urban History* 5 (1979): 308–39.

29. *Report of the Board of Health of New Orleans* (New Orleans: 1900), 166–67.

30. *The New Orleans Sewerage System, Inaugural Ceremonies, 18 April 1894* (New Orleans: Graham and Sons, 1894), 2–7. The New Orleans system was to employ a "separate" sewer system that would carry only sewerage and not surface runoff.

31. George Earl, "Drainage, Sewerage, and Water Supply of New Orleans," paper presented to the 54th Annual Meeting of the American Medical Association (1903), 17, Drainage and Paving vertical file, Jones Library, Tulane University, New Orleans.

32. Roy, Report on Drainage and Sewerage, 7; New Orleans Auxiliary Sanitary Association, *Report of the Flushing Committee,* 13–14.

33. S. S. Herrick, "Numerical Sanitation: A Calculus of Subsoil Drainage in New Orleans," *Public Health Papers and Reports* 6 (1880): 345–46.

34. Joseph Jones, *Quarantine and Sanitary Operations of the Board of Health of the State of Louisiana* (Baton Rouge: Jastremski, 1884), 281–87.

35. Herrick, "Numerical Sanitation," 346; Roy, *Report on Sewerage and Drainage,* 20.

36. Edward Fenner and J. O. Nixon, The Origin and Objects of the New Orleans Draining and Paving Association (New Orleans: Graham and Sons, 1886), 6.

37. Breeden, "Joseph Jones and Public Health in the New South"; Jackson, *New Orleans in the Gilded Age,* 172–77.

38. The batture is the area between the artificial levee and the river. Edward H. Barton, "Report of the Sanitary Commission," 390.

39. Barton, "Report upon the Sanitary Condition," 390.

40. Leovy, *General Ordinances of the City of New Orleans,* articles 508 and 529, 175–76.

41. Henry Leovy and C. H. Luzenberg, *The Laws and General Ordinances of the City of New Orleans* (New Orleans: Simmons, 1870), article 435, 179.

42. *Ibid.*

43. *Annual Report of the Board of Health, 1874* (New Orleans: Republican, 1875), 85.

44. Holt, "History of the Yellow Fever Epidemic."

45. *Annual Report, 1879,* 153.

46. Act 40 of 1882, cited in *Report of the Board of Health of the City of New Orleans, 1900–1901* (New Orleans: 1901), 166–67.

47. J. Q. Flynn, *Flynn's Digest of City Ordinances* (New Orleans: Graham and Son, 1896), Ordinance 7860, 370–77.

48. Louisiana Board of Health, *Biennial Report of the Board of Health to the General Assembly, 1894–1895* (Baton Rouge: Daily Advocate, 1896), 95.

49. Jackson, *New Orleans in the Gilded Age,* 138–39, 160; Gordon Gilson, *Louisiana State Board of Health: The Progressive Years* (Baton Rouge: Moran Industries, 1976), 70; "Coming Closer to a Garbage Decision," *New Orleans Daily Picayune,* 26 August 1897, 3; John Kendall, *History of New Orleans,* vol. 2 (Chicago: Lewis, 1922), 509.

50. Robert M. Lewis, "New Orleans Municipal Waste Collection and Disposal: Public and Private Cost Alternatives" (master's paper, University of New Orleans, 1978), 18–20.

51. Roger Baudier, "Sanitation in New Orleans: First Water Works in New Orleans," *Southern Plumbing and Heating Retailer* (February 1955): 10–12; "Sanitation in New Orleans: First Board of Health and First Health Ordinance," *Southern Plumbing and Heating Retailer* (March 1955): n.p.; Gary Donaldson, "Bringing Water to the Crescent City: Benjamin Latrobe and the New Orleans Waterworks System," *Louisiana History* 28:4 (1987): 381–96.

52. *Annual Report by the Commissioners of the City Water Works, 1869* (New Orleans: Caxton, 1870), 8; Louisiana Board of Health, *Annual Report, 1880,* 47–193.

53. Louisiana Board of Health, *Annual Report, 1880,* 16, 46; New Orleans Board of Health, *Report, 1900–1901* (New Orleans: 1901), 66–77.

54. *Annual Report, 1879,* 74, 160.

55. *Annual Report, 1879,* 46–193; Louisiana Board of Health, *Biennial Report to the General Assembly, 1894–1895,* 98.

56. Barton, "Report upon the Sanitary Condition," 429–30.

57. Louisiana Board of Health, *Annual Report of the Board of Health, 1871* (New Orleans: 1872), 31.

58. Holt, "History of the Yellow Fever Epidemic," 10.

59. Louisiana House of Representatives, Special Committee on the Removal of Slaughter Houses, Minute Book, 1867, MS 1037, Hill Memorial Library, Louisiana State University, Baton Rouge.

60. Leovy and Luzenberg, *Laws and General Ordinances,* 184–85.

61. *Annual Report by the Commissioners of the City Water Works, 1869,* 8.

62. Holt, "History of the Yellow Fever Epidemic," 10.

63. New Orleans Department of Water Works and Public Buildings, *Report, 1877* (New Orleans: Hyatt, 1878), 5–10.

64. Although most cities were moving towards centralized municipal control of their public works, New Orleans's chronic fiscal crisis inhibited this move. See Melosi, *Sanitary City,* 75–79, and Jackson, *New Orleans in the Gilded Age,* 203.

65. New Orleans Water Works, *Annual Report, 1879* (New Orleans: Hansell, 1879), 1–2.

66. See legislative Act 85 passed in 1882, Louisiana Department of Health, *Supplement to the Annual Report: Laws and Ordinances Relating to Health and Sanitation* (New Orleans: 1896), 38–39.

67. New Orleans Water Works, *Annual Report, 1882* (New Orleans: Hyatt, 1882); New Orleans Water Works, *Annual Report, 1883* (New Orleans: Hyatt, 1883); New Orleans Water Works, *Annual Report, 1884* (New Orleans: Hyatt, 1884); Jewell, *Digest of the City Ordinances,* 381–83.

68. See Melosi, *Sanitary City,* esp. chap. 4. New York's water system is discussed in Matthew Gandy, *Concrete and Clay: Reworking Nature in New York City* (Cambridge: MIT Press, 2002), chap. 1.

69. New Orleans Water Works, *Annual Report, 1883,* 6; Joseph Jones, *Quarantine and Sanitary Operations of the Board of Health of the State of Louisiana during 1881–1883* (Baton Rouge: Leon Jastremski, 1884), 382–93.

70. Filtration systems were still very experimental; in 1880 only three municipalities had viable sand filtration systems in place. Melosi, *Sanitary City,* 87.

71. New Orleans Water Works, *Eleventh Annual Report* (New Orleans: Hyatt, 1889), 3; *Fourteenth Annual Report* (New Orleans: Hyatt, 1892), 3; and New Orleans Water Works, *Seventeenth Annual Report* (New Orleans: Hyatt, 1895), 4.

72. New Orleans Water Works, *Fourteenth Annual Report,* 8–9.

73. New Orleans Water Works, *Sixteenth Annual Report* (New Orleans: Hyatt, 1894), 3–4; New Orleans Water Works, *Seventeenth Annual Report,* 1.

74. Louisiana Board of Health, *Biennial Report to the General Assembly, 1896–1897* (Baton Rouge: Baton Rouge News Publishing Company, 1898), 105; New Orleans Board of Health, *Report, 1900–1901,* 67–68.

75. Louisiana legislature, *Investigation of the New Orleans Water Works Company* (New Orleans: Picayune, 1898).

76. Barton, "Report upon the Sanitary Condition," 391.

77. Jones, *Quarantine and Sanitary Operations,* 333–36.

78. *A Digest of the Ordinances, Resolutions, By-Laws and Regulations of the Corporation of New Orleans* (New Orleans: Gaston, 1836), 65–71; Mary Louise Christovich et al., eds., *New Orleans Architecture,* vol. 3, *The Cemeteries* (Gretna, LA: Pelican, 1974), 5–16.

79. Louisiana Board of Health, *Annual Report, 1870* (New Orleans: 1871), 31.

80. The changing geography of cemetery locations is recounted in David C. Sloane, *The Last Great Necessity: Cemeteries in American History* (Baltimore: Johns Hopkins University Press, 1991), 34–38, 44–68, and in William Pattison, "The Cemeteries of Chicago: A Phase of Land Utilization," *Annals of the Association of American Geographers* 45 (1955): 245–57.

81. Jones, *Quarantine and Sanitary Operations*, 328; Leovy, *Laws and General Ordinances*, 36.

82. Louisiana Board of Health, *Biennial Report to the General Assembly, 1888–1889* (Baton Rouge: Advocate Book, 1890), quote from 127–29.

83. Holt, "History of the Yellow Fever Epidemic," 12.

84. Barton, "Report upon the Sanitary Condition," 391.

85. Leovy, *Laws and General Ordinances*, 89–90.

86. Leovy and Luzenberg, *Laws and General Ordinances*, 261.

87. Gustavus Devron, "Abattiors," *Public Health Papers and Reports* 6 (1880): 219–20.

88. E. S. Lewis testimony, in Louisiana House of Representatives, Special Committee on the Removal of Slaughterhouses, Minute Book, MS 1037, Hill Memorial Library, Louisiana State University, Baton Rouge, quoted in Ronald Labbe, "New Light on the Slaughterhouse Monopoly Act of 1869," in *Louisiana's Legal Heritage*, ed. Edward F. Haas (Pensacola, FL: Perdido Bay Press for the Louisiana State Museum, 1983), 143–61.

89. Devron, "Abattiors," 219–20.

90. A recent analysis of the slaughterhouse cases argues that the charges of monopoly and corruption were largely rhetorical. See Michael Ross, "Justice Miller's Reconstruction: The *Slaughter-House Cases*, Health Codes, and Civil Rights in New Orleans, 1861–1873," *Journal of Southern History* 64 (1998): 649–76.

91. For discussion of the slaughterhouse cases see, Wendy E. Parmet, "From Slaughter-House to Lochner: The Rise and Fall of the Constitutionalization of Public Health," *American Journal of Legal History* 40 (1996): 476–505, and Slaughter-House Cases, 83 US 36 (1872) and 16 Wall 36.

92. Devron, "Abattiors," 221–24; Louisiana Board of Health, *Annual Report of the Board of Health of the State of Louisiana, 1875* (New Orleans: Republican, 1876), 247–53.

93. Sanborn Map Company, *New Orleans*, vols. 1–4 (Pelham, NY: Sanborn Map, 1885, 1887, and 1893).

94. *Flynn's Digest of City Ordinances* (New Orleans: L. Graham and Son, 1896), 296–98, 361–65, 991–96, and 998–1001.

95. New Orleans Conseil de Ville, Ordinance 19 May 1812, New Orleans Municipal Archives, microform AB 311, New Orleans Public Library, New Orleans. For a full discussion of the park, see Elizabeth Honecker, "Jackson Square: A Look at Its Social and Physical Development as an Urban Open Space," (master's thesis, Louisiana State University, 1982).

96. New Orleans First Municipality Surveyor's Office, 5 March 1850, New Orleans Municipal Archives, microform KG 440, New Orleans Public Library, New Orleans.

97. "Washington Park," *New Orleans Times-Picayune*, 14 May 1976, n.p., in New Orleans—Parks, vertical file, Hill Memorial Library, Louisiana State University, Baton Rouge.

98. Kendall, *History of New Orleans*, 679; Mary Louise Christovich et al., eds., *New Orleans Architecture*, vol. 2, *The American Sector* (Gretna, LA: Pelican, 1972), 119.

99. Benjamin M. Norman, *Norman's New Orleans and Environs* (1845; Baton Rouge: Louisiana State University Press, 1976), 182–83. A thorough history of Congo Square's function is Jerah Johnson, "New Orleans's Congo Square: An Urban Setting for Early Afro-American Culture Formation," *Louisiana History* 72 (1991): 117–57.

100. Letters to the mayor, 6 February 1810, 11 June 1810, 27 August 1810, New Orleans Municipal Records Collection, Surveyor's Reports, Collection T-57, Hill Memorial Library, Louisiana State University, Baton Rouge; letter to the mayor from the Conseil de Ville, 30 January 1813, New Orleans Municipal Records Collection, Surveyor's Reports, Collection T-57, Hill Memorial Library, Louisiana State University, Baton Rouge.

101. Norman, *New Orleans and Environs,* 181.

102. Henry Lawrence, "Origins of the Tree-Lined Boulevard," *Geographical Review* 78:1 (1988): 355-74.

103. E. H. Barton, *Report to the Louisiana Medical Society on the Meteorology, Vital Statistics, and Hygiene of Louisiana* (New Orleans: Davies and Son, 1851), 40.

104. *Historical Souvenir: City Park* (New Orleans: New Orleans City Park Improvement Association, 1895), n.p.

105. Louisiana Writers' Project, *New Orleans City Park: Its First Fifty Years* (New Orleans: Board of Commissioners, 1941), 17-18. See also Sally K. Evans Reeves and William D. Reeves, *Historic City Park, New Orleans* (New Orleans: Friends of City Park, 1982).

106. Carolyn Galloway, "The Acquisition and Early Development of New Orleans's Audubon Park, 1871-1929," (master's thesis, University of New Orleans, 1977), 6-16; L. Ronald Forman and Joseph Logsdon with John Wilds, *Audubon Park: An Urban Eden* (Baton Rouge: Friends of the Zoo, 1985): 86-88.

107. Galloway, "Acquisition and Early Development," 17-21.

108. Audubon Park Improvement Association, *Yearbook* (New Orleans: 1891), 14-18.

109. Commissioners of Audubon Park, *Yearbook* (New Orleans: 1898), 21.

110. Audubon Park Association, *Yearbook* (New Orleans: 1897, 1898, 1900); Forman, Logsdon, and Wilds, *Audubon Park,* 110-21; Reeves and Reeves, *Historic City Park,* 18-19; Louisiana Writers' Project, *New Orleans City Park* (New Orleans: Gulf Printing, 1941), 7-11.

NOTES TO CHAPTER 3

Portions of this chapter appeared previously in the *Journal of Historical Geography* 28 (2002): 237-57. It is reprinted here with permission.

1. Peirce F. Lewis, *New Orleans: The Making of an Urban Landscape,* 2nd ed. (Santa Fe: Center for American Places in association with University of Virginia Press, 2003).

2. Originally Congo Square was a market for produce raised by the enslaved population; it was a popular gathering place for African Americans during the nineteenth century and fell into disuse as a public space by the 1890s. See Jerah Johnson, "New Orleans's Congo Square: An Urban Setting for Early Afro-American Culture Formation," *Louisiana History* 32 (1991): 117-57.

3. Susan Cutter defines environmental inequity as "the disproportionate effects of environmental degradation on people and places." See Susan Cutter, "Race, Class, and Environmental Justice," *Progress in Human Geography* 19:1 (1995): 111-22, esp. 112.

4. The concept of environmental development was presented in Christine M. Rosen, *The Limits of Power* (Cambridge: Cambridge University Press, 1986).

5. For a full discussion of urban sanitation history, see Martin V. Melosi, *The Sanitary City: Urban Infrastructure in America from Colonial Times to the Present* (Baltimore: Johns Hopkins University Press, 2000), esp. chaps. 6–9, pp. 103–75.

6. Daphne Spain, "Race Relations and Residential Segregation in New Orleans: Two Centuries of Paradox," *Annals of the American Academy of Political and Social Science* 441 (January 1979): 82–96.

7. For discussions of late-nineteenth-century public works see Joel A. Tarr, "The Separate vs. Combined Sewer Problem: A Case Study in Urban Technology Design Choice," *Journal of Urban History* 5 (May 1979): 308–39, Jon A. Peterson, "The Impact of Sanitary Reform upon American Urban Planning, 1840–1890," *Journal of Social History* 13 (Fall 1979): 83–103, and Stanley K. Schultz and Clay McShane, "To Engineer the Metropolis: Sewers, Sanitation, and City Planning in Late-Nineteenth-Century America," *Journal of American History* 65 (1978): 389–411.

8. C. Vann Woodward, *The Strange Career of Jim Crow*, 3rd rev. ed. (New York: Oxford University Press, 1974), 91.

9. For an overview of environmental equity justice literature see Cutter, "Race, Class, and Environmental Justice," 112–22. This discussion was sparked by R. D. Bullard, "Solid Waste Sites and the Black Houston Community," *Sociological Inquiry* 53 (1983): 273–88. See also V. Been, "Locally Undesirable Land Uses in Minority Neighborhoods: Disproportionate Siting or Market Dynamics," *Yale Law Journal* 10 (1994): 1383–422, Feng Liu, "Dynamics and Causation of Environmental Equity, Locally Unwanted Land Uses, and Neighborhood Change," *Environmental Management* 21(1997): 643–56, and Laura Pulido, Steve Sidawi, and Robert Vos, "An Archeology of Environmental Racism in Los Angeles," *Urban Geography* 17 (1996): 419–39.

10. Joy J. Jackson, *New Orleans in the Gilded Age: Politics and Urban Progress, 1880–1896* (Baton Rouge: Louisiana State University Press, 1969); Carl V. Harris, *Political Power in Birmingham, 1871–1921* (Knoxville: University of Tennessee Press, 1977); and Louis P. Cain, *Sanitation Strategy for a Lakefront Metropolis: The Case of Chicago* (Dekalb: Northern Illinois University Press, 1978).

11. Laura Pulido argues that not all racist activity is *deliberate* and that racism is the product of "those practices and ideologies, carried out by structures, institutions, and individuals that reproduce racial inequality and systematically undermine the well-being of racially subordinated people." See Laura Pulido, "Rethinking Environmental Racism: White Privilege and Urban Development in Southern California," *Annals of the Association of American Geographers* 90 (2000): 12–40.

12. John Kellog, "Negro Clusters in the Postbellum South," *Geographical Review* 67 (1977): 313–21. Milton Newton found similar patterns in small towns; see "Settlement Patterns as Artifacts of Social Structure," in *The Human Mirror*, ed. Miles Richardson (Baton Rouge: Louisiana State University Press, 1974), 339–62.

13. Blaine A. Brownell, "The Urban South Comes of Age, 1900–1940," in *The City in Southern History*, ed. Blaine Brownell and David Goldfield (Port Washington, NY: Kennikat, 1977), 123–58.

14. For a discussion of the emergence and perpetuation of ideas about race and sanitation see Kay Anderson, "The Idea of Chinatown: The Power of Place and Institutional Practice in Making of a Racial Category," *Annals of the Association of American Geographers* 77 (1987): 580–98.

15. Harris, *Political Power in Birmingham,* 179–80.

16. Stuart Galishoff, "Germs Know No Color Line: Black Health and Public Policy in Atlanta, 1900–1918," *Journal of the History of Medicine and Allied Sciences* 40:1 (1985): 22–41.

17. George M. Fredrickson, *Black Liberation: A Comparative History of Black Ideologies in the United States* (New York: Oxford University Press, 1995), 95–105.

18. A thorough discussion of restrictions on housing options can be found in David Delaney, *Race, Place, and the Law, 1836–1948* (Austin: University of Texas Press, 1998).

19. H. W. Gilmore, "The Old New Orleans and the New: A Case for Ecology," *American Sociological Review* 9 (1944): 385–94; Roger A. Fisher, "Racial Segregation in Ante Bellum New Orleans," *American Historical Review* 74 (1969): 926–37; Spain, "Race Relations and Residential Segregation in New Orleans," 82–96.

20. Fisher, "Racial Segregation in Ante Bellum New Orleans," 926–37; Dale Somers, "Black and White in New Orleans: A Study of Urban Race Relations," *Journal of Southern History* 40 (1974): 19–42.

21. Roger A. Fisher, "A Pioneer Protest: The New Orleans Street-Car Controversy of 1867," *Journal of Negro History* 53 (1968): 219–33.

22. Zane L. Miller, "Urban Blacks in the South, 1865–1920: The Richmond, Savannah, New Orleans, Louisville, and Birmingham Experience," in *The New Urban History,* ed. L. F. Schnore (Princeton: Princeton University Press, 1975), 184–204.

23. Forrest E. Laviolette, "The Negro in New Orleans," in *Studies in Housing and Minority Groups,* ed. Nathan Glazer and Davis McIntire (Princeton: Princeton University Press, 1975), 385–94. The first census tract data for New Orleans became available in 1940, and it illustrates a well-defined pattern of African American neighborhoods that had been developing but was far less obvious in the pre-1940 ward-based census information.

24. Gilmore, "The Old New Orleans and the New," 385–94. Others have argued that poorly drained areas became the residential areas for blacks throughout the south, Kellog, "Negro Urban Clusters in the Postbellum South," 310–21.

25. New Orleans Board of Engineers, *Drainage Report* (New Orleans: New Orleans Board of Engineers, 1868), 5.

26. *Annual Report of the Board of Health of the State of Louisiana, 1879* (New Orleans: Graham, 1880). The "bottom of the bowl" is identified by topographic maps prepared by the Sewerage and Water Board as the "21-foot contour." The mean level of Lake Pontchartrain (sea level) on this map was 21.26 feet and the low-water mark for the Mississippi River was 20.7 feet. Thus the bottom of the bowl was below both sea level and normal river stages and occupied an area in the center of the crescent. Most of the area north of the ridges was virtually flat and stood roughly at sea level.

27. New Orleans Advisory Board on Drainage, *Report on the Drainage of the City of New Orleans* (New Orleans: Fitzwilliam and Co., 1895), 5.

28. *Ibid.,* present drainage system map insert.

29. *Ibid.*, 18.

30. *Ibid.*, 24–28.

31. For a discussion of the development of New Orleans's downtown area, see Anne Mosher, Barry Keim, and Susan Franques, "Downtown Dynamics," *Geographical Review* 85:4 (1995): 497–517.

32. New Orleans Advisory Board on Drainage, *Report on the Drainage*, 32.

33. George Earl, "Drainage, Sewerage, and Water Supply of New Orleans," paper read at the 54th Annual Session of the American Medical Association, 1903, 8–9, Drainage and Paving vertical file, Jones Library, Tulane University, New Orleans.

34. Martin Behrman (mayor of New Orleans), "New Orleans: A History of Three Great Utilities," presented to the Convention of the League of American Municipalities, Milwaukee, Wisconsin, 1914, 6.

35. Henry Lawrence, "Changing Forms and Persistent Values: Historical Perspectives on the Urban Forest," in *Urban Forest Landscapes*, ed. Gordon A. Bradley (Seattle: University of Washington Press, 1995), 17–40; Henry W. Lawrence, "Origins of the Tree-Lined Boulevard," *Geographical Review* 78 (October 1988): 355–74.

36. Letter to the mayor from the Conseil de Ville, 30 January 1813, New Orleans Municipal Records Collection, Surveyor's Reports, Collection T-57, Hill Memorial Library, Louisiana State University, Baton Rouge; P. Maverick, engraver, Plan of the City of New Orleans (New York: F. B. Ogden, 1829), Historic New Orleans Collection, New Orleans; *Southern Travels: Journal of John H. B. Labrobe, 1834*, ed. Sam Wilson (New Orleans: Historic New Orleans Collection, 1986), 49.

37. New Orleans Municipal Surveyor's Office, record entries for 8 March 1850, 12 February 1852, and 28 March 1852, New Orleans Municipal Archives, microform KG 440, New Orleans Public Library, New Orleans.

38. "Citizens Irate Oaks Cut on St. Charles," *New Orleans Times-Democrat*, 14 January 1891, 3; "Tree Cutters Convicted," *New Orleans Times-Democrat*, 19 February 1891, 3.

39. New Orleans Sewerage and Water Board, *Twenty-First Semi-Annual Report* (New Orleans: 1910), 23.

40. New Orleans Sewerage and Water Board, *Twenty-Sixth Semi-Annual Report* (New Orleans: 1912), 48–49.

41. Louisiana State Board of Health, *Biennial Report, 1906–1907* (Baton Rouge: Daily State Press, 1908). In New Orleans, the annual malaria death rate per 100,000 was 55 for whites and 82 for blacks. For typhoid, the rates per 100,000 were 7 for whites and 31 for blacks. Mortality rates by ward are unavailable, hampering any assessment of more localized impacts of the drainage system.

42. Louisiana State Board of Health, *Biennial Report, 1906–1907*, 119.

43. New Orleans Sewerage and Water Board, *Twenty-First Semi-Annual Report*, 10.

44. New Orleans Sewerage and Water Board, *Semi-Annual Report* (New Orleans: 1900), 12–13.

45. New Orleans Sewerage and Water Board, *Twelfth Semi-Annual Report* (New Orleans:

1905), and New Orleans Sewerage and Water Board, *Thirteenth Semi-Annual Report* (New Orleans: 1906), water system map inserts.

46. New Orleans Sewerage and Water Board, *Fourteenth Semi-Annual Report* (New Orleans: 1906); New Orleans Sewerage and Water Board, *Sixteenth Semi-Annual Report* (New Orleans: 1907), map inserts of water system construction; New Orleans Sewerage and Water Board, *Twenty-First Semi-Annual Report*, 14–15 and map insert of water system construction progress.

47. New Orleans Parking Commission, Reports, 1909, 10, New Orleans Municipal Archives, microform LO 200, New Orleans Public Library, New Orleans.

48. New Orleans Parking Commission, Reports, 1910, 9, New Orleans Municipal Archives, microform LO 200, New Orleans Public Library, New Orleans.

49. New Orleans wards covered sizable territories that were not yet cleared of cypress or drained and therefore were uninhabitable. The ward maps presented here attempt to show population within the built-up areas of the administrative units. Also, the wards were the smallest unit available for presenting population information through 1930, and it is not possible to map white and black population concentrations at a finer resolution before census tract information was published in 1940.

50. "Friday Night Storm Was Handled All Right," *New Orleans Times-Picayune*, 12 May 1912, 6.

51. Named after their inventor, Albert B. Wood, the "Wood" pumps represented a breakthrough in technology and pumping efficiency. New Orleans Sewerage and Water Board, *Twenty-Sixth Semi-Annual Report;* New Orleans Sewerage and Water Board, *Thirty-Sixth Semi-Annual Report* (New Orleans: 1917).

52. New Orleans Sewerage and Water Board, *Forty-Second Semi-Annual Report* (New Orleans: 1920), 21.

53. Board of Health for the Parish of Orleans and the City of New Orleans, *Biennial Report, 1914–1915* (New Orleans: Brandao Printing, 1915), Table 1.

54. New Orleans Sewerage and Water Board, *Twenty-Third Semi-Annual Report* (New Orleans: 1911), 23–25.

55. New Orleans Sewerage and Water Board, *Twenty-Sixth Semi-Annual Report*, 75.

56. Behrman, "New Orleans: A History of Three Great Utilities," 7; New Orleans Sewerage and Water Board, *Forty-Second Semi-Annual Report*, 21.

57. New Orleans Sewerage and Water Board, *Forty-Second Semi-Annual Report*, 33.

58. New Orleans Sewerage and Water Board, *Twenty-First Semi-Annual Report*, 14–15 and insert map of water system; New Orleans Sewerage and Water Board, *Twenty-Sixth Semi-Annual Report*, 47; New Orleans Sewerage and Water Board, *Forty-Second Semi-Annual Report*, 25 and map insert of water system.

59. Orleans Board of Health and Metropolitan Life Insurance Company, *Report of the Health Survey of the City of New Orleans* (New Orleans: Brandao Printing, 1919), 46–49.

60. "Spirit of Revolt Is Rampant All along Esplanade Avenue," *New Orleans Times-Picayune*, 6 February 1920, 2; "Indignant Public Saves Old Trees," *New Orleans Times-Picayune*, 7 February 1920, 2.

61. New Orleans Sewerage and Water Board, *Fifty-Sixth Annual Report* (New Orleans: 1927), 113.

62. "South Is Deluged as City Suffers Heavy Downpour," *New Orleans Times-Picayune,* 14 February 1927, 1; "Heavy Rain Paralyzes Traffic; Bares Drainage System's Inadequacy," *New Orleans Times-Picayune,* 16 April 1927, 1; "Water Still Deep in Many Sections Long after Rain," *New Orleans Times-Picayune,* 17 April 1927, 1.

63. New Orleans Sewerage and Water Board, *Sixty-Sixth Semi-Annual Report* (New Orleans: 1932), map insert.

64. New Orleans Sewerage and Water Board, *Forty-Eighth Semi-Annual Report* (New Orleans: 1923), 24.

65. Orleans Parish and City of New Orleans, *Biennial Report of the Board of Health* (New Orleans: Palfrey, Rodd, Pursell, 1926).

66. New Orleans Sewerage and Water Board, *Forty-Eighth Semi-Annual Report,* 12–13.

67. New Orleans Sewerage and Water Board, *Fifty-Sixth Semi-Annual Report,* 10–11, 87, and water system map insert.

68. Spain, "Race Relations and Residential Segregation in New Orleans," 89.

69. Louisiana Act No. 117 (1912) authorized municipalities to enact segregation ordinances, and Act No. 118 (1924) prohibited racial mixing by neighborhood. New Orleans ordinance 8037, Common Council Series (1924), implemented the state acts in the city. The major challenge to this act dealt with a rental property. Louisiana Land Development Company v. New Orleans, Case File, City Attorney's Records, 1926, Box 1, New Orleans Municipal Archives, New Orleans Public Library, New Orleans.

70. Louisiana Land Development Company v. New Orleans, 13 F.2nd 898 (1926).

71. Delaney, *Race, Place, and Law,* 151–53.

72. New Orleans Conveyance Office, COB 340 / FOL 446, 1921.

73. "Petition to City Planning and Zoning Commission, " 29 November 1923, by the law firm of Williams and Williams, New Orleans Planning and Zoning Commission, Minute Book, vol. 7, October–December 1930, New Orleans Municipal Archives, New Orleans Public Library, New Orleans.

74. Clement E. Vose, *Caucasians Only: The Supreme Court, the NAACP, and the Restrictive Covenant Cases* (Berkeley: University of California Press, 1959), 6; *Queensborough Land Company v. Cazeaux* 67 So. 641 (1917).

75. Laviolette, "Negro in New Orleans," 110–34.

76. New Orleans Sewerage and Water Board, *Fifty-Sixth Semi-Annual Report,* 27–47.

77. New Orleans Sewerage and Water Board, *Sixty-Sixty Semi-Annual Report,* 48.

78. New Orleans Parks and Parkways Commission, Scrapbook, 1928–1930, newspaper clipping, August 1928, New Orleans.

79. Juliette Landphair, "Sewerage, Sidewalks, and Schools: The New Orleans Ninth Ward and Public School Desegregation," *Louisiana History* 40:1 (1999): 35–62.

80. New Orleans Sewerage and Water Board, *Eighty-Second Semi-Annual Report* (New Orleans: 1940), 11.

81. New Orleans Sewerage and Water Board, *Eighty-Forth Semi-Annual Report* (New Orleans: 1941), 8.

82. New Orleans Sewerage and Water Board, *Eighty-Second Semi-Annual Report,* 12; New Orleans Sewerage and Water Board, *Eighty-Fourth Semi-Annual Report,* 9.

83. New Orleans Sewerage and Water Board, *Eighty-Second Semi-Annual Report,* 39, 11.

84. *Ibid.,* 40.

85. Landphair, "Sewerage, Sidewalks, and Schools," 35–62.

86. Parkway Commission of New Orleans, *Fortieth Anniversary Report, 1909–1949* (New Orleans: 1949), 18–22.

87. U.S. Department of Commerce, Bureau of the Census, *Population and Housing Statistics for Centracts: New Orleans, Louisiana* (Washington: Government Printing Office, 1942), 4–5.

NOTES TO CHAPTER 4

1. Samuel P. Hays, *Beauty, Health, and Permanence: Environmental Politics in the United States, 1955–1985* (New York: Cambridge University Press, 1987), 2–4; Hugh S. Gorman, *Redefining Efficiency: Pollution Concerns, Regulatory Mechanisms, and Technological Change in the U.S. Petroleum Industry* (Akron: University of Akron Press, 2001), 1–4.

2. Discussions of environmental policy and law include Paul Portney, ed., *Public Policies for Environmental Protection* (Washington: Resources for the Future, 1990), and Rutherford H. Platt, *Land Use and Society: Geography, Law, and Public Policy* (Washington: Island, 1996).

3. A previous version of this section appeared as "Environmental Justice in the Big Easy? The Agriculture Street Tragedy," *Environmental Practice* 3:1 (2001): 19–26. It is reprinted here by permission of Oxford University Press and the National Association of Environmental Professionals.

4. Martin Melosi points out that in the latter part of the century cities began to assume responsibility for waste disposal. See Martin V. Melosi, *Garbage in the Cities: Refuse, Reform, and the Environment, 1880–1980* (College Station: Texas A&M University Press, 1981), esp. chap. 1, pp. 21–50.

5. New Orleans Board of Health, *Biennial Report* (New Orleans: 1902–3), 167–69.

6. Robert Lewis, "New Orleans Municipal Waste Collection and Disposal: Public and Private Cost Alternatives," (master's thesis, University of New Orleans, 1978), 19.

7. City of New Orleans, *Laws and Ordinances Relating to Health and Sanitation,* part 1 (New Orleans: 1908), 167.

8. Lewis, "New Orleans Municipal Waste Collection and Disposal," 20.

9. Louis Dodge, "The Public Belt Railroad of New Orleans," *American City* 5 (1911): 330.

10. New Orleans Department of Public Sanitation, *Report on Refuse Disposal Study for New Orleans, 1951* (New Orleans: 1951), 1.

11. New Orleans Division of Public Works, *Monthly Reports, 1912–1921,* KDW204, City Archives, New Orleans Public Library, New Orleans, Louisiana.

12. New Orleans Department of Public Sanitation, *Report on Refuse Disposal,* 2.

13. Act 464, *Acts Passed by the Legislature of the State of Louisiana at the Regular Session, 1948* (Baton Rouge: 1948), 1281–82.

14. Carl Schneider, "New Orleans Uses Sanitary Landfill in Marshy Areas . . . Successfully," *American City* 64 (December 1949): 110–11. In addition to converting the Agriculture Street dump into a landfill, the city also opened a new dump seven miles away.

15. "Term City Dump 'Unbearable'; Ask Grand Jury Move," *New Orleans States*, 13 December 1949, 1.

16. "Says Dump Is Not Health Menace," *New Orleans States*, 14 December 1949, 4.

17. Carl Schneider, "Sanitary Fill Re-Used Safely," *American City* 68 (October 1953): 83–84.

18. "Dump Nuisance Suit Reopened in Civil Court," *New Orleans States*, 6 September 1951, 15.

19. "Use of Garbage Dump is Upheld," *New Orleans Times-Picayune*, 4 January 1952, 21.

20. Schneider, "Sanitary Fill Re-Used Safely," 83–84.

21. "Flies Disrupt School Work," *New Orleans Times-Picayune*, 4 October 1953, 22; "Residents Protest 'City Dump' Road," *New Orleans Item*, 26 March 1954, 1.

22. "Agriculture Street Dump Departing," *New Orleans Item*, 27 January 1958, 21.

23. "City to Move Dump Fill in Asthma Fight," *New Orleans States-Item*, 22 October 1962, 17.

24. U.S. Environmental Protection Agency (EPA), *Agriculture Street Landfill: Factsheet* (Dallas: U.S. EPA, Region 6, 1999).

25. The idea of landscapes of tragedy is developed by Kenneth Foote, *Shadowed Ground: America's Landscapes of Violence and Tragedy* (Austin: University of Texas Press, 1997).

26. U.S. Department of Commerce, Bureau of the Census, *1950 Population: New Orleans, Louisiana, Census Tracts* (Washington: 1952), 32; U.S. Department of Commerce, Bureau of the Census, *1980 Census of Population and Housing: New Orleans, Louisiana, Census Tracts* (Washington: 1983), 79.

27. Robert Bullard, "Solid Waste Sites and the Black Houston Community," *Sociological Inquiry* 53 (1983), 273–88; United Church of Christ, Commission for Racial Justice, *Toxic Wastes and Race in the United States* (New York: United Church of Christ, 1987).

28. For a review see Susan Cutter, "Race, Class, and Environmental Justice," *Progress in Human Geography* 19:1 (1995): 111–22. A recent critique of that literature is Laura Pulido, "Rethinking Environmental Racism: White Privilege and Urban Development," *Annals of the Association of American Geographers* 90 (2000): 12–40.

29. C. M. Browner, "The EPA's Environmental Justice Strategy," http://www.epa.gov/docs/oejpubs/strategy/strategy.txt.html, 1995 (accessed August 2000). Early development of the environmental justice movement is discussed in Eileen McGurty, "From NIMBY to Civil Rights: The Origins of the Environmental Justice Movement," *Environmental History* 2 (1997): 301–23.

30. Juliette Landphair, "Sewerage, Sidewalks, and Schools: The New Orleans Ninth Ward and Public School Desegregation," *Louisiana History* 40 (1999): 35–62.

31. "Term City Dump 'Unbearable,'" 1.

32. Pulido, "Rethinking Environmental Racism," 12–40.

33. "Good Intentions Doom Press Park," *New Orleans Times-Picayune*, 24 April 1995, A1; U.S. EPA, *Agriculture Street Landfill: Factsheet*; U.S. EPA, *Community Relations Plan: A Guide to*

Public Involvement in the Agriculture Street Landfill Remedial Removal Integrated Investigation (Dallas: U.S. EPA, Region 6, 1994).

34. U.S. EPA, preface to *Superfund: 20 Years of Protecting Human Health and the Environment* (2000), http://www.epa.gov/superfund/action/20years/preface (accessed June 2002); U.S. EPA, "Superfund Cleanup Figures" (2001), http://www.epa.gov/superfund/action/process/mgmtrpt (accessed June 2002).

35. "Federal Actions to Address Environmental Justice in Minority Populations and Low-Income Populations: Executive Order 128" (11 February 1994), http://www.epa.gov/swerosps/ej/html-doc/execordr.htm (accessed August 2000).

36. "Scientists Dispute Dangers of Pollution," *New Orleans Times-Picayune,* 23 April 1995, A19.

37. "Federal Actions to Address Environmental Justice."

38. "Scientists Dispute Dangers of Pollution," *New Orleans Times-Picayune,* 23 April 1995, A19.

39. Foote, *Shadowed Ground,* 8–27. Not all landscapes of tragedy are places of massive loss of life, and although Superfund sites seldom produce fatalities, neighbors view them in much the same manner. In addition, affected residents retain attachments to their homes or neighborhoods despite their proximity to sites of calamitous events. This point was first made by Rebecca A. Sheehan, "Attachment to Place and Superfund Communities," paper presented to the Southwest Association of American Geographers meeting, San Marcos, Texas, October 22, 1999.

40. National Environmental Justice Advisory Council, *The Model Plan for Public Participation* (Washington: U.S. EPA, 1996).

41. Discussions of Superfund sites as historical sites include Donald Hardesty, "Issues in Preserving Toxic Wastes as Heritage Sites," *Public Historian* 23:2 (2001): 19–28, and Fredric Quivik, "Integrating the Preservation of Cultural Resources with Remediation of Hazardous Materials: An Assessment of Superfund's Record," *Public Historian* 23:2 (2001): 47–61.

42. "School Site Subject of Closed Session," *New Orleans Times-Picayune,* 12 February 1985.

43. "Desire Residents want Moton School Despite Dump Site," *New Orleans Times-Picayune,* 27 February 1985.

44. "Lead Tests for Kids Ordered," *New Orleans Times-Picayune,* 2 October 1996.

45. *Ibid.*

46. "Scientists Dispute Dangers of Pollution," A19.

47. U.S. EPA, *Community Relations Plan.*

48. National Environmental Justice Advisory Council, *Model Plan,* 2.

49. U.S. EPA, *Remedial Removal Integrated Investigation: Agriculture Street Landfill* (Dallas: U.S. EPA, Region 6, 1995).

50. U.S. EPA, *Record of Decision: Agriculture Street Landfill Superfund Site* (Dallas: U.S. EPA, Region 6, 1997).

51. "Scientists Dispute Dangers of Pollution," A19. Toxicologists attributed the reduction in the number of children with high lead levels in their blood to a federal ban on leaded gasoline

that would have reduced emissions from vehicles traveling on the major artery adjacent to the neighborhood.

52. Louisiana Office of Public Health, *Public Health Assessment for Agriculture Street Landfill* (New Orleans: Louisiana Office of Public Health, 1996); Louisiana Department of Health and Hospitals, *Review of Health Outcome Data for the Agriculture Street Landfill Site* (New Orleans: Louisiana Department of Health and Hospitals, 1997).

53. "Superfund Site Residents Seek Government Buyout," *New Orleans Times-Picayune,* 28 September 1995, B3. According to Elizabeth Blum, females typically express concern with environmental issues in maternal terms, and men employ financial rhetoric. See Elizabeth Blum, "Pink and Green: A Comparative Study of Black and White Women's Urban Environmental Activism" (Ph. D. diss., University of Houston, 2000). Comments made by members of the Agriculture Street community are similar to comments made by Blum's subjects.

54. Nationally, the EPA had relocated residents at only 14 sites, while it had undertaken emergency removal/response actions at over 2,000 sites and completed over 700 remediation efforts as of 1998. U.S. EPA, "Cleanup Responses at Hazardous Waste Sites" (December 1, 1998), http://www.epa.gov/superfund/accomp/ei/cleanup.htm (accessed May 2000).

55. "EPA Might Scrape Away Tainted Soil in 9th Ward," *New Orleans Times-Picayune,* 9 April 1996, A1 and "EPA 9th Ward Cleanup Easier than Relocation," *New Orleans Times-Picayune,* 17 April 1996, A1.

56. "Fix or Flee: Residents Are at Odds," *New Orleans Times-Picayune,* 19 May 1997, B1.

57. "End Agriculture Dump Deadlock," *New Orleans Times-Picayune,* 26 May 1997, B6.

58. "Not All Oppose Life on Superfund Site," *New Orleans Times-Picayune,* 20 March 1997, B1; "9th Ward Superfund Cleanup Site Grows," *New Orleans Times-Picayune,* 7 July 1997, A1.

59. "Cleanup Proposal Called Too Little," *New Orleans Times-Picayune,* 3 September 1997, A1.

60. "Morial Seeks Gore's Help in EPA Cleanup," *New Orleans Times-Picayune,* 27 September 1997, B3.

61. "Council Wants U.S. to Pay Homeowners," *New Orleans Times-Picayune,* 4 October 1997, B1.

62. "Delay Could Revive Buyout," *New Orleans Times-Picayune,* 2 November 1997, B1.

63. "9th Ward Neighbors Sue to Stop EPA," *New Orleans Times-Picayune,* 16 January 1998, B1.

64. "Soil Suit Thrown Out by Judge," *New Orleans Times-Picayune,* 12 March 1998, B1.

65. "EPA Vows to Begin Landfill Cleanup," *New Orleans Times-Picayune,* 26 February 1999, B1.

66. U.S. EPA, "Administrative Order: In the Matter of City of New Orleans Regarding Agriculture Street Landfill," USEPA Docket No. CERCLA 6-10-99 (2 February 1999).

67. "Judge Stops Landfill Cleanup on City Land," *New Orleans Times-Picayune,* 9 March 1999, B1.

68. "Judge OKs Landfill Cleanup in 9th Ward," *New Orleans Times-Picayune,* 2 April 1999, B1.

69. "Louisiana Delegation to Testify about Discrimination," *New Orleans Times-Picayune,* 3 April 1999, A14; "EPA May Help Landfill Residents Move," *New Orleans Times-Picayune,* 25 May 1999, B1.

70. "Residents Protest Cleanup," *New Orleans Times-Picayune,* 24 June 1999, B1.

71. "Ag Street Residents Livid over EPA Ruling," *New Orleans Times-Picayune,* 10 July 1999, A1.

72. "Living a Nightmare," *New Orleans Times-Picayune,* 23 May 2000.

73. "Landfill Suit OK'd as Class Action," *New Orleans Times-Picayune,* 21 September 1999, A1.

74. "School Built over Landfill to be Reopened," *New Orleans Times-Picayune,* 12 June 2001, Metro 1; "Cleanup Declared Complete at Dump's 95 Acre Site," *New Orleans Times-Picayune,* 3 May 2002, Metro 1. An active unit is one under remediation.

75. "Cleanup Declared Complete," Metro 1.

76. "Residents Say Land Making Them Ill," *New Orleans Times-Picayune,* 2 June 2002, Metro 1.

77. The controversy over the riverfront batture is another prime example. See Ari Kelman, *A River and Its City: The Nature of Landscape in New Orleans* (Berkeley: University of California Press, 2003), 19–49.

78. Several ideas in this section appeared in an entirely different form in Craig E. Colten, "Too Much of a Good Thing: Industrial Pollution in the Lower Mississippi," in *Transforming New Orleans and Its Environs: Centuries of Change,* ed. Craig E. Colten (Pittsburgh: University of Pittsburgh Press, 2000), 141–59.

79. The law specified that "the proprietor above can do nothing whereby the natural service due by the estate below may be rendered more burthensome." *A Digest of the Civil Laws Now in Force in the Territory of Orleans (1808); Containing Manuscript References to Its Source and Other Civil Laws on the Same Subjects,* De la Vergne volume (New Orleans: Bradford and Anderson, 1808; Baton Rouge: Claitor's, 1971), 128.

80. For a summary of early pollution case law see, Colten, "Too Much of a Good Thing," 144–48.

81. "Act 183: An Act to Protect the Rice Planters . . . ," *Acts Passed by the General Assembly of the State of Louisiana, 1910* (Baton Rouge: New Advocate, 1910), 272–73.

82. "Act 133: An Act to Protect all the Natural Waterways and Canals . . . ," *Acts Passed by the Legislature of the State of Louisiana, 1924* (Baton Rouge: Ramires-Jones, 1924), 199–200. The conservation agency had responsibilities to safeguard the state's wildlife.

83. New Orleans Sewerage and Water Board, *Semi-Annual Report* (New Orleans: 1900), 29–30.

84. Robert McMichael, "Plant Location Factors in the Petrochemical Industry in Louisiana" (Ph. D. diss., Louisiana State University, 1961), 76–86.

85. U.S. Public Health Service (USPHS), *Summary Report on Water Pollution: Southwest-Lower Mississippi Drainage Basins* (Washington: USPHS, Division of Water Pollution, 1951).

86. U.S. Department of Commerce, Bureau of the Census, *Census of Manufacturers: 1947,*

vol. 3, *Statistics by States* (Washington: Bureau of the Census, 1950); U.S. Department of Commerce, Bureau of the Census, *Census of Manufacturers: 1954*, vol. 3, *Area Statistics* (Washington: Bureau of the Census, 1955); U.S. Department of Commerce, Bureau of the Census, *Census of Manufacturers: 1958*, vol. 3, *Area Statistics* (Washington: Bureau of the Census, 1961); U.S. Department of Commerce, Bureau of the Census, 1963 *Census of Manufacturers*, vol. 3, *Area Statistics* (Washington: Bureau of the Census, 1965); U.S. Department of Commerce, Bureau of the Census, 1967 *Census of Manufacturers*, vol. 3, *Area Statistics* (Washington: Bureau of the Census, 1971). Also see McMichael, "Plant Location Factors," 5.

87. U.S. EPA, *Industrial Pollution of the Lower Mississippi River* (Dallas: U.S. EPA, Region 6, 1972).

88. "Act 367: An Act to Create a Stream Control Commission," *Acts Passed by th Legislature of the State of Louisiana, 1940* (Baton Rouge: 1940).

89. Texas Company v. Montgomery 73 F. Supp. 527 (1948).

90. Louisiana Department of Conservation, *Fifteenth Biennial Report, 1940–1941* (Baton Rouge: 1941), 139–41.

91. Louisiana Department of Wild Life and Fisheries, *Second Biennial Report (1946–1947)* (Baton Rouge: 1947), 328–29; and Louisiana Department of Wild Life and Fisheries, *Third Biennial Report (1948–1949)* (Baton Rouge: 1950), 352–53.

92. Joseph Pratt, "Letting the Grandchildren Do It: Environmental Planning during the Ascent of Oil as a Major Oil Source," *Public Historian* 2:4 (Summer 1980): 28–61; Craig E. Colten, "Texas v. the Petrochemical Industry: Contesting Pollution in an Era of Industrial Growth," in *The Second Wave: Southern Industrialization, 1940–1970*, ed. Philip Scranton (Athens: University of Georgia Press, 2001), 146–67.

93. Louisiana Department of Conservation, *Fifteenth Biennial Report, 1940–1941*, 136; Louisiana Department of Conservation, *Sixteenth Biennial Report, 1942–1943* (New Orleans: 1944), 166–87.

94. Louisiana Board of Health, *Biennial Report, 1942–1943* (Baton Rouge: 1943), 166–67.

95. Louisiana Department of Wild Life and Fisheries, *Third Biennial Report, 1948–1949*, 368–69.

96. USPHS, *Summary Report on Water Pollution*, 132–33.

97. For several years, the SCC kept no written records of the permit application process, but it began publishing the proceedings in 1958. Louisiana Stream Control Commission, *Proceedings of Meeting* (Baton Rouge: May 15, 1958, through September 22, 1966), Louisiana Department of Environmental Quality, Baton Rouge.

98. USPHS, *Summary Report on Water Pollution;* U.S. Department of Health, Education, and Welfare, USPHS, Inventory: Municipal and Industrial Waste Facilities, 1957 (Washington: U.S. Department of Health Education, and Welfare, USPHS, 1958). Louisiana compiled its data in 1953.

99. M. L. Eddards, L. R. Kister, and Glenn Scarcia, *Water Resources of the New Orlean Area, Louisiana,* Geological Survey Circular 374 (Washington: U.S. Geological Survey, 1956); Louisiana Stream Control Commission, *Proceedings of Meeting* (Baton Rouge: May 15, 1958, through September 22, 1966). See also Colten, "Too Much of a Good Thing," 149. For the one rejection

see, Louisiana Stream Control Commission, *Proceedings of Meeting* (Baton Rouge: June 30, 1961), 15–25.

100. Louisiana Wildlife and Fisheries Commission, *Eighth Biennial Report (1958–1959)* (New Orleans: 1960), 170–71.

101. Surveys of state water pollution laws led to the rapid revamping of statutes in the postwar period. Anthony Anable and R. P. Kite, "Pollution Abatement: Appraisal of Current Regulations," *Chemical and Engineering Progress* 44 (January 1948): 3–16; Marvin Weiss, *Industrial Pollution: Survey of Legislation and Regulations* (New York: Chemonics, 1951); Manufacturing Chemists' Association, *Water Pollution Abatement Manual: Compendium of Water Pollution Laws* (Washington: Manufacturing Chemists' Association, 1959).

102. In a review of industrial waste practices in the oil industry, Hugh Gorman argues that an efficiency ethic guided early-twentieth-century efforts that reduced pollution indirectly by salvaging by-products from the waste stream. By the second half of the twentieth century, he suggests that the most viable waste recovery techniques had been put into practice. Gorman, *Redefining Efficiency.*

103. Kenneth Biglane, "Industry and the Mississippi River," *Proceedings of the Sixth Annual Water Symposium* (Baton Rouge: Louisiana State University, Engineering Experiment Station, 1957), 30–34; Louisiana Wild Life and Fisheries Commission, "Mississippi River Survey," *Eighth Biennial Report (1958–1959),* 183–86.

104. Louisiana Wild Life and Fisheries Commission, *Ninth Biennial Report (1960–1961)* (New Orleans: 1962), 203–4; Louisiana Stream Control Commission, *Proceedings of Meeting* (Baton Rouge: April 5, 1960), 2–3.

105. Eddards, Kister, and Scarcia, *Water Resources of the New Orleans Area;* U.S. Geological Survey, *Quality of Surface Waters of the United States, 1959,* parts 7 and 8, Water Supply Paper 1644 (Washington: U.S. Geological Survey, 1965).

106. U.S. Department of Health, Education, and Welfare, *Inventory.*

107. U.S. Department of Health, Education, and Welfare, *Water Pollution Surveillance System: Annual Compilation of Data, October 1, 1962–September 30, 1963,* vol. 8 (Washington: U.S. Department of Health, Education, and Welfare, Public Health Service, 1963).

108. Louisiana Wild Life and Fisheries Commission, *Ninth Biennial Report (1960–1961),* 197.

109. Rachael Carson, *Silent Spring* (Boston: Houghton-Mifflin, 1962). See also Linda Lear, "Rachael Carson's *Silent Spring,*" *Environmental History Review* 17:2 (1993): 23–47.

110. Louisiana Wild Life and Fisheries Commission, *Eighth Biennial Report (1958–1959),* 187; U.S. Department of the Interior, Federal Water Pollution Control Administration (FWPCA), *Endrin Pollution in the Lower Mississippi River Basin* (Dallas: U.S. Department of the Interior, FWPCA, 1969), 61.

111. See "Poisons Kill Fish in the Mississippi," *New York Times,* 22 March 1964, 79; other articles appeared in the *Times* on 24 March 1964, 32; 7 April 1964, 55; 8 April 1964, 23; 10 April 1964, 27; 23 April 1964, 41; 24 April 1964, 35; 26 April 1964, 60; 6 May 1964, 52. See also U.S. Senate, Committee on Government Operations, *Interagency Coordination in Environmental Hazards (Pesticides),* 88th Cong., 2nd sess., April 7, 8, and 15, 1964.

112. USPHS, Report on Investigation of Fish Kills in Lower Mississippi River, Atchafalaya

River, and Gulf of Mexico (Washington: U.S. Department of Health, Education, and Welfare, 1964), reprinted as exhibit 160 in U.S. Senate, Committee on Government Operations, *Interagency Coordination in Environmental Hazards (Pesticides)*, 1698–1701.

113. FWPCA, *Endrin Pollution in the Lower Mississippi River Basin*, 71.

114. Alfred D. Grzenda, "Statement," *Conference in the Matter of Pollution of the Interstate Waters of the Mississippi River: Proceedings*, vol. 2, *May 5–6* (Washington: U.S. Department of Health, Education, and Welfare, 1964), 182–258.

115. The notion of regularly diverting wastes from one sink to another appears in Joel A. Tarr, "The Search for the Ultimate Sink: Urban Air, Land, and Water Pollution in Historical Perspective," *Records of the Columbia Historical Society of Washington* 51 (1984): 1–29. Consequences of the Velsicol diversion are discussed in Craig E. Colten, "The Big Kill: Endrin in the Mississippi and the Search for a New Sink," *Bulletin of the Illinois Geographical Society* 43 (Spring 2001): 30–37.

116. Bernard Lorant (vice president, Velsicol Chemical Corporation), "Statement," in *Conference in the Matter of Pollution of the Interstate Waters of the Lower Mississippi River: Proceedings*, vol. 3, 487–91; FWPCA, *Endrin Pollution*.

117. FWPCA, *Endrin Pollution*, 85.

118. Louisiana Board of Health, *Biennial Report, 1966–1967* (New Orleans: 1967), 92.

119. Lucia Dunham, Roger O'Gara, and Floyd Taylor, "Studies on Pollutants from Processed Water: Collection from Three Stations and Biologic Testing for Toxicity and Carcinogenesis," *American Journal of Public Health* 57:12 (1967): 2178–85.

120. U.S. EPA, *Industrial Pollution of the Lower Mississippi River*. For earlier SCC evaluations see, Louisiana Stream Control Commission, *Proceedings of Meeting* (Baton Rouge: 1958–1966).

121. U.S. EPA, *Industrial Pollution of the Lower Mississippi River*, 6–7.

122. James F. Coerver, "New Orleans Study," unpublished paper presented to the Conference of State Sanitary Engineers, Austin, Texas, May 18, 1976, 4–5.

123. Joel B. Goldsteen, *Danger All Around: Waste Storage Crisis on the Texas and Louisiana Gulf Coast* (Austin: University of Texas Press, 1993), 142–51; James Friloux, "Petrochemical Wastes as a Water Pollution Problem in the Lower Mississippi River," unpublished paper submitted to the Senate Subcommittee on Air and Water Pollution, 5 April 1971 (from the personal collection of the author). See also Robert T. Denbo, "Program for Improvement of Waste Effluent at Humble's Baton Rouge Refinery," *Proceedings of the 25th Industrial Waste Conference*, part 1 (Lafayette, IN: Purdue University, 1970), 274–82.

124. Ralph Nader, statement, *Safe Drinking Water Act of 1963: Hearing Before the Subcommittee on the Environment of the U.S. Senate Committee on Commerce*, before the Senate Subcommittee on the Environment, 93rd Cong., 1st sess., May 31, 1973, 88–104.

125. Robert H. Harris and Edward M. Brecher, "Is the Water Safe to Drink," *Consumer Reports* 39 (June, July, and August 1974): 436–42, 538–42, 623–27. The claim that New Orleans residents suffered bladder and urinary cancer at an elevated rate stemmed from a 1958 USPHS report that did not attribute an environmental source for the illnesses. The study's authors puzzled over the fact that urinary tract cancer was higher among males and nonwhite females. It also noted that Louisiana had a high rate of lung cancer—not explained by drinking water.

See Harold Dorn and Sidney Cutler, *Morbidity from Cancer in the United States*, Public Health Monogram 56 (Washington: USPHS, 1958).

126. "Treat Water, End 50 Orleans Cancer Deaths Yearly," *New Orleans Times-Picayune*, 8 November 1974, 1; T. A. DeRouen and J. E. Diem, "New Orleans Drinking Water Controversy: A Statistical Perspective," *American Journal of Public Health* 65:10 (1975): 1060-62.

127. "Drinking Water Poses No Imminent Hazard—EPA," *New Orleans Times-Picayune*, 20 July 1974, 1.

128. "No Detectable Threshold for Chemical Carcinogen," *New Orleans Times-Picayune*, 4 July 1974, 26; "Bottled Water Sales Flow," *New Orleans Times-Picayune*, 9 November 1974, 4.

129. Betty Dowty, D. R. Carlisle, and J. L. Laseter, "New Orleans Drinking Water Sources Tested by Gas Chromatography-Mass Spectrometry," *Environmental Science and Technology* 9:8 (August 1975): 762-65; Robert W. Miller, chief, Epidemiology Branch, National Cancer Institute, memorandum, 18 December 1974, historical files of the Louisiana Department of Health, New Orleans; Robert E. Tarone and John J. Gart, unpublished review of "The Implications of Cancer-Causing Substances in Mississippi River Water," by Robert H. Harris, prepared for the Applied Mathematics Section of the National Cancer Institute, 10 January 1975, historical files of the Louisiana Department of Health, New Orleans.

130. Frank C. Wells, *Hydrology and Water Quality of the Lower Mississippi River*, Water Resources Technical Report 21 (Baton Rouge: Louisiana Department of Transportation and Development, 1980), 76.

131. New Orleans Sewerage and Water Board, *Annual Report* (New Orleans: 1975), 8; New Orleans Sewerage and Water Board, *Annual Report* (New Orleans: 1978), 8-9; New Orleans Sewerage and Water Board, *Annual Report* (New Orleans: 1980), 10.

132. New Orleans Sewerage and Water Board, *Annual Report* (New Orleans: 1981), 4.

133. "Science Adds Taste That Nature Left Out," *New Orleans Times-Picayune*, 13 June 1984, 1 and 4.

134. "N.O. Water Tapped as the Best Tasting," *New Orleans Times-Picayune*, 11 June 1984, 1, 5; "Science Adds Taste That Nature Left Out," 1, 4.

135. Abita Springs has long had a reputation for pure spring waters and is the namesake of one of the leading bottled water suppliers to the Crescent City. "Law May Keep Well Water out of Dixie Beer," *New Orleans Times-Picayune*, 3 March 1984, 13; "Franklinton Water Going to Dixie," *New Orleans Times-Picayune*, 8 March 1984, 18.

NOTES TO CHAPTER 5

1. The most complete discussion of environmental consequences of suburbanization is Adam Rome, *The Bulldozer in the Countryside: Suburban Sprawl and the Rise of American Environmentalism* (New York: Cambridge University Press, 2001). Peirce Lewis coined the term "galactic city." See Peirce Lewis, "The Galactic Metropolis," in *Beyond the Urban Fringe: Land Use Issues of Nonmetropolitan America*, ed. Rutherford Platt and George Macinko (Minneapolis: University of Minnesota Press, 1983). An overview of American suburban development appears in Peter O. Muller, *Contemporary Suburban America* (Englewood Cliffs, NJ: Prentice-Hall, 1981).

2. Gilbert White et al., *Changes in Urban Occupance of Flood Plains in the United States,* Department of Geography Research Paper 57 (Chicago: University of Chicago, 1958). See also Burrell Montz and Eve C. Gruntfest, "Changes in American Urban Floodplain Occupancy since 1958: The Experiences of Nine Cities," *Applied Geography* 6 (1986): 325–38, and Steven Driver and Danny Vaughn, "Flood Hazard in Kansas since 1880," *Geographical Review* 78 (1988): 1–19.

3. Martin V. Melosi, *The Sanitary City: Urban Infrastructure in America from Colonial Times to the Present* (Baltimore: Johns Hopkins University Press, 2000), 8–14.

4. George Waring and George Cable, *History and Present Condition of New Orleans, Louisiana* (Washington: U.S. Department of the Interior, 1881); Tenth Census of the United States: Social Statistics of Cities (Washington: U.S. Department of the Interior, 1881), 68–69.

5. Selecting a flood protection technology in the nineteenth century established a "path dependent" course of action into the next two centuries. See Melosi, *Sanitary City,* 8–14.

6. D. O. Elliot, *The Improvement of the Lower Mississippi River for Flood Control and Navigation* (Vicksburg: U.S. Waterways Experiment Station, 1932), 170–79.

7. The flood of 1927 is a story worthy of extended treatment. Others have provided excellent accounts: see John M. Barry, *Rising Tide: The Great Mississippi Flood of 1927 and How It Changed America* (New York: Simon and Schuster, 1997); Gay M. Gomez, "Perspectives, Power, and Priorities: New Orleans and the Mississippi River Flood of 1927," in *Transforming New Orleans and Its Environs: Centuries of Change,* ed. C. E. Colten (Pittsburgh: University of Pittsburgh Press, 2000), 109–20; and Ari Kelman, *A River and Its City: The Nature of Landscape in New Orleans* (Berkeley: University of California Press, 2003), 157–96.

8. "South Is Deluged as City Suffers Heavy Downpour," *New Orleans Times-Picayune,* 14 February 1927, 1–2; "Heavy Rain Paralyzes Traffic; Bares Drainage System's Inadequacy," *New Orleans Times-Picayune,* 16 April 1927, 1–2; and "Water Still Deep in Many Sections Long after Rain," *New Orleans Times-Picayune,* 17 April 1927, 1, 14; and "Deluges and Drainage," *New Orleans Times-Picayune,* 17 April 1927, 1.

9. The general guidelines for the New Orleans system are outlined in New Orleans Advisory Board on Drainage, *Report on the Drainage of the City of New Orleans* (New Orleans: Fitzwilliam and Co., 1895), 5–12.

10. New Orleans Sewerage and Water Board, A Report on Storm Water Drainage with Special Emphasis on the Period May 1978 to June 1981 and Problems Encountered (New Orleans: New Orleans Sewerage and Water Board, 1981), p. 2–8.

11. Barry D. Keim and Robert A. Muller, "Temporal Fluctuation of Heavy Rainfall Magnitudes in New Orleans, Louisiana: 1871–1991," *Water Resources Bulletin* 28:4 (1992): 721–30. There were some major storms, but a lull in urban expansion during the 1930s and 1940s minimized the impacts.

12. The lakefront project was part of Long's attempt to take charge of public works in New Orleans while building his political base. After his death, federal prosecutors indicted several of Long's associates including levee board president Abraham Shushan on tax fraud charges. A jury found Shushan guilty. See T. Harry Williams, *Huey Long* (New York: Knopf, 1969), 795–99, and Harnett T. Kane, *Louisiana Hayride: The American Rehearsal for Dictatorship, 1928–1940* (New York: Morrow and Co., 1941), 166.

13. Judy Filipich and Lee Taylor, *Lakefront New Orleans: Planning and Development, 1926–1971* (New Orleans: Louisiana State University in New Orleans, Urban Studies Institute, 1971), 9–15; Burke and Lamantia Architects and Barnard and Burk Engineers, *East Lakefront Flood Protection and Reclamation* (New Orleans: Orleans Levee Board, 1962), 6–9; Orleans Levee Board, *Building a Great City* (New Orleans: Orleans Levee Board, 1954), n.p.

14. Burk and Associates, *East Bank Master Drainage Plan: Jefferson Parish, Louisiana*, vol. 1 (Gretna, LA: Jefferson Parish, 1980), 5.

15. U.S. Army Corps of Engineers, *Lake Pontchartrain, Louisiana, and Vicinity Hurricane Protection Project: Reevaluation Study*, vol. 1, *Main Report and Final Supplement I to the Environmental Impact Statement* (New Orleans: U.S. Army Corps of Engineers, New Orleans District, 1983), 22; Burk and Associates, *East Bank Master Drainage Plan*, 5.

16. U.S. Army Corps of Engineers, *Lake Pontchartrain, Louisiana, and Vicinity Hurricane Protection Project: Final Environmental Impact Statement* (New Orleans: U.S. Army Corps of Engineers, New Orleans District, 1974), 7–8.

17. U.S. Army Corps of Engineers, *Memorandum Report: Hurricane Flossy* (New Orleans: U.S. Army Corps of Engineers, New Orleans District, 1957), 5–6.

18. U.S. Army Corps of Engineers, *Hurricane Hilda* (New Orleans: U.S. Army Corps of Engineers, New Orleans District, 1966), 11.

19. U.S. Army Corps of Engineers, *Report on Hurricane Betsy* (New Orleans: U.S. Army Corps of Engineers, New Orleans District, 1965), 24–28, 35.

20. U.S. Army Corps of Engineers, *Report on Hurricane Camille* (New Orleans: U.S. Army Corps of Engineers, New Orleans District, 1970), 92–99.

21. Most of the post-1927 flood protection system throughout the Mississippi River valley relied on levees and outlets—both structural approaches. See Albert E. Cowdrey, *Land's End: A History of the New Orleans District, U.S. Army Corps of Engineers* (New Orleans: U.S. Army Corps of Engineers, 1977).

22. A discussion of conditions before the 1967 federal act appears in White et al., *Changes in Urban Occupance of Floodplains.* Also see R. J. Burby and S. P. French, "Coping with Floods: The Land Use Management Paradox," *Journal of the American Planning Association* 47:3 (1981): 289–300.

23. New Orleans Sewerage and Water Board, De-watering and Rewatering the City of New Orleans, 1899–1950 (New Orleans: New Orleans Sewerage and Water Board, 1950), n.p.; and Daniel, Mann, Johnson, and Mendenhall, *Master Plan for Orleans Parish Drainage Improvements*, vol. 1 (New Orleans: New Orleans Sewerage and Water Board, 1983), 5.

24. A brief summary of the National Flood Insurance Program appears in Rutherford H. Platt, *Land Use and Society: Geography, Law, and Public Policy* (Washington: Island, 1996), 418–34.

25. A 100-year flood plain has a 1 percent chance of flooding each year. For a brief description of the flood program see Platt, *Land Use and Society*, 418–34.

26. Federal Emergency Management Agency (FEMA), *Flood Insurance Rate Map, New Orleans and Orleans Parish, Louisiana* (Washington, D.C.: FEMA, 1984); FEMA, *Flood Insurance Rate Map, Jefferson Parish and Incorporated Areas, Louisiana* (Washington, D.C.: FEMA, 1995).

27. This is "path dependence" at its finest. See Melosi, *Sanitary City*, 8–14.

28. New Orleans Sewerage and Water Board, Report on Storm Water Drainage, fig. 3.

29. New Orleans Sewerage and Water Board, Drainage Improvements to the Broadmoor Neighborhood: Pre-Application to the Statewide Flood Control Program (New Orleans: New Orleans Sewerage and Water Board, 1998), p. 4–3.

30. Old Metairie is in neighboring Jefferson Parish, but it is served by canals that flow into Orleans Parish and the New Orleans drainage system.

31. "Area Flood Price Tag $240 Million," *New Orleans Times-Picayune,* 6 May 1978, 1.

32. "Hundreds of Area Homes Flooded," *New Orleans Times-Picayune,* 7 February 1979, 1; "City Waters Recede; Flood Damage Minor," *New Orleans Times-Picayune,* 8 February 1979, 3.

33. "Killer Floods Inundate Area," *New Orleans Times-Picayune,* 14 April 1980, 1, 12; "16 Billion Gallons of Water Handled by Pumps," *New Orleans Times-Picayune,* 15 April 1980, 6.

34. New Orleans Sewerage and Water Board, *Drainage Improvements to the Broadmoor Neighborhood,* p. 4–3.

35. "Uptown, Broadmoor Streets Flooded by Thunderstorms," *New Orleans Times-Picayune,* 30 April 1981, 1.

36. Investigators note that the storms of the late 1920s and the late 1970s and early 1980s stand out in the long-term pattern of New Orleans rainfall events. Keim and Muller, "Temporal Fluctuation of Heavy Rainfall Magnitudes."

37. "2 Uptown Businessmen are Fed Up with Rising Frequency of Flooding," *New Orleans Times-Picayune,* 30 April 1981, 19.

38. "Millage Proposals Pass Easily," *New Orleans Times-Picayune,* 17 May 1981, 1, 5.

39. "Frustration Builds in Rain-Soaked City," *New Orleans Times-Picayune,* 26 April 1982, 13; New Orleans Sewerage and Water Board, *Report on Storm Water Drainage,* 14.

40. New Orleans Sewerage and Water Board, *Drainage Improvements to the Broadmoor Neighborhood,* p. 4–3.

41. "Spring Storm Floods, Isolates Metro Area," *New Orleans Times-Picayune,* 8 April 1983, 1; "Uptown Flood Victims Find Strength in Numbers," *New Orleans Times-Picayune,* 12 June 1983, 25.

42. "Discussion on Flooding Set in Metairie," *New Orleans Times-Picayune,* 19 April 1983, 15; Linfield, Hunter, and Gibbons, Inc., Seventeenth Street Canal Drainage Basin Study (New Orleans: New Orleans Sewerage and Water Board, 1983).

43. Daniel, Mann, Johnson, and Mendenhall, Master Plan for Orleans Drainage Improvements (New Orleans: New Orleans Sewerage and Water Board, 1983).

44. "Rain: Adds Up to Street Flooding," *New Orleans Times-Picayune,* 17 October 1985, 33; "Downpour Floods Streets, Knocks Out Electricity," *New Orleans Times-Picayune,* 22 March 1989, 1; "Flood Takes N.O. by Surprise," *New Orleans Times-Picayune,* 14 May 1990, 1.

45. New Orleans Sewerage and Water Board, Drainage Improvements to the Broadmoor Neighborhood, p. 4–3.

46. Gulf Engineers and Consultants, May 1995 Post Flood Report: Flood Damage Assessment (New Orleans: U.S. Army Corps of Engineers, New Orleans District, 1996), 7.

47. "Rain Overwhelmed Pumps S&WB Says," *New Orleans Times-Picayune*, 11 May 1995, B-2.

48. New Orleans Planning Commission, *Floodplain Management Plan for the City of New Orleans* (New Orleans: New Orleans Planning Commission, 1992), 12–13.

49. New Orleans Sewerage and Water Board, *Drainage Improvements to the Broadmoor Neighborhood.*

50. U.S. Army Corps of Engineers, Southeast Louisiana Project: Technical Report (New Orleans: U.S. Army Corps of Engineers, New Orleans District, 1996), pp. 3-4 to 3-8.

51. New Orleans Building Code and Related Regulations (New Orleans: City of New Orleans, 1958 and 1980 editions), sec. 202.

52. Michael Centieneo, director, New Orleans Department of Safety and Permits, personal communication, 2 April 2002; S Z S Consultants, Inc., Monthly Inspection Report to New Orleans Department of Safety and Permits (New Orleans: S Z S Consultants, 2000); New Orleans Planning Commission, *Floodplain Management Plan,* 44–45.

53. New Orleans Department of Safety and Permits, Building Inspection Section, Monthly Reports for 1964 and 1985, New Orleans Municipal Archives, New Orleans Public Library, New Orleans; New Orleans Department of Safety and Permits, Annual Building Permits, 1996–2001, New Orleans.

54. "New Orleans Is Awarded $1.25 Million Flood Grant," *New Orleans Times-Picayune*, 8 September 2001, 4.

55. "Flood Project Rattles Residents," *New Orleans Times-Picayune*, 17 May 2001, Metro section, 1.

56. "Streets Turn Soggy as Allison Hits Land," *New Orleans Times-Picayune*, 7 June 2001, 1; "Wringing Out," *New Orleans Times-Picayune*, 10 June 2001, Metro section, 1.

57. "Isidore Drenching New Orleans Area," *New Orleans Times-Picayune*, 26 September 2002, 1; "Adios, Isidore," *New Orleans Times-Picayune*, 27 September 2002, 1; "Money Down the Drain," *New Orleans Times-Picayune*, 29 September 2002, 1.

58. Juliette Landphair, "Sewerage, Sidewalks, and Schools: The New Orleans Ninth Ward and Public School Desegregation," *Louisiana History* 40 (1999): 35–62.

59. "Desire Residents Angered by Floods, Lack of Warning," *New Orleans Times-Picayune*, 21 January 1983, 6; "New Orleans Residents File $10 Million Lawsuit," *New Orleans Times-Picayune*, 25 January 1983, 9.

60. Burk and Associates, *East Bank Master Drainage Plan*, vol. 1 (Gretna, LA: Jefferson Parish Public Works, 1980), p. 2–6. For a discussion of subsidence see J. O. Snowden, W. C. Ward, and J. R. J. Studlick, *Geology of Greater New Orleans: Its Relationship to Land Subsidence and Flooding* (New Orleans: New Orleans Geological Society, 1980).

61. URS Company, *West Bank Master Drainage Study*, vol. 1, *Report* (Gretna, LA: Jefferson Parish Public Works, 1981), pp. 1-1 through 1-3.

62. FEMA, Insurance Overview: Jefferson Parish (computer printout), 31 July 1993 (Dallas: FEMA Regional Office, 1993).

63. "Flood Insurance Program Termed Injurious to Area," *New Orleans Times-Picayune*, 14 April 1970, 1, 3. Over 44 percent of Louisiana's flood-prone communities were participating

in the federal program, compared with participation rates of about 21 percent nationally. "Louisiana's Communities Take to Flood Insurance," *New Orleans Times-Picayune*, 2 February 1974, 15. Jefferson had submitted over $74 million in claims, while Orleans Parish ranked second with $44 million. "Jeff, Orleans Top Nation in Flood Claims," *New Orleans Times-Picayune*, 20 October 1982, 13.

64. "Area Flood Price Tag $240 Million," *New Orleans Times-Picayune*, 6 May 1978, 1; "Must Limit West Bank," *New Orleans Times-Picayune*, 10 May 1978, 1, 22; "Floods Not the Only Problem in Marrero Disaster Area," *New Orleans Times-Picayune*, 12 May 1978, 2.

65. "Disaster Hits Coubra Again," *New Orleans Times-Picayune*, 7 February 1979, 1; "Flooded Again," *New Orleans States-Item*, 9 February, 1979, 1; "City Waters Recede," *New Orleans Times-Picayune*, 8 February 1979, 1.

66. "Jeff Streets Closed," *New Orleans Times-Picayune*, 3 April 1980, 1.

67. "May 3 Yardstick in Jeff Replaced," *New Orleans Times-Picayune*, 14 April 1980, 1, 2; "Floods Plague West Bank Areas," *New Orleans Times-Picayune*, 16 April 1980, 1.

68. Ted Steinberg offers an extensive discussion of the "act of God" defense for hazards planners in *Acts of God: The Unnatural History of Natural Disasters* (New York: Oxford University Press, 2000).

69. "Parishes Get Break in U.S. Flood Case," *New Orleans Times-Picayune*, 9 April 1985, 1; "Court Overturns Liability," *New Orleans Times-Picayune*, 17 April 1985, 1; U.S. v. Jefferson Parish et al., "Settlement Agreement," U.S. District Court for the Eastern District of Louisiana, case nos. 81–1810 and 83–2077 (1987).

70. Burk and Associates, *East Jefferson Flood Reduction Study*, vol. 1 (Gretna, LA: Jefferson Parish Department of Public Works, 1989).

71. Jefferson Parish, Amendments to the Adopted Standard Codes (Gretna, LA: Jefferson Parish, 1998), secs. 113.1.4 and 113.1.5.

72. Jefferson Parish Ordinance 21409, 10 October 2001.

73. Meyer Engineers, Jefferson Parish Floodplain Management/Repetitive Loss Plan, A/E Project 20–0113 (Metairie: 2001), 1–10.

74. "Drenching Takes Soggy Toll on Area," *New Orleans Times-Picayune*, 3 April 1988, 1–2.

75. "West Bank Dries Out," *New Orleans Times-Picayune*, 4 April 1988, 1, 4; "Neighborhoods Start to Mop Up," *New Orleans Times-Picayune*, 5 April 1988, 1, 4.

76. "State Supreme Court Squashed Class Action Suit," *New Orleans Times-Picayune*, 28 November 1997, B-1.

77. "$4 Million Settlement Approved," *New Orleans Times-Picayune*, 16 March 2000, A-1; "Legacy of the May Flood," *New Orleans Times-Picayune*, 8 May 2000, B-4.

78. U.S. Army Corps of Engineers, New Orleans District, *Southeast Louisiana Project: Jefferson Parish Technical Report* (New Orleans: U.S. Army Corps of Engineers, New Orleans District, 1996), 10–54.

79. Jefferson Parish was seeking funds to raise twenty-three of its most vulnerable houses by fall 2001. "New Orleans Is Awarded $1.25 Million Flood Grant," 4.

80. U.S. Army Corps of Engineers, *Southeast Louisiana Project*, 18.

81. "Streets Turn Soggy as Allison Hits Land," 1; "Wringing Out," 1.

82. "Isidore Drenching New Orleans Area," 1; "Adios Isidore," 1; "Money Down the Drain," 1. The economic impact of the storm was felt the most in disruptions to tourism and the off-shore oil industry.

83. The tendency to plan for the last flood has been discussed by Ron Hagelman, "Spatial Evolution of Flood Hazards in San Antonio, Texas" (Ph.D. diss., Southwest Texas State University, 2001).

84. New Orleans Planning Commission, *Floodplain Management Plan for the City of New Orleans* (New Orleans: New Orleans Planning Commission, 1992), 42.

85. "Corps Hearing Views on Permit," *New Orleans Times-Picayune*, 29 June 2001, Metro section, 1.

NOTES TO CHAPTER 6

A previous version of this chapter was published in *Environmental History* 7:2 (January 2002): 226–46. *Environmental History* is jointly published by the Forest History Society, Durham, North Carolina, and the American Society of Environmental History. It is reprinted here with permission, and thanks to Adam Rome, editor.

1. An excellent overview of New Orleans's geographic development is Peirce Lewis, *New Orleans: The Making of an Urban Landscape*, 2nd ed. (Santa Fe: Center for American Places in association with University of Virginia Press, 2003), esp. 37–100.

2. A lengthy treatment of urban open space preservation appears in John B. Wright, *Rocky Mountain Divide: Selling and Saving the West* (Austin: University of Texas Press, 1993), and a lively discussion of the persistence of nature in the city can be found in Anne Matthews, *Wild Nights: Nature Returns to the City* (New York: North Point Press, 2001).

3. Several recent works exemplify the growing body of wetland scholarship. Ann Vileisis, *Discovering the Unknown Landscape: A History of America's Wetlands* (Washington: Island Press, 1997); Hugh Prince, *Wetlands of the American Midwest: A Historical Geography of Changing Attitudes* (Chicago: University of Chicago Press, 1997); Martin Reuss, *Designing the Bayous: The Control of Water in the Atchafalaya Basin, 1800–1995* (Alexandria, VA: U.S. Army Corps of Engineers, Office of History, 1998); Gay Gomez, *A Wetland Biography: Seasons on Louisiana's Chenier Plain* (Austin: University of Texas Press, 1998); David McCally, *The Everglades: An Environmental History* (Gainesville: University of Florida Press, 1999).

4. See William Cronon, *Nature's Metropolis: Chicago and the Great West* (New York: W. W. Norton, 1991); Vileisis, *Discovering the Unknown Landscape*, chaps. 7 and 8; Daniel W. Schneider, "Enclosing the Floodplain: Resource Conflict on the Illinois River, 1880–1920," *Environmental History* 1 (1996): 70–96; John Thompson, *Wetlands Drainage, River Modification, and Sectoral Conflict in the Lower Illinois Valley, 1890–1930* (Carbondale, IL: Southern Illinois University Press, 2002); Christopher Meindl, "Past Perceptions of the Great American Wetland: Florida's Everglades during the Early Twentieth Century," *Environmental History* 5 (2000): 378–95.

5. Discussions of the environmental conditions and industrialization of the Calumet wetland can be found in Alfred H. Meyer, "Circulation and Settlement Patterns of the Calumet Region

of Northwest Indiana and Northeast Illinois," part 1, *Annals of the Association of American Geographers* 44 (1954): 245–74, and part 2, *Annals of the Association of American Geographers* 46 (1956): 312–26, and in Craig E. Colten, *Industrial Wastes in the Calumet Area, 1869–1970: An Historical Geography,* Research Report 1 (Champaign, IL: Hazardous Waste Research and Information Center, 1985). An assessment of the threats to this urban wetland and plans to preserve it appears in National Park Service, Midwest Region, *Calumet Ecological Park Feasibility Study,* http://www.lincolnnet.net/environment/feasibility/calumet1.html, 1998, and in Joel Greenberg, *A Natural History of the Chicago Region* (Chicago: University of Chicago Press, 2002).

6. Private donations from E. A. McIlhenny, Mrs. Russell Sage, and the Rockefeller Foundation became the core of the state's refuge system. See Gomez, *Wetland Biography,* 120–23.

7. In 1964, New Orleans established the Mosquito Control Board, which used chemical control, source reduction (habitat destruction), and biological control. See George T. Carmichael, *An Evaluation of Salt Marsh Mosquito Problems in Orleans Parish, Louisiana, With Recommendations for a Comprehensive Mosquito Control Program* (Atlanta: U.S. Public Health Service, 1963), and New Orleans Mosquito Control Board, *Mosquito Control* (New Orleans: New Orleans Mosquito Control Board, 1991).

8. Ari Kelman, "A River and Its City: Critical Episodes in the Environmental History of New Orleans" (Ph.D. diss., Brown University, 1998), 11–12. Levees, jetties, and floodways are some of the tools Kelman discusses. See also Kelman's *A River and Its City: The Nature of Landscape in New Orleans* (Berkeley: University of California Press, 2003). Efforts to manage the highly urbanized Los Angeles River are discussed in Blake Gumprecht, *The Los Angeles River: Its Life, Death, and Possible Rebirth* (Baltimore: Johns Hopkins University Press, 1999).

9. Several essays consider the persistence of nonhuman systems within New Orleans in *Transforming New Orleans and Its Environs: Centuries of Change,* ed. Craig E. Colten (Pittsburgh: University of Pittsburgh Press, 2000). See especially the essays by Don Davis, Guy Gomez, and Todd Shallat.

10. Rutherford H. Platt, "From Commons to Commons: Evolving Concepts of Open Space in North American Cities," in *The Ecological City: Preserving and Restoring Urban Biodiversity,* ed. Rutherford H. Platt, Rowan A. Rowntree, and Pamela C. Muick (Amherst: University of Massachusetts Press, 1994), 21–39.

11. The evolutionary stages of urban green space in England are chronicled in Henry W. Lawrence, "The Greening of the Squares of London: Transformation of Urban Landscapes and Ideals," *Annals of the Association of American Geographers* 83 (March 1993): 90–118. A discussion of space use within American parks is presented by Terence Young in "Modern Urban Parks," *Geographical Review* 85 (October 1995): 535–51. The contribution of Frederick Law Olmsted to the development of urban natural spaces is discussed in Anne Whiston Spirn, "Constructing Nature: The Legacy of Frederick Law Olmsted," in *Uncommon Ground: Toward Reinventing Nature,* ed. William Cronon (New York: W. W. Norton, 1995), 91–113.

12. See L. Ronald Forman and Joseph Logsdon, *Audubon Park: An Urban Eden* (New Orleans: Friends of the Zoo, 1985).

13. The recreational value of wetlands is treated in Hugh Prince, "A Marshland Chronicle, 1830–1960: From Artificial Drainage to Outdoor Recreation," *Journal of Historical Geography* 21 (1995): 3–22, and Don Davis and Randall Detro, "Louisiana's Marsh as a Recreation Resource," *Geoscience and Man* 12 (1975): 91–98.

14. National Park Service, *Calumet Ecological Park Feasibility Study;* New Jersey Meadowlands Commission, *Meadowlands Environmental Center,* http://www.hwdc.state.nj.us/ec/environment_center.htm, 2001. See also Lisa Cameron, "Experimental Park Grows on a Landfill," *Public Works* 126 (June 1995): 48–52.

15. William Cronon, "The Trouble with Wilderness; or Getting Back to the Wrong Nature," in *Uncommon Ground: Toward Reinventing Nature,* ed. William Cronon (New York: W. W. Norton, 1995), 80–81.

16. See Platt, "From Commons to Commons," and Julie Tuason, "*Rus* in *Urbe:* The Spatial Evolution of Urban Parks in the United States," *Historical Geography* 25 (1997): 124–47, esp. 126–27.

17. *Historical Sketch Book and Guide to New Orleans and Environs* (1885; reprint, New York: W. H. Coleman, 1924), 245. Algiers is a west bank suburb of New Orleans.

18. Henry Wadsworth Longfellow, *The Poetical Works of Henry Wadsworth Longfellow,* vol. 2 (New York: AMS Press, 1966), 67.

19. See David C. Miller, *Dark Eden: The Swamp in Nineteenth-Century American Culture* (Cambridge: Cambridge University Press, 1989), 32–33, 57–68.

20. George A. Coulon, *350 Miles in a Skiff through the Louisiana Swamps* (New Orleans: George Coulon, 1888), 1–2.

21. Federal Writers' Project, *The WPA Guide to New Orleans* (1938; reprint, New Orleans: Historic New Orleans Collection, 1983), 87, 391–92.

22. Stanley Clisby Arthur, *Louisiana Tours: A Guide to Places of Historic and General Interest, Where to Go, How to Go, What to See* (New Orleans: Harmanson, 1950), 55 and 86. See also Oliver Wendell Evans, *New Orleans* (New York: Macmillan, 1959), 136–39, and Thomas Kurtz Griffin, *New Orleans: A Guide to America's Most Interesting City* (Garden City, N.Y.: Doubleday, 1961), 93–95.

23. *Southern Bell Telephone Directory: New Orleans, Louisiana* (New Orleans: Southern Bell, 1955–1961).

24. For a detailed discussion of this controversy see Reuss, *Designing the Bayous,* esp. chaps. 8 and 9.

25. Jack Rudloe and Anne Rudloe, "Trouble in Bayou Country," *National Geographic* 182 (September 1979): 377–97; C. C. Lockwood, *Atchafalaya: America's Largest River Basin Swamp* (Baton Rouge: Beauregard, 1981).

26. For example, see John P. Sevenair, *Guide to Louisiana Wilderness Trails and the Delta Country* (New Orleans: New Orleans Group of the Sierra Club, 1978).

27. *South Central Bell Telephone Directory: Greater New Orleans* (New Orleans: South Central Bell, 1977–1999) and brochures obtained in New Orleans hotel information racks.

28. Samuel P. Hays, *Beauty, Health, and Permanence: Environmental Politics in the United*

States, 1955–1985 (New York: Cambridge University Press, 1987). On concerns about wetlands in particular, see Vileisis, *Discovering the Unknown Landscape,* esp. 211–48.

29. Samuel P. Shaw and C. Gordon Fredine, *Wetlands of the United States: Their Extent and Their Value to Waterfowl and Other Wildlife,* Circular 39 (Washington: U.S. Department of the Interior, Fish and Wildlife Service, 1956), 28.

30. Outdoor Recreation Resources Review Commission, *Outdoor Recreation for America: A Report to the President and Congress* (Washington: Outdoor Recreation Resources Review Commission, 1962), 81.

31. Frank J. Tysen, "Nature and the Urban Dweller," *Man and Nature in the City: A Symposium* (Washington: U.S. Department of the Interior, Bureau of Sport Fisheries and Wildlife, 1968), 12. A thorough discussion of suburbanization and environmentalism is found in Adam Rome, *The Bulldozer in the Countryside: Suburban Sprawl and the Rise of American Environmentalism* (New York: Cambridge University Press, 2001).

32. The notion that the South responded slowly to the environmental movement appears in James C. Cobb, *Industrialization and Southern Society, 1877–1984* (Lexington: University Press of Kentucky, 1984). Additional discussions of environmental action in the South appear in Jeffery Stine, *Mixing the Waters: Environment, Politics, and the Building of the Tennessee-Tombigbee Waterway* (Akron: University of Akron Press, 1993); Richard A. Bartlett, *Troubled Waters: Champion International and the Pigeon River Controversy* (Knoxville: University of Tennessee Press, 1995); Reuss, *Designing the Bayous;* McCally, *The Everglades.*

33. Faith McNulty, *The Whooping Crane: The Bird That Defies Extinction* (New York: E. P. Dutton, 1966), 18.

34. Herschel Miller, "The Angry Animals," *New Orleans* 3 (October 1968): 17–20, 38–41.

35. McNulty, *Whooping Crane,* 18.

36. The zoo revitalization program also represented a significant political and financial shift. Friends of the Zoo, an Uptown not-for-profit support group, effectively assumed control by shifting funding from municipal appropriations to private sources and boosting attendance. See Jonathan Mark Souther, "City in Amber: Race, Culture, and the Tourist Transformation of New Orleans, 1945–1995" (Ph.D. diss., Tulane University, 2002), 321–22.

37. Major zoos elsewhere, such as those in San Diego and St. Louis and the National Zoo in Washington, D.C., had already begun converting old barred cages to open-air habitats for their exotic animals.

38. Bureau of Government Research, *Audubon Park Zoo Study,* part 1, *Zoo Improvement Plan* (New Orleans: Bureau of Government Research, 1971), 2.

39. The Brown Pelican was completely eliminated from the state during the 1960s. Donald Norman and Robert Purrington, "Demise of the Brown Pelican in Louisiana," *Louisiana Ornithological Society News* 55 (15 August 1970): 3–6; U.S. Fish and Wildlife Service, Division of Endangered Species, "Brown Pelican," *Endangered and Threatened Species of the Southeastern United States,* http://endangered.fws.gov/i/b/sab2s.html, 1995. Also, Joseph E. Brown, *The Return of the Brown Pelican* (Baton Rouge: Louisiana State University Press, 1983).

40. A lively discussion of efforts to study and protect alligators appears in Gomez, *Wetland Biography,* 81.

41. Bureau of Government Research, *Audubon Park Zoo Study*, 56.

42. The inspiration for the exhibit came from the Arizona-Sonora Desert Museum outside Tucson, which situated a zoo in the midst of a relatively undisturbed saguaro cactus stand. Rick Atkinson, Curator of the Audubon Zoo Swamp Exhibit, interview with the author, 21 December 2000.

43. Marjorie Roehl, "Swamp to Open at Zoo," *New Orleans Times-Picayune*, 6 April 1984, 15.

44. Atkinson, interview.

45. A critical assessment of zoos as social institutions appears in Kay Anderson, "Culture and Nature at the Adelaide Zoo: At the Frontiers of 'Human Geography,'" *Transactions of the Institute of British Geographers*, n.s., 20 (1995): 275–94.

46. Now operated by the Audubon Institute, the same organization that manages the Audubon Zoo, the nature center acquired a new name in 2000, the Audubon Louisiana Nature Center.

47. *Louisiana Nature Center* (New Orleans: Louisiana Nature Center, 1977), 1–2.

48. "Swamp Scene," *Louisiana Nature Center News* 1 (Winter 1980–81): 1. This location was drained during the second decade of the twentieth century as part of a private wetland reclamation project for which the Sewerage and Water Board assumed responsibility in 1919. Robert Harrison and Walter Kollmorgen, "Drainage Reclamation in the Coastal Marshlands of the Mississippi River Delta," *Louisiana Historical Quarterly* 30 (1947): 654–709; New Orleans Sewerage and Water Board, *Fortieth Semi-Annual Report* (New Orleans: New Orleans Sewerage and Water Board, 1919), 77.

49. Louisiana Nature Center, *Concept Master Plan* (New Orleans: Louisiana Nature Center, 1979–80).

50. Vileisis, *Discovering the Unknown Landscape*, esp. chaps. 12 and 13; see also Reuss, *Designing the Bayous*, esp. chaps. 9–10.

51. Two landmark cases that significantly expanded the Clean Water Act's influence over wetlands were *Natural Resources Council v. Calloway*, 392 F. Supp. 685 (1975), and *U.S. v. Riverside Bayview Homes*, 474 US 121 (1985). For a general discussion of these cases, see Rutherford H. Platt, *Land Use and Society: Geography, Law, and Public Policy* (Washington: Island, 1996), 436–41.

52. Willie Fontenot, Louisiana Attorney General's Office, personal conversation with the author, January 2001. Decline in the Louisiana oil industry also undercut development pressures in the 1980s.

53. Sherwood M. Gagliano, Klaus J. Meyer-Arendt, and Karen Wicker, "Land Loss in the Mississippi River Deltaic Plain," *Transactions: Gulf Coast Association of Geological Societies*, 31st meeting (Corpus Christi, TX: October 1981), 295–300.

54. Changing attitudes toward rural wetlands is treated by Prince, *Wetlands of the American Midwest*, esp. chap. 9. A popular account of rediscovering urban wetlands is Robert Sullivan, *The Meadowlands: Wilderness Adventures at the Edge of a City* (New York: Scribner, 1998). Preservation of another New Jersey suburban wetland is chronicled in Cam Cavanaugh, *Saving the Great Swamp: The People, the Power Brokers, and an Urban Wilderness* (Frenchtown, NJ: Columbia, 1978).

55. Gomez, *Wetland Biography*, 122–23.

56. J. O. Snowden, W. C. Ward, and J. R. J. Studlick, *Geology of Greater New Orleans: Its Relationship to Land Subsidence and Flooding* (New Orleans: New Orleans Geological Society, 1980).

57. National Park Service (NPS), *Proposed Jean Lafitte National Cultural Park, Louisiana* (Washington: NPS, 1972), 60–73. "Natural" is a term commonly used by agencies such as the NPS to refer to the nonhuman world, even when it has been altered by human activity.

58. U.S. Congress, Senate, Subcommittee on Parks and Recreation of the Committee on Energy and Natural Resources, *Hearings: Jean Lafitte National Park,* 95th Cong., 2nd sess., Publication 95–97, 1978.

59. The enabling legislation specifically provides solutions attentive to local interests for all these concerns. See Jean Lafitte National Historical Park and Preserve, Public Law 95–625, 1978, 92 Stat. 3534.

60. Jean Lafitte National Historical Park, Public Law 95–625. The historical park included property in the historic French Quarter and at the Chalmette battlefield site. The Barataria segment constituted the preserve component.

61. Jean Lafitte National Historical Park, Public Law 95–625.

62. See Betsy Swanson et al., *Terre Haute de Barataria: An Historic Upland on an Old River Distributary Overtaken by Forest in the Barataria Unit of the Jean Lafitte National Historical Park and Preserve,* Monograph 11 (Harahan, LA: Jefferson Parish Historical Commission, 1991).

63. Discussions of wildlife management in the national parks appear in William Halvorson and Gary Davis, eds., *Science and Ecosystem Management in the National Parks* (Tucson: University of Arizona Press, 1996), and R. Gerald Wright, *Wildlife Research and Management in the National Parks* (Urbana: University of Illinois Press, 1992).

64. NPS, *Jean Lafitte National Historical Park: Land Protection Plan* (New Orleans: NPS, 1984).

65. NPS, *Land Protection Plan: Jean Lafitte National Historical Park and Preserve* (New Orleans: NPS, 1989), 15–16.

66. Traînasses are small canals dug by trappers for passing through the marsh grass in traditional boats known as pirogues.

67. Jean Lafitte National Heritage Park and Preserve, Barataria Preserve Trapping Season Summary, 1992, Jean Lafitte National Heritage Park and Preserve Collection, MS 294, Box 11, folder 859, University of New Orleans Archives, New Orleans. Nutria are rodents of South American origin introduced to Louisiana in the early twentieth century. They have become both competitors with native species such as muskrats and prey for fur trappers. See Shane Bernard, "*M'sieu* Ned's Rat? Reconsidering the Origin of Nutria in Louisiana: The E. A. McIlhenny Collection, Avery Island, Louisiana," *Louisiana History* 43 (2002): 281–93.

68. NPS, *Jean Lafitte National Heritage Park and Preserve: Amendment to the General Management Plan* (Denver: NPS, Denver Service Center, 1995).

69. Impact Assessment, Inc., *Traditional Use Study: Barataria Preserve, Final Report* (New Orleans: National Park Service, 1998).

70. U.S. Congress, House of Representatives, Subcommittee on Fisheries and Wildlife of the Committee on Merchant Marine and Fisheries, *Hearings: Bayou Sauvage Urban National Wildlife Refuge*, Serial 99–55, 99th Cong., 2nd sess., 1986, esp. testimony of John A. Hilton, 18–21. Also see Todd Shallat, "In the Wake of Hurricane Betsy," in Colten, *Transforming New Orleans and Its Environs*, 134–35.

71. The wetland tract was sinking, and only through human intervention could this process be reversed. Testimony of Sherwood Gagliano in U.S. Congress, *Hearings: Bayou Sauvage*, 21–24.

72. Under the Endangered Species Act, critical habitat is an area necessary for a species' survival. Testimony of James Pulliam in U.S. Congress, *Hearings: Bayou Sauvage*, 10–11.

73. Cashio, Cochran, and Torre/Design Consortium et al., *Bayou Sauvage National Wildlife Refuge: Master Plan* (New Orleans: U.S. Fish and Wildlife Service, 1994), 3.

74. Cashio, Cochran, and Torre/Design Consortium et al., *Bayou Sauvage National Wildlife Refuge: Final Environmental Impact Statement* (Atlanta: U.S. Fish and Wildlife Service, 1994), 3–9.

75. Cashio, Cochran, and Torre/Design Consortium et al., *Bayou Sauvage National Wildlife Refuge: Master Plan*, 38, 83–89.

76. Two additional wetland preserves include Bayou Segnette State Park in Westwego, not far from the Barataria Preserve, and the LaBranche Wetland, just west of Kenner along Lake Pontchartrain. The LaBranche Wetland, a failed early-twentieth-century agricultural drainage project, is undergoing extensive rehabilitation with cooperation between state and federal agencies. See Coastal Environments, Inc., *Remote-Sensing Survey of the Bayou LaBranche Wetlands Restoration Borrow Area, St. Charles Parish, Louisiana* (New Orleans: U.S. Army Corps of Engineers, New Orleans District, 1993).

77. *Everybody Needs a Home: A Curriculum-Based Education Program for Grades 4–5* (Marrero, LA: Jean Lafitte National Historical Park and Preserve, n.d.); *Vanishing Wetlands: Curriculum-Based Education Program for Grades 6–8* (Marrero, LA: Jean Lafitte National Historical Park and Preserve, n.d.).

78. Fish and Wildlife Service, Southeast Louisiana Refuges, "Bayou Medley," "Habitat Is Where It's At," and "Water We Have Here" educational packets (Slidell, LA: U.S. Department of the Interior, Fish and Wildlife Service, n.d.).

79. I took tours on the Cypress Swamp Tours in Westwego, Louisiana, and the New Orleans Swamp Tours in the Bayou Sauvage Wildlife Refuge in the summer of 1999 and the Alligator Bayou tour near Baton Rouge in 2000.

80. Mary Swerczek, "Demand Increasing for Heads, Claws of Alligators," *Baton Rouge Advocate*, 8 September 2000, 7B. Most body parts come from farm-raised alligators bred primarily for their skins and not from animals taken in the wild.

81. These are the very contradictions that by their presence humans negate. See William Cronon, "The Trouble with Wilderness; or Getting Back to the Wrong Nature," in Cronon, *Uncommon Ground*, 80–81.

NOTES TO EPILOGUE

1. It is no surprise New Orleans has inspired several recent volumes on its environmental history. See Ari Kelman, *A River and Its City: The Nature of Landscape in New Orleans* (Berkeley: University of California Press, 2003), and Craig E. Colten, ed., *Transforming New Orleans and Its Environs: Centuries of Change* (Pittsburgh: University of Pittsburgh Press, 2000).

2. Craig E. Colten, "Industrial Topography, Groundwater, and the Contours of Environmental Knowledge," *Geographical Review* 88:2 (1998): 199–218.

3. James E. Vance, *The Continuing City: Urban Morphology in Western Civilization* (Baltimore: Johns Hopkins University Press, 1990).

4. See David Harvey, *The Urban Experience* (Baltimore: Johns Hopkins University Press, 1989).

5. Michael Dear and Steven Flusty, "Postmodern Urbanism," *Annals of the Association of American Geographers* 88 (1998): 50–72; Edward Soja, *Postmetropolis: Critical Studies of Cities and Regions* (Malden, MA: Blackwell, 2000).

6. Recent efforts to unite social and ecological sciences in the study of the city have been gaining attention. See Brian J. L. Berry, "A New Urban Ecology?" *Urban Geography* 22 (2001): 699–701.

7. "Nothing's Easy for New Orleans Flood Control," *New York Times,* 30 April 2002; Mark Fischetti, "Drowning New Orleans," *Scientific American* 285:4 (October 2001): 77–85.

8. "Mayor: N.O. Location 'Lousy Place to Put a City,'" *Baton Rouge Advocate,* 17 May 2001, 14A.

INDEX

Abita Springs, 138

Agriculture, 20

Agriculture Street Landfill: addition to National Priorities List, 138; adjacent to Moton elementary school, 118–19; and class action suit, 125; closure, 113; conversion from dump to landfill, 112; EPA involvement, 116, 119–25, 138; as example of environmental ethic, 109, 139, 189; high soil lead levels and, 118–19; as "landscape of tragedy," 117, 118, 138; location, 110–11; possible link to breast cancer, 120–21; reclassification as hazard, 138; remediation/relocation of, 121–24; residential opposition to, 112–13; as site for public housing, 114–15. *See also* U.S. Environmental Protection Agency (EPA)

Agriculture Street Superfund site. *See* Agriculture Street Landfill

Algiers, Louisiana, 69, 167

Alligators, 17, 167–68, 172, 179, 183, 184, 190

Almonaster Avenue, 110

American Sector, 71, 89

Arpent survey system, 20

Atchafalaya Basin, 29, 168, 169, 171, 173

Atchafalaya River, 25, 29

Atlanta, Georgia, 80

Audubon Louisiana Nature Center. *See* Louisiana Nature Center

Audubon Park, 1, 73, 74, 75, 84, 105, 166

Audubon Park Improvement Association, 75

Audubon Zoo, 163, 166, 171, 174, 175

Auxiliary Sanitary Association, 54

Barataria, Louisiana, 168, 177

Barataria Preserve, 163, 166–67, 168, 170, 177, 178, 179, 180, 183, 184, 190. *See also* Jean Lafitte National Historical Park and Preserve

Barton, E. H., 35, 36, 42, 47, 48, 50, 57, 66, 72

Basin Street, 77, 87, 90, 106

Baton Rouge, Louisiana, 3, 21, 126, 130, 134

Battle of New Orleans, 71

Batture, 17, 57, 60, 73

Bayou in Moonlight. See Hamilton, James

Bayou Manchac, 6

Bayou Sauvage National Wildlife Refuge, 163, 166–67, 170, 174, 180–82, 183, 185, 190

Bayou Segnette State Park, 170

Bayou St. John, 2, 4, 10, 28, 38, 41, 64, 67, 77, 82, 84, 143

Bay St. Louis, Mississippi, 43

Bienville, Jean Baptiste Le Moyne de, 2, 3, 96

Birmingham, Alabama, 80

Blackstone, William, 50

Bogue Falaya River, 64

Bonnet Carré crevasse, 29, 31

Bonnet Carré spillway, 155, 161, 190

Brackenridge, Henry, 23

Brecher, Edward, 136

Broadmoor: description, 147, 154, 160; effect of flooding in 1980, 150; effect of Tropical Storm Allison in, 153; effect of Tropical Storm Isidore in, 153–54; effects of 1978 storm in, 149; flood damage in 1995, 151; flood prevention in, 152–53; improving drainage in, 151, 153

Broad Street, 92

Brooks, Elizabeth, 12

Brown pelican, 171

Bubonic plague, 110

Buffalo, New York, 74

Burgundy Street, 66

Butler, General Benjamin F., 51

Butte, Montana, 117

Caernarvon, 142

Canal Street, 67, 70, 82, 89, 91, 169

Carondelet Canal, 38, 39, 77, 87

Carrollton neighborhood, 24, 25, 40, 73, 82, 84

Carson, Rachel, 131, 132

Cemeteries: as nuisances, 66, 68, 70–71, 112; relocating, 66. *See also* specific cemeteries

Central Park, 9. *See also* New York City

Charity Hospital Cemetery, 67

Chicago, Illinois, 5, 165

Chicago fire, 117

Chicago River, 5

Cholera, 66

Cisterns: in helping prevent disease, 65; for rainwater collection, 61; water company campaign to discredit, 64–65

City Beautiful Movement, 165, 166, 171

City of New Orleans (government), 122, 123, 124

City Park, 74, 75, 105

Civil War, 30, 31, 51, 73, 125, 188

Claiborne Avenue, 91, 97, 102, 153

Clean Water Act, 136, 166, 175. *See also* Water

Climatic conditions and disease, 34, 35

Company of the Indies, 19

Comprehensive Environmental Response, Compensation, and Liability Act (CERCLA). *See* Superfund

Comprehensive Environmental Response, Compensation, and Liability Information System (CERCLIS), 115

Congo Square, 72, 77, 105

Conseil de Ville, 21

Consumer Reports, 136

Coubra Drive (Marrero), 158

Coulon, George, 168

Cronon, William, 5

Cypress: planting to prevent disease, 35, 36; as resource, 18

Cypress Grove Cemetery, 67

Darby, William, 17, 22, 34
Dauphine Street, 24
Demographic change, 113–14
De Russy, Lewis, 42
Dichloro-diphenyl-trichloroethane (DDT), 112
Dixie Brewing Company, 138
Duffy, John, 36
Dunbar, George, 41
Du Plantier, M., 39

Earl, George, 87
Egypt, 33
Eighth Ward, 100
Eleventh Ward, 91, 95, 100, 104
Emel, Jacque, 12
Endangered Species Act, 166
Endrin: 131–34. *See also* Pollution
Environment: and cancer rates, 136; changing attitudes toward, 163, 167; and disease, 12, 19, 33, 34, 35, 47, 188; impacts of suburbanization on, 140; laws to protect, 166; management of, generally, 6, 11; management of, in nineteenth-century New Orleans, 12, 48; rediscovery of, 14; role of, 9; transformation of in New Orleans, 15, 48, 50, 89, 91; twentieth-century redefinition of, 109. *See also* Water; Pollution; Mississippi River
Environmental activism, 169, 170, 175, 180, 184
Environmental Defense Fund, 136
Environmental equity and inequity, 78–82
Environmental justice, 114, 115, 124
Environmental problems as municipal concerns, 51
Environmental quality, 12
EPA. *See* U.S. Environmental Protection Agency (EPA)
Esplanade Avenue, 89, 91, 95, 96
Evangeline (Longfellow), 168

Federal Emergency Management Agency (FEMA), 149, 153, 158, 160
Federal Water Pollution Control Act. *See* Clean Water Act
Federal Water Pollution Control Administration (FWPCA), 134–35
Federal Writers' Project, 168
Felicity Street, 83
Fenner, Edward, 24, 35, 41
Fields, Timothy, 124
Fifth Ward, 104
Flint, Timothy, 35, 39, 43
Flooding: capital improvement projects to prevent, 150–51; and construction standards, 152–53, 154; controlling in nineteenth century, 17, 19; diversion of floodwaters, 29, 142; during Spanish occupation, 23; and economic success, 20, 30; federal responsibility, 31, 32; French response to, 19; historic around New Orleans, 4, 5, 16; in 1735, 19; in 1785, 23; in 1816, 24; in 1828, 25; in 1874, 31; in 1890, 32; in 1927, 96–97, 105–6, 142–43; in 1978, 149; in 1979, 150; in 1980, 150; in 1981, 150; in 1982, 151; in 1983, 151; in 1995, 151; influence of, 19; land-use controls, 152, 159, 160; municipal ordinance to prevent, 23; patterns in New Orleans, 149, 160; prevention in Barataria Preserve, 178; protection, 11, 20, 141–42, 152; and public works program (1899), 87, 90; as result of urban sprawl, 146; resulting from hurricanes, 145, 146; structural methods to control, 160, 161. *See also* Broadmoor; Jefferson Parish; Ninth Ward
Florida Parishes, 64, 161
Foote, Kenneth, 116
Formosa termites, 191
Fourteenth Ward, 100, 105
French Quarter, 1, 24, 27, 38, 49, 70, 71, 72, 82, 83, 84, 89, 91, 95, 100, 104, 167, 191. *See also* Eighth Ward; Ninth Ward
Freret Street, 68

Gandy, Matthew, 6, 9

Garbage: burning of, outlawed, 112; city responsibility for, 110; conditions in 1853, 58; dumps and racial discrimination, 114; as fertilizer, 59; inadequate disposal of, 70, 75; and "nuisance wharves," 58, 59; opposition to policy on disposal of, 112–13

Garden District, 82, 89, 90, 91

Gentilly neighborhood, 145

Gentilly Ridge, 4, 98

Gert Town, 150

Gettysburg, 116

Girod Cemetery, 67

Gordon Plaza, 115, 124

Gravier neighborhood, 24

Gravier Square, 72

Great Invitational Water-Tasting Challenge, 137

Greenpeace, 123

Gretna, Louisiana, 128

Groundwater, 60–61

Gulf Distilling, 128

Gulf of Mexico, 6, 10, 43, 109, 153, 178

Hamilton, James, 168

Harris, Robert, 136

Harvey, David, 188

Hazards: dealing with in New Orleans, 11, 13, 19, 44, 45; distinguished from nuisances, 47; influence of, 19; in nineteenth-century New Orleans, 33, 47; and metropolitan sprawl, 13; river pollution as, 138; sanitary landfills as, 112; swamps as source of, 17, 18, 33. *See also* Agriculture Street Landfill

Hazeur-Distance, Ellen, 122

Hebert, P. O., 25, 26

Herrick, S. S., 56

Heustis, Jabez, 34

Historical geography: of New Orleans, 6

Holt, Joseph, 53, 56, 58, 61, 68

Hurricane Betsy, 113, 145, 146, 154

Hurricane Camille, 145, 146

Hurricane Flossy, 145

Hurricane Hilda, 145

Iberville, Lemoyne d', 2

Industrial Canal, 144, 145, 146, 154

Inner Harbor Navigation Canal. *See* Industrial Canal

Irish immigrants, 42

Isle of Orleans, 6

Jackson Square, 3, 28, 16, 71, 77

Jean Lafitte National Historical Park and Preserve, 177. *See also* Barataria Preserve

Jefferson, Louisiana, 69

Jefferson, Thomas, 39

Jefferson, William, 122

Jefferson Parish: building codes in, 159; characteristics of, 155–56; current construction patterns in, 160, 161, 190; development of drainage canals in, 146–47; development of tract housing in, 141; drainage in, 155, 156; and effectiveness of flood insurance program, 149; effect of 1978 storm in, 157–58; effect of 1980 flood in, 158; FEMA suit against, 158; flood insurance in, 156–57; homeowners' class action suit against, 159; lakefront levee construction in, 144; land subsidence in, 155; lobbying for flood protection by, 151; location of, 155; NFIP guidelines in, 157, 158; rejection of drainage system improvements in, 158; requirement to provide flood reduction plan in, 158–59; storm damage in, 159–60; storm surge in, 145; suburbanization in, 6, 14, 144, 146, 147, 155; U.S. Corps of Engineers' work in, 160; wetland drainage in, 162–63, 176

Jim Crow, 78, 79, 81, 97, 105, 106–7, 189

Johnstown flood, 117

Jones, Joseph, 57

Kansas City, 135
Kelman, Ari, 165
Kenner, Louisiana, 176

LaBranche wetlands, 190
Lafayette, Marquis de, 72
Lafayette Square, 71
Lafitte, Louisiana, 168
La Harpe, Jean Baptiste Bernard de, 33
Lake Borgne, 33, 84, 87, 90
Lake Calumet (Illinois), 164, 166
Lake Maurepas, 6
Lake Ponchartrain, 1, 2, 4, 6, 14, 24, 28, 29, 31,
    33, 36, 38, 39, 40, 42, 43, 56, 64, 77, 82, 84,
    87, 128, 140, 142, 144, 155, 162, 176, 190, 191
"Landscapes of tragedy," 116, 117, 118, 189
Latrobe, Benjamin, 43, 60
Lawrence, Henry, 6
Le Page du Pratz, Antoine-Simon, 3, 34
Leprous Road, 66
Levees, 1, 2, 3, 4, 10, 11, 12, 14, 17, 141, 188; in
    antebellum years, 24; construction, 19, 20;
    and crevasses, 26, 28, 29, 32; defined, 19;
    effectiveness during hurricanes, 145, 146;
    effectiveness of, 22, 24, 25, 29, 31, 32, 45,
    142, 191; as flood protection in nineteenth
    century, 29, 30, 40, 42; under French
    and Spanish rule, 20; maintenance of, in
    Territory of Louisiana, 21; maintenance
    through taxation, 21, 22; municipal re-
    sponsibility for, 25, 28, 45, 141; as naviga-
    tional aids, 31; rural landholders responsi-
    bility for, 20, 21, 29, 45
Lewis, Peirce, 2
Lockwood, C. C., 169
Locust Street, 68
Long, Huey, 144
Longfellow, Henry Wadsworth, 168
Long-lot survey system, 20
Louisiana Board of Health, 54, 57, 59, 64, 65,
    67, 82, 110

Louisiana Department of Health, 97, 120
Louisiana Department of Wild Life and
    Fisheries, 130
Louisiana Nature Center, 163, 166, 173–74
Louisiana Purchase, 45, 125
Louisiana Supreme Court, 159
Louisiana Territory, 21, 125
Love Canal (New York), 115

Madisonville, Louisiana, 43
Manufacturing: as a nuisance, 68–69; regu-
    lation of, 69
Marigny (Faubourg), 24, 71, 72
Marigny Canal, 39
Marrero, Louisiana, 157, 159, 160. *See also*
    Jefferson Parish
McDonough, John, 73
McNulty, Faith, 171
Melosi, Martin, 13, 142
Melpomene Canal, 39
Memphis, Tennessee, 133
Metairie, Louisiana, 149, 151
Metarie Bayou, 75
Metairie Ridge, 4, 27, 32, 41, 43, 66, 67, 70,
    73, 98, 155
Miasmas, 11, 17, 33, 34, 35, 188
Mid-City neighborhood, 97
Minneapolis, Minnesota, 135
Mississippi River, 2, 6, 10, 51, 64, 163, 165,
    178; basin, 6, 14; delta, 1, 3, 17; diluting
    power of, 88–89, 126; drainage of, 5; engi-
    neering work stabilization, 169; and envi-
    ronmental problems, 131, 138–39; flooding,
    16, 142; flooding in 1823, 25; as garbage
    sink, 59, 60, 109, 110; levees on, in 1812,
    21; as municipal water supply, 109, 126,
    129, 134; as navigable waterway, 125; in
    nineteenth-century New Orleans, 17, 18;
    oil industry and, 127; reclamation of lower,
    30, 140–41; as resource, 18; as sewage sink,
    52; as site of New Orleans, 3, 16, 141, 155;

Mississippi River (*continued*)
wetland drainage and, 162. *See also*
Pollution
Mississippi River Commission, 31, 32, 45,
142, 188
Mississippi Valley, 133
Missouri River, 5
Morial, Mark, 2, 122, 192
Mosquitoes, 6, 17, 36, 37, 38, 51, 53, 82, 90,
112, 141, 165, 182, 184, 191
Moton Elementary School, 120, 124–25. *See
also* Agriculture Street Landfill
Mumford, Lewis, 6
Muskrats, 142

Nader, Ralph, 135–36
Napoleon Avenue, 153
National Environmental Justice Advisory
Council, 120
National Flood Insurance Program (NFIP),
146, 147, 152, 154, 157, 158, 159, 161
National Park Service (NPS), 176, 177, 178,
183, 185
National Priorities List (NPL), 115, 116, 117,
118, 119, 120
Native Americans, 10
New Basin Canal (New Orleans Navigation
Canal), 87, 144
New Canal, 28, 31, 39, 40
New Jersey Meadowlands, 166
New Orleans, City of. *See* City of New
Orleans
New Orleans Board of Health, 35
New Orleans Canal and Banking Com-
pany, 40
New Orleans Chemical and Fertilizer Com-
pany, 59, 60
New Orleans Common Council, 83
New Orleans Draining Company, 40
New Orleans Medical and Surgical Associa-
tion, 53

New Orleans Navigation Canal (New Basin
Canal), 87, 144
New Orleans Park Commission, 73
New Orleans Sewerage and Water Board,
88, 90, 92, 94, 96, 97, 99, 100, 101, 105, 106,
137, 143, 151, 152, 153
New Orleans Sewerage Company, 56
New Orleans Swamp Land Reclamation
Company, 99
New Orleans Water Works, 60, 63
New York City, 9, 64. *See also* Central Park
New York Times, 132–33
NFIP. *See* National Flood Insurance
Program
Ninth Ward: African American population
in, 104; description of, 154, 160; and drain-
age system in, 147, 154; flood control in,
154–55; flooding from Hurricane Betsy in,
154; public services in, 114, 154; residents file
suit in, 154; sewer system in, 100; structural
damage in, 154; white population in, 105
Norman, Benjamin, 72
North Shore, 43–44
NPL. *See* National Priorities List
NPS. *See* National Park Service
Nuisances: defined, 49–50, 113, 138; elimination of, 188; garbage dumps, 108, 110,
112; putrefying matter, 52; regulation of,
71. *See also* Cemeteries; Manufacturing;
Slaughterhouses
Nutria, 179

Ohio River, 5, 135
Olmsted, John Charles, 75
Orleans Levee Board, 144
Orleans Parish, 6, 23, 145, 152, 160, 176
Orleans Parish School Board, 118
Orleans Parish seawall, 144–45

Parking Commission, 91, 95–96, 100
Parks: description of, in 1850s, 72; establish-

ment of, 71–72, 75, 78, 189; and idea of wetland, 176; as open spaces, 165–66; original purpose of, 72, 74; and preservation of public health, 72–73. *See also* Audubon Park; Barataria Preserve; Bayou Sauvage National Wildlife Refuge; Louisiana Nature Center; Wetlands

Parks and Parkway Commission, 100, 102

Philadelphia, Pennsylvania, 64

Pile, Louis, 43

Pilgrim's Progress (Bunyan), 32

Pitot, James, 33, 34

Pittsburgh, Pennsylvania, 135

Place d'Armes. *See* Jackson Square

Platt, Rutherford, 165, 166

Pollution (of Mississippi River): as cancer causing agent, 136; congressional hearings on, 133; efforts to control, 129, 137; EPA findings on, 135; federal involvement in monitoring of, 134–35, 136; fish kills and, 128, 130, 131, 13233, 134; laws and protection of traditional economies, 126, 139; petrochemical industry waste as source of, 127–29, 133–34, 139; and sugarcane cultivation, 133; toxic chemicals, 131–35; upstream control of, 126, 130, 135, 136, 138; and Velsicol Chemical Company, 133–34; water quality and, 130–31, 136, 139

Potentially Responsible Party (PRP). *See* City of New Orleans

Potomac River, 5

Poydras Canal, 39

Poydras Street, 40

Press Park, 115

Privies: poor maintenance of, 52; in Progressive Era, 80; specifications for, 52, 54; and surface water pollution, 53

PRP (Potentially Responsible Party). *See* City of New Orleans

Public works: and African American neighborhoods, 79–80, 81–82, 96, 97, 99, 105, 189; and city growth, 98, 99; and drainage issues, 82–83, 92–93, 96, 100–101, 141, 142; to eliminate nuisances, 188–89; and environmental inequity, 78–79; expansion of, into high-risk areas, 146, 154; federal funding of, 100–101, 106; under Huey Long, 144; program of 1899, 84–85, 87, 89–90; as Progressive Era reforms, 78, 105, 106

Public Works Department, 110

Pulido, Laura, 114

Pulliam, James, 180

Rampart Street, 19, 27, 66, 91

Reconstruction, 51, 60, 73, 77, 79

Red River, 21, 25

Ribicoff, Abraham, 133

Rigolets, 4

Robin, C. C., 35

Rocky Mountains, 10

Safe Drinking Water Act (1974), 135, 136. *See also* Water

San Francisco, California, 74

Sauvé Crevasse, 26, 28, 29, 31, 40

Second Municipality, 28

Second Ward, 95, 100, 104

Segregation: and access to public works, 83, 89–90, 91, 94, 95, 97, 99, 102, 105, 106, 141, 189; and disease, 90, 93, 94–95, 97; residential, 81, 82, 99, 100, 104, 106, 107, 189. *See also* Public works

Seventh Ward, 91, 95, 96, 104

Sewage: as nuisance, 53, 82; and canal dredging, 50–51; economic effects of, 56–57, 83; effective cleansing of, 51; and sewerage system, 56, 78, 83, 90, 93–94, 97, 101, 105, 106

Shell Oil Company, 128–29

Sixteenth Ward, 91, 104

Slaughterhouses, 62, 69–70, 87–89, 90

Southeast Louisiana Flood Control project, 160

Stafford, Andrew, 99

Standard Oil Company, 127–28

St. Bernard Parish, 142

St. Charles Avenue, 89, 91, 104

St. Charles Parish, 161, 190

St. John neighborhood, 24

St. Louis Cathedral, 77

St. Louis Cemetery No. 1, 66

St. Louis Cemetery No. 2, 66

St. Louis Cemetery No. 3, 67

St. Mary (Faubourg), 24

St. Patrick's Cemetery, 67

St. Peter Street, 66

Stream Control Commission (SCC), 127, 129

St. Roche Avenue, 91

St. Tammany Parish, 190

Suburbanization, 11, 97, 140–41, 144, 189

Superfund, 113, 114, 115–16, 117, 119, 121, 122, 124, 125, 135, 189. *See also* Agriculture Street Landfill

Survey systems, 20

Swamp Lands Act: of 1849, 30, 45; of 1950, 30, 45

Tangipahoa River, 64

Tchefuncte River, 64

Tenth Ward, 95, 100, 104

Texas City explosion, 117

Texas Company, 127–28

Tickfaw River, 64

Topography, 17, 27, 154, 190

Toulouse Street, 66

Tourism: summer retreats 43–44; swamp tours, 168–70

Tremé neighborhood, 24, 72

Tropical Storm Allison, 153, 159, 160

Tropical Storm Isidore, 153, 160

Underground burial, prohibition of, 66–67

United Nations, 123

Uptown (New Orleans), 149, 150

Uptown Flood Association, 151

U.S. Army Corp of Engineers, 142, 145, 152, 155, 160, 161, 169, 175, 181, 188

U.S. Congress, 22, 31, 136

U.S. Department of Housing and Urban Development, 158

U.S. Environmental Protection Agency (EPA), 114, 115, 116, 117, 119, 120, 121, 122, 123, 124, 125, 135, 136, 138

U.S. Fish and Wildlife Service, 170, 171, 180, 181, 182, 183, 185

U.S. Geological Survey, 129

U.S. Public Health Service (USPHS), 110–11, 129, 130, 133

U.S. Senate, 30

U.S. Supreme Court, 99

Urbanization: as ecological system, 9; as economic process, 7, 8

Valley of the Drums (Kentucky), 115

Vance, James, 8, 18

Velsicol Chemical Company: *see* Pollution

Venetian Isles subdivision, 146

Vicksburg, Mississippi, 116, 133

Vidangeurs, 52, 53, 56, 58

Vieux Carré. *See* French Quarter

Vileisis, Anne, 32

Ward One, 94

Ward Three, 94

Ward Two, 94

Washington, D.C., 5

Washington, George, 72

Water: federal involvement in monitoring of, 134–35, 136, 189; Mississippi River as source of, 109, 129, 131, 134; monitoring of quality of, 130, 133, 136; pollution as cause of cancer, 136; problems with supply, 60, 63, 65–66, 78; rainwater, 61; service during late nineteenth century, 83, 89; supplier responsibilities for quality of,

131; taste of, 134, 137, 139; treatment of, 137, 139

Waterman, Charles M., 73

Water Pollution Control Division, 131

Webster, Noah, 33

West Nile Virus, 191

Westwego, Louisiana, 158

Wetlands: artistic impressions of, 168; bayou trips, 168–69; changing attitudes toward, 163, 175, 190; coastal erosion and, 175, 176, 185; display at Audubon Zoo, 173, 184; display at Louisiana Nature Center, 174, 184; drainage of, 32–44, 164, 176; as educational tools, 163, 166, 167, 171, 182, 183; establishment of preserves for, by National Park Service, 177–79; hunting in, 167–68, 177, 179; laws protecting, 175, 182, 184, 190; perceived as health hazards, 33–37; perception of, in nineteenth century, 168; preservation of, 166; protection of flora and fauna in, 172–73; real estate development in, 39, 40, 176; rural, 165, 167, 169, 170; swamp tours, 169–70, 184; as tourist destinations, 167, 168, 169, 184; urban, 164–65; value of, 163; vulnerability of, 170. *See also* Barataria Preserve; Bayou Sauvage National Wildlife Refuge

White, Gilbert, 141

White privilege, 114

Whooping crane, 171

Woodward, C. Vann, 79

Wooldridge, A. D., 29

World War II, 13, 112, 130

World's Industrial and Cotton Centennial Exposition, 73

WPA (Works Progress Administration), 100, 111

Yellow fever, 33, 36, 38, 42, 44, 47, 51, 52, 57, 61